Praise for

"Madison Young is living a double life—running a DIY queer, feminist art space in San Francisco by day, and jetting off to Europe to get tied up, smacked up, and glamour-shot by night. Or is she hosting trans-inclusive dirty spoken word events by night and being a world-famous bondage model by day? And when does she find the time to shoot her own blue movies? 'Cause she does. This lady has done more in the first quarter of her life than most people do in a generation."

MICHELLE TEA, author of *Valencia* and *The Chelsea Whistle*

"Madison Young is one of the most important feminist artists and pornographers working today. She's brave, brilliant, and one of a kind!"

TRISTAN TAORMINO, author of *Opening Up* and
The Ultimate Guide to Kink

"Madison Young: Twinkly-eyed, mischievous provocateur, carrying on the flame that burns in the soul of San Francisco. With impish glee and preternatural charm, she's carved out a much needed space-time continuum for art and life in a city nearly suffocated in recent days by conventional concerns. Keep an eye on this sexy little devil!"

MIDORI

"In my twenty-five years as both an entertainer and educator of adults, I've met very few women as compelling as Madison Young. I've worked with many attractive, artistic, creative, intelligent, ambitious, strong, and driven women. I've rarely, however, experienced all of those traits in one person as I do in Ms. Young."

NINA HARTLEY

"Madison has the ability to blend these worlds while maintaining both eroticism and intellect."

DAVE NAVARRO

Madison Young is an incredible and singular force in the world of art, and her talent, spirit, and energy never fail to impress me. She's dedicated to changing the game for women, queers, kinksters—and now moms—with her individualism, innovation, insight, and innate intelligence. She is downright inspirational. Madison is the real deal, the whole package. We need her voice now more than ever, and I know that supporting her work means to support the needs of women, indie women, queer women, women who want more—women everywhere. I am a longtime fan of Madison Young, both artistically and personally, and I cannot wait for each new project. She is devoted to the truth, and that—after motherhood—truly is the noblest profession."

MARGARET CHO, author of *I Have Chosen to Stay and Fight*

"A fascinating insight into the mind and work of a modern day icon. Madison wrestles with the ultimate struggle modern women face—the public body versus the private body—and as usual comes out on top."

DR. BROOKE MAGNATI, author of *Belle de Jour*, adapted for *The Secret Diary of a Call Girl*

"Young says early in her book that her motto in life is 'reveal all, fear nothing'. She has produced a memoir that does exactly this, painting an engaging and fascinating picture of an erotic life filled with complexity, self-awareness and a good chunk of humour that will challenge preconceptions of porn performers, Daddy/Little Girl relationships and even kinky parents trying to juggle family life with playtime. *Daddy* is unflinchingly honest, hot and with much to say about feminism, sexuality, porn and relationships. It is exactly the kind of unapologetic yet nuanced book you'd imagine a woman as articulate as Madison Young would write, explaining in an engaging way exactly what a self-assured capable feminist would get out of BDSM and the Daddy/Little Girl dynamic. The world she brings to life flows between the universal concerns of an everywoman to an Alice/*Through the Looking-Glass* insight into the porn industry, full of character and erotic detail. At all points her writing is honest, fascinating, hot and at points romantic without being schmaltzy, an all round great read."

SOPHIE MORGAN, *Sunday Times* bestselling author of *The Diary of a Submissive*

Daddy

a memoir

Daddy

a memoir

.

Madison Young

with a foreword by **Annie Sprinkle**

THIS IS A GENUINE BARNACLE BOOK

A Barnacle Book | Rare Bird Books
453 South Spring Street, Suite 531
Los Angeles, CA 90013
abarnaclebook.com
rarebirdbooks.com

Set in Goudy Old Style
Printed in the United States
Distributed in the U.S. by Publishers Group West

10 9 8 7 6 5 4 3 2 1

Publisher's Cataloging-in-Publication data

Young, Madison.
    Daddy : a memoir / Madison Young / with a foreword by Annie
Sprinkle.
    p. cm.
    ISBN 978-0-9854902-8-7

1. Young, Madison. 2. Pornography—United States—Case studies. 3.
Sex-oriented businesses—United States—Employees—Biography. 4.
Bondage (Sexual behavior). 5. Fetishism (Sexual behavior). 6. Sex
customs—United States—Case studies. 7. Fathers and daughters—Biog-
raphy. 8. Feminism—United States. 9. Sexual minorities—United States.
I. Sprinkle, Annie. II. Title.

HQ472.U6 Y68 2013
363.4/7—dc23

*For the quiet girl in the corner waiting for the moment
to sound her voice. Follow your truth.*

"We are like sculptors, constantly carving out of others the image we long for, need, love or desire, often against reality, against their benefit, and always, in the end, a disappointment, because it does not fit them."

—Anaïs Nin

Foreword

H<small>I</small>. I'M A<small>NNIE</small> S<small>PRINKLE</small> and I'll be your guide into the journey that is this book. Think of me as your sparkly good witch welcoming you to a magical, kinky kingdom where a beautiful feminist porn princess, Madison Young, tries to win the heart—and cock—of a handsome, charming, sexy prince, Sir James Mogul. There are no lions, tigers, or bears. That's kids stuff. This kingdom is for adults only. There are sex slaves, bondage babes, and fire breathing green-eyed monsters. Oh my! We are going way, way, way over the rainbow. Just wait until you find out who is really running the show from behind the curtain! And it's not Daddy!

So why did Madison Young ask me to be the one to welcome you into her life story and first book? First, I am Madison's "kinky fairy godmother," and she is my darling "porn-art daughter." We met nine years ago when she was curating an exhibit for her very own art gallery, Femina Potens. She called me up and asked to show some of my work. I loaned her a large photograph I had made of a naked woman with a full beard, crucified on a cross. We have been collaborating in art, and in life, ever since, and have become family. I adore her! Second, a long time ago (1973-1995), on the isle of Manhattan, I was a reigning "Queen of Kink." I made porn movies, fetish videos, and worked at the Hell Hole Hospital as a dom, sub, and nasty nurse. On weekends I haunted the Hell Fire Club where I cast many sexy spells. Eventually I transitioned into a life of experimental art, sex education, and doing theater about my life. You see, I helped pave the kinky brick road that Madison would follow, follow, follow early in her career. Madison has since paved an all-new kinky brick road uniquely her own. It's a vastly improved, high-tech super highway, which many newbie pleasure artists today follow, follow, follow. Madison has gone from a bondage princess to today's reigning Queen of Kink, and a premier body based performance artist and successful gallerist of edgy art. She carries the fiery torch with great pride, wisdom, and grace.

So, before you slip into this bedtime story and fondle its sensuous pages...before you savor its juicy details... allow me to make a few suggestions. Take what you like and leave the rest.

Have no expectations. Because this book probably won't be what you expect.

Keep an open mind. Taboos will be broken. Gettin' all judgmental is no fun, and it doesn't feel good. So try and keep an open mind, at least until you get to the end of the story.

Open your heart and feel Madison Young's love flow from these pages. This book is Madison's gift to you. Let yourself receive it.

Savor the "naughty bits." Warning! Parts of this tale/tail are sexually explicit! Go ahead, enjoy 'em!

Be grateful for your freedoms. There are plenty of countries whose governments absolutely would not allow this material into the hands of its citizens. How privileged are we?

Don't let this book make you feel sexually inadequate. Few people can outkink my darling porn daughter! She's a fierce BDSM gladiator, boldly going where few women dare. James is a master alchemist of sexual ecstasy. Do not compare yourself. Few of us are at their level.

Wear sexy outfits while reading this book. Especially glittery red high heeled slippers you can click together. Or simply wear rope. You will feel like you are there!

Check out Madison and James' work online. You can actually view the erotica, porn, and art Madison writes about. You will know the real life back-stories.

If after you read this book, you would like to meet Madison and James in the flesh, check out their workshops, appearances, and performances. Mail them a card, pop them an email, offer them gigs, send them presents! They are mythic characters but relatively accessible—if you are worthy.

Do not try these advanced BDSM techniques at home, unless you are properly trained. They can be dangerous! This said, the training is a helluva lot of fun, so sign up!

Now just follow the kinky brick road, and see what happens. Can Madison Young win the heart of Sir James? How does Sir James get so many women to kneel at his feet and submit to his titillating tortures? How does James' magic camera spin digital images into gold? Can Madison maintain her feminist identity and woman of power status while bottoming to a man? Will Sir James drink the potion and fall down the rabbit hole? What will Madison do when she gets pregnant? A baby in the life of the royal couple of kink? That's really edgy! Who's Daddy anyway?

This is a story about sexual fantasies becoming realities. It is a rare peek into the life of one very special woman who has made sexuality her life's path and work. This is also very much a story about family, self-awareness, and about gaining wisdom through excess. I can vouch for its authenticity. I was there. This story is honest, and true.

It has been my honor to be your good witch to welcome you on this journey. Now go! Before the Wicked Witch shows up.

—Annie Sprinkle

With Your Consent

I WILL TAKE YOU on a journey. We will journey together, giving and taking, experiencing pain and pleasure; you as the reader, I as the read. I lay my heart bare, simple, raw, beating, human, and emotional with truth of honesty and vulnerability, fear and heroism. I offer you myself—a piece of me, not all of me—a slice to connect with, to touch, to feel. I cannot hear the consenting "yes" seep from your lips, but by the simple turn of this page you will be physically consenting to this journey, to this scene, between you and I. I feel your eyes upon my words. Consider carefully the risks, the beauty, the parts of your psyche that you will be allowing me into; the energy that you will be sharing with me as you clutch these pages in your damp, sweaty hands and go further, exploring your depths and mine. Know that this is a carefully constructed container in which you and I are equals. We play different roles and have different histories written on our hearts, but in the construction of this, here in these negotiations of consent, we are equals. If in your reading things get too intense, if you want to slow down, if you need to dog-ear my pages and get a drink of water, do so. Listen to your body; we will pace ourselves as we explore our edges. If you need to use a safeword, do so, close the book, leave the room, go for a walk, and breathe deeply. I will not take offense. Instead, I will respect you even more for knowing yourself, for communicating your needs and meeting them. I give of myself in these pages with trust, honesty, intimacy, and respect. I write because I am a writer. I speak because too many are silent. I make space for human error because we are flesh and blood. With love we grow.

Part 1

1

W ITH THE FIRST BLUSH of sunrise seeping through the clouds outside the airplane window, I settle my heavy, sleepless eyes on the horizon. Between my toddler's teething and late-night preparations for the coming weekend's conference, sleep is far away from my reality. I take slow sips from a plastic cup fizzing with an iced energy drink, and gaze over at my fifteen-month-old daughter peacefully asleep in her father's arms. This is a rare moment of solitude in the flurry of activity that constitutes our lives. Hopeful for a moment like this, I had armed myself with a stack of magazines to browse during the flight. I thumb through my stash: *Entrepreneur* ("How to Launch a Disruptive Company"), *Parents* ("No-Scream Discipline"), *Bloomberg Businessweek* ("XXX: Three letters could make the Internet safe from porn and more lucrative for pornographers," with neon illustrations of women in fishnets and handcuffs pole dancing around the large pink X's of the cover headline). I settle on a copy of *The Atlantic* with a photograph of a working mother in a tweed skirt holding a briefcase;

a ten-month-old doe-eyed, shirtless baby with chestnut colored ringlets sits in the briefcase, staring at the reader.

On the plane, sitting in the aisle seat, I feel my body tense. My stomach knots and suddenly lurches. I reach for a stiff white paper bag in the seat back pocket in front of me and open it, just in time. The taste of acid sours my mouth, burning my gums. I sit back and, with my eyes closed, take a deep swig of the fizzing energy drink. A passenger in the row across from me leans over and says, "Keeping your eyes on the horizon helps with air sickness."

I nod—"Hey, thanks"—and take another pull from the sweet, icy beverage, then ring for the flight attendant to remove the sloshing bag of vomit from my lap before it triggers another round of nausea. I look over at my daughter, still sound asleep. James is cradling Emma close to his chest, her drool wets his T-shirt as his drool soaks the airline provided pillow.

Paging through the magazine, I land on an essay about Jacqueline Bouvier Kennedy and John F. Kennedy that details recently released audio interviews with Jackie about their relationship. It's a flawed fairytale that feels achingly familiar. *Why is it that it feels so easy, so natural, to fall in love with Camelot?* Jackie's descriptions of John as a dashing daddy, a hero, and a beloved Prince, mirrors the words that I might use to describe the father of my child: Jackie spoke of John as an excellent father. He would read to the children at night and the Oval Office was always open for them to pop into. Even castles house families.

When the world feels like it's just too much to bear, like it would take a superhero to handle the chaos of everyday life, it seems essential to have an entity to look up to, someone that can make everything okay with the touch of their powerful hand and a kiss on the forehead. Some people have prayer; they believe in God or a higher power. I believe in Daddy.

My heart begins to race as I read further into the article knowing that the author will remind me of my shattered fairytale fantasy. I look over at Daddy as tears well up in my eyes. I read about one of John's mistresses, Mimi Alford, a secretarial intern for the president. The president's indiscretions remind me of my partner's not so distant infidelity. It's been nearly a year and a half since the incident, but we are still healing, and in this moment I feel the pain and betrayal that Jackie must have felt, that my own mother must have felt when my father strayed from their marriage. I feel the pain, jagged and hard to swallow, catching in my airway, making it hard to breathe.

I continue to read, but I want to stop. I want to close my eyes and escape into the safe, fantasy world that has protected me so many times in the past. I know how to get there. It's an escape that I am familiar with, blocking out everything around me and transcending to a safe space, enveloped in safe arms. I finish the article and close the magazine, tucking it into the pocket of the airplane seat in front of me. I exhale, close my eyes, and quietly whisper to myself:

Be gentle with yourself. Be gentle with others. Be gentle with the world around you.

It is a mantra I'd first come up with while navigating my new baby girl through emotional peaks and tantrums. I found the phrases mutually beneficial for my own turmoil and my own fresh wounds.

I recall the words of the therapist that I have been seeing for about six months. Alex would say, "Name the feeling. Allow it to exist. Recognize its existence and how it is affecting your body. Breathe, and give yourself permission to let go of that feeling." It is painful to venture forward with a partner with whom trust must slowly rebuild. I recognize Jackie's pain as my own and as I exhale a deep breath, I feel that emotion leave my body, plunging the toxic residue of past resentment, jealousy, and fear from my body. I close my eyes knowing that it will take many a deep breath before this ache is dull, before I can fully accept the words "I love you" from my partner again without doubt. But there is a space opening in my heart, a small crevice, and with every deep breath, with every deep kiss and long embrace, the space opens a little more. In that space there is a new us growing, fumbling awkwardly at times through date nights and dark bedrooms, with buttons on blouses and impossible bra straps. But when his hands find their way to my quivering body, we fit neatly, passionately together. We are lovers from a past life with muscle memory in our fingers and hips and lips and cock, which all know just how to dance with one another. I breathe and I make space for the us that exists now because I believe in love.

I want to believe that we are all a little more heroic than we are flawed, that the honorable role of Daddy does exist. I believe in my Daddy.

SOME OF MY EARLIEST memories are of my parents' divorce. My father left when I was four. In response, my mother threw things and screamed, and my dad tried to deflect her beating fists and flailing legs. I hid behind the couch with Miss Piggy earmuffs over my ears and closed my eyes. I hoped I could make all of the fighting disappear by wiping away the sights and sounds of their brawl.

When my dad left, I somehow knew he wasn't coming back. I cried, and burrowed my head and body under pink covers, sobbing until I fell asleep. Hours later, I groggily awoke to the scent of pork chops, fresh buttermilk biscuits, and au gratin potatoes. I was hungry, my young body worn out from the emotional hurricane and grasping for an understanding of what had just happened. My baby brother, only a year old, was always crying. My only memory of him from this time is of a loud, faceless being that pulled my mom's attention away from me.

When my mom had screamed at my dad earlier, she swore. There were profanities and words that flew over my four-year-old head, but the one word that stuck with me was *prostitute*. It felt full of power and shame, and I saw how it enraged my mother as it fell with disgust from her trembling mouth.

"Mom? Mom? Hey, Mom?" I reached across the round oak kitchen table and tugged at my mom's magenta satin sleeve while my mother spooned mashed sweet potatoes into my sobbing baby brother's mouth.

"Yes, Tina. What is it?" My mother sighed deeply and closed her eyes, emotionally exhausted, not really ready for the question itching at my young curious mouth.

"What's prostitute?" I asked, biting my lip and squinting my eyes as I struggled to pronounce the awkward word. It sounded a bit like a church or a deadly disease.

"What? Where did you hear that word, Tina?" My mother dropped the sweet potatoes onto the table and pointed the baby spoon in my direction with great concern.

"You yelling at Dad." I diverted my eyes in shame and stared into a plate full of now unappetizing dinner. My stomach was unsettled by the tension I'd inadvertently started.

"Hmmph...your dad has paid a woman to sleep with him. When a man pays a woman to sleep with him in his bed that makes her a prostitute." My mother's tone was bitter and pained, sharp and prickly. Perhaps she was too exhausted to play make-believe or feed me a story.

"Why's Dad sleepin' with a prostitute? Daddy sleeps in our house. Right, Mom?" In my four-year-old mind I imagined my charitable father extending our family bed in the same fashion I had shared a sleeping bag with one of my Girl Scout members or friends from kindergarten. I hoped this prostitute didn't mind Dad's snoring.

"That's a good question, Tina. Your dad seems to think he's in love." My mother's voice was pained as the palms of her hands ran up the landscape of her face, grasping at the roots of her platinum blonde hair.

"Maybe she's poor? Maybe Dad is helping?" It seemed obvious to me that my father was providing a place to sleep for a woman who didn't have a home. *Right?* Why couldn't my mother see that? Why was she so upset?

"Your father just wants to help himself! Can we please talk about this later, Tina? Finish your dinner and head off to bed, ya hear?"

"Mom! I want Daddy! Call him, please? I wanna tell him something. I wanna tell him good night."

My mom led me into her bedroom to the rotary phone and dialed a long string of numbers that she had scribbled down on a sheet of paper, numbers that might reach my dad. I needed to hear my dad's voice, I wanted to hear him say, "Tina, everything is going to be okay, I promise." I watched the phone with bated breath as the rotary dial made its slow way around in circles, hoping to conjure up comfort from my dad.

"Come on, Richard, pick up," my mom mumbled under her breath. The phone rang, but there was no answer.

"Tina, your dad isn't there." I glared at her in disbelief and ran to my room. I sat on my bed sobbing and holding a photo of my dad and me playing in the autumn leaves earlier that year. Suddenly, the world felt cold and snowy and everything had changed.

I BREATHE DEEPLY IN an attempt to settle my recently emptied stomach. Out the window now, I can see light, doughy formations suspended by the dozen in clear blue sky. I imagine sinking my teeth into them, envisioning the buttermilk biscuits my mother made the night my dad had left. That taste always makes me yearn for one of my dad's big bear hugs.

After having watched me regurgitate my morning muffin, the woman sitting across the aisle on our international flight felt shared intimacy. She sensed my physical vulnerability and, somewhere over Washington state, decided she wanted to talk. I sensed the need for human contact boiling up inside. She couldn't contain herself.

Harmless airplane small talk can be a dangerous situation for me. The first questions out of strangers' mouths tend to be: "Are you from here?" and "How old is your little girl?" and "What do you do?" Our family identity is complicated. For me, the phrase Little Girl conjures different imagery than it probably does for this upbeat new mother of two from Los Angeles. She recently became a grandmother. Her youngest daughter is thirty-two and her granddaughter is five weeks old. After the birth of her two daughters, she decided to stay home and raise the kids, and now she is full of pride and excitement over the arrival of her daughter's little girl and wants to know, "How old is your little girl?"

The Little Girl inside me is eight years old; she never ages. She is a symbolic element of innocence of a time when sitting at Daddy's feet or on Daddy's lap really did solve all of your problems, a time when Daddy could make the world better. My Daddy and I have been in a relationship for seven years.

Daddy and Little Girl are dominant/submissive dynamics that define my relationship with my partner, James. I am my Daddy's Little Girl. James is my Daddy. Emma is our daughter, which is something else entirely. For James and me, this relationship reflects a part of our psyche that desires to be nurturing and accepting of the love and care a skillful guiding mentor can provide while he leads his Little Girl through life's lessons. Daddy creates a space for me to feel safe in my Little Girl role. He holds a space for surrender, a space for unconditional love, and the expression of my truest self.

We embrace our desires in these roles, as well as the roles of the authoritarian and disciplinarian. I feel warmth in my cunt when I earn a gold star on our discipline and behavior chart. My nipples tingle while we shop for back to school clothes at Bloomingdale's, Daddy's eyes surveying my body as he zips up my dress in the dressing room. There is power that I surrender to in this role. There is also power gained. I am able to abandon my outside world responsibilities in exchange for an hour or two of being completely present and connected with Daddy. We construct a safe space for our unorthodox, mutually pleasurable power exchange to exist in, and it feels incredibly true to slip into these natural roles. There is comfort in obedience and following our own rules, a dependable structure that allows us to explore each other.

With dominant/submissive power play—specifically within our Daddy and Little Girl dynamic—we revel in cerebral stimulation. By slipping into these well-defined roles of our relational dynamic, we deconstruct society's imposed power dynamics for our erotic pleasure. This happens well before Daddy has physically penetrated any of my available orifices. For me, this role of Little Girl provides a sense of comfort, excitement, and arousal all at the same time.

When I was nineteen, my first boyfriend gave me a birthday card that read, *Eight is great. Never lose your magic and love of play.* He nurtured my Little Girl with stuffed animals and trinkets from the Winnie-the-Pooh store, trips to the ice cream parlor, jungle gym adventures at the nearby park, and playing hopscotch with pigtails. Eight felt like a magical age for me, a time when I was little enough to be Daddy's Little Girl, but not so young that I couldn't earn Daddy's approving kiss on the forehead or express my frustrations and disappointments through tantrums.

I'm not always a Little Girl, and I'm not always honest with strangers. So, "What do I do?" There isn't a clear job description for my line of work, or a box that I fit in neatly. I'm an entrepreneur, president of a sex toy company, sole proprietor of a production company that makes feminist erotic films for couples, and artistic director of a nonprofit arts organization that focuses on the intersections of sexuality and identity. In short, I'm a Sex Expert.

The flight attendant interrupts my musing with a customs form.

"Are you all one family? You only need one customs form per family."

I smile and nod, "We are a family."

The airplane loudspeaker informs us that the plane will land momentarily and asks us to return our tray tables and seats to their upright positions. The woman across from me waits expectantly for my answers. Emma starts to stir and whimper; her slight sounds and movements wake up James and she starts to cry, her ears beginning to pop from the descent. The shaggy-haired blue-eyed toddler looks at me: "Ma ma ma ma."

"Come here, sweetheart." I say. "Shhhhhh...shhhh, I know. It hurts Emma's ears, huh?"

Emma rubs her ears and nuzzles into my chest, trying to suckle. I remove my left breast from my low cut, V-neck shirt and offer it to her. I look at my daughter, with love, and kiss her on the forehead. With a deep inhale I look up at the woman in the row across from ours.

"Well, I'm an artist who works on surreal landscapes and this little lady here is the love of my life, my daughter, Emma. She is fifteen months old," I say.

Having crossed through clouds and sky and country lines, we start our descent into Vancouver

International Airport. Thousands of miles away, in the heartland of America, my dad is starting his workday with his new family. He probably kisses his wife and now four-month-old daughter goodbye and grabs a cold Coca-Cola for the road, his car already warming up in the driveway. He knows better than to drink soda for breakfast. His body has warned him time and time again with numerous painful kidney stones. My dad is a man whose rough, calloused hands tell the story of his life. He drives a company pickup truck, large enough for a car seat in the back, and with a bed hearty enough to carry the tree limbs and brush that's hauled away after a day of work. Knowing him, the cab of the truck is encrusted with sawdust and bits of dried leaves. The truck displays the Madison Tree Service emblem—the family business of landscaping and tree care. It will be humid today; it's the middle of August in southern Ohio, which means he's surely dressed in a T-shirt and jeans. After a morning spent paying visits to lifelong clients, he will eat salted homegrown tomatoes for lunch, then prune a couple of pear or magnolia trees before checking up on the crews he sent out to do the big jobs and check for rookie mistakes.

My dad's short, curly, blond hair and reddish-blond beard give him a coarse appearance—an amusing counterpoint to his jester-like antics and a vocabulary that rivals that of Lewis Carroll. He used to refer to me and my brother as Lizard Lips and Snaggletooth, and could recite rhymes and riddles about Old Dan Tucker. I have been known to break into limericks of my own, much to my friends' amusement. I still remember my dad's riddles, and they have come in handy now that I have a child of my own. My father is a hero to me, he taught me the value of hard work and a love of play. Though our lives have drifted far apart, one thing connects us—we're always armed with a bag full of rope.

My rope is neatly coiled and rests patiently in my carry-on bag, waiting for James—my Daddy—to hold it in his skilled and calloused hands and cinch its toothy texture around my naked skin.

Whenever we travel, the security agents at the airport examine the fine jute rope coiled in my carry-on bag.

"Are you into rock climbing?"

DADDY AND I SPOONED close to one another on our queen size mattress. The warmth of his long, slender body felt comforting to my small, curvy frame. His arms cradled me close to his furry chest and I felt the scruff on his face against the nape of my neck. I slowly opened my eyes. Sometime in the night I stole the covers, nothing new, but my feet were still cold. They're always cold. I rubbed my icy toes up and down Daddy's scruffy calves. Daddy stirred in bed and his hands traced my neck down to my back and grabbed ahold of my hips tightly. Daddy ground his cock against my ass and I felt it pulsing, throbbing. His hand grasped a chunk of my thick strawberry-blonde hair as he pulled my head back and whispered into my ear, "Get your ass in the air, Slut."

"Yes, Daddy."

I turned over and stuck my ass high in the air, folded my arms behind my back and faced the side. Daddy threw a single strand of fibrous jute rope down beside my face. He rubbed my face in the rope, teasing me. We both knew that we didn't have time for bondage that morning, but he indulged my senses in the scent and taste of one of my favorite sensuous pleasures: rope. My eyes closed and Daddy's heavy hands came down on my ass, hard.

"Thank you, Sir. Thank you, Daddy. God that feels so good, Daddy. You're making my cunt so wet, my love." His hands found their way between my legs and he filled my hole one finger at a time, then he flipped me over onto my back.

"Would my Little Girl like a nice hard fuck from Daddy?" he said as he stretched my legs back toward my head.

"Yes, Daddy. Please fuck me, Daddy," I said as his long, hard cock penetrated my wet cunt. Those first long, slow strokes caused me to sink my nails into our covers, reveling in the teasing pleasure of having his delicious cock inside of me. Then his fucking gained momentum, pounding deep. He lowered his mouth to my breast and sucked with great pressure.

"Please, Daddy. Please, may I come?" I begged of him.

"Yes, come for Daddy, Slut."

My cunt clenched tightly around his cock and I screamed out in deep pleasure. Daddy continued to push hard and deep in my cunt as his breathing escalated in speed and he released a deep moaning orgasm and came onto my belly, all over the stretch marks from the birth of our daughter. I scooped up his come and fisted it into my mouth with love and devotion. I looked up with puppy dog eyes, "I love you, Daddy."

"I love you, too, Slut." He kissed my head and mouth, sending me off with a gentle, loving slap on my face. "Now go jump in the shower. Our Em will be up any minute."

I headed off to shower, covered in my Daddy's juices and dripping in my own. The hot shower washed over me, steam filling up the bathroom, and I lathered citrus scented body wash in my hands and over my body.

Toweling off and slipping into a navy blue polka dot vintage dress, I heard Emma start to cry, "Down. Down. Ma ma ma ma. Down," from her room.

"Mama's coming, sweetheart. Did my little muffin have a good sleep?" I asked as I picked her up from her crib and placed her on the changing table.

"Book. Mama. Go. Book." *She knows what she wants!* I laughed and changed her diaper as she squirmed, relentless in her pursuit to get to the bookshelf.

Emma reached for a colorful orange book. I pulled it off the shelf and thumbed through it, trying to read each page before she turned to the next. The book, *10,000 Dresses*, features a young, transgender girl who wants to wear dresses, but her parents don't understand. Emma pointed at the illustrations.

"'S zatt?" Emma's finger landed on a dress made of lilies that hangs from a red valentine staircase.

"That is a dress made of flowers. This little girl dreams that she can have a dress just like that one. That dress will make her feel pretty and cozy. It's magic," I said. Emma picked up the book and brought it to her nose, inhaling and exhaling in rapid succession, attempting to smell the picture of the flower dress.

"'S zatt?" Emma quickly turned the page, almost ripping it clear out of the book.

"A mommy. I'm your mommy. Ma-ma. Everyone has different types of parents or people who care for them. Not everyone has a mommy, but this character does, and you do. We all have people who love us. And I love, love, love you!"

"'S zatt?" Emma pointed to the image of the dad outside mowing the lawn.

"Well, that is a daddy. Da-da. You have a da-da." I lift Emma up so she can peek out her window at her da-da in the garden. "A daddy loves you and protects you and lets you know that everything is going to be okay. But sometimes da-da will fall and go boom."

Emma opened her mouth wide, "Ooooo. No boom!"

"Yes. Sometimes we all go boom. Even daddies. But we get back up because we are brave. This daddy in the book is falling down right now." I tried to explain as best I could and she seemed to understand, nodding and flipping to the next page.

"What's that?" she asked, pointing to an illustration of the protagonist's hippie seamstress neighbor, the first person who honors the young girl's gender identity.

"That is 'chosen family.'" I told her. I knew she didn't comprehend this term yet, but I wanted her to know that family does not only exist among blood relatives, and that in queer communities and families such as ours we often search for belonging. "That person makes the little girl feel really cozy."

2

JAMES PUSHES THE CART full of luggage through the Vancouver airport: suitcases, backpacks, bags full of children's toys, and toys for Mommy and Daddy. Emma's car seat teeters on the mountain of essential objects for work and play, for the care of both a toddler and her parents. Since Emma's birth, I have been slowly reintroducing myself to the public as my identity, work priorities, and availability shift from my postpartum stage to some version of working motherhood. This is our first work trip attempting to travel as a family and we're headed to Vancouver Edge, a weekend-long event featuring workshops, presentations, and roundtable discussions on the topics of relationships, gender, and sexuality.

My first attempts at heading back to work were comical. At six weeks postpartum my stretch marks and pregnancy weight lingered like battle scars. I stood before the camera naked and awkward, attempting to seduce the viewer with my eyes and suppress the insecurities that were flaring through my psyche as I touched my furry red cunt and leaked milk from heavy, lopsided, and engorged breasts. I found my stride again on the other side of the camera and in a lecture hall of eager university students. I was a new, more maternal creature, no longer the girl next door, and I didn't need to pretend to be.

When Emma turned a year of age, I began traveling from city to city a week out of the month, teaching sexuality workshops and directing erotic films. Daddy stayed home, caring for Emma, splashing in the baby pool, and planting tomatoes in the desert sun of Southern California—where we built an island of family, far from the intrusive gaze of fans and the supportive encouragement of his community. We were finding who we were again in that quiet desert.

The Vancouver Edge BDSM—bondage, dominance/submission, sadism/masochism—conference is a chance for me and Daddy to be together as a family, to go to work together building community again, and to return from work together (to our temporary home, the hotel) greeted by our little bean, Emma. I'm excited for Daddy and for us; we deserve this.

"Do we know who is picking us up or what they look like?" James asks, scanning the crowd.

"No. I'm not sure. But they know what we look like." I smile, trying to steer toward a clear, visible area where our ride might recognize us. I'm unsure if they'll recognize me. I have glasses on and my hair pulled back; my face is free of makeup. I'm wearing a pink seventies vintage T-shirt that read "Daddy's Little Girl" over form-fitting skinny jeans and a kelly green hoodie. Not exactly the femme fatale my film image projects. James, luckily, is clearly the Mr. Mogul of his many on-screen performances. It's impossible not to notice his tall, slender 6'1" frame. My petite body often gets lost among the crowd.

Our driver is a conference volunteer, Daniel, a tall gentleman with short dark hair and a gentle demeanor. Daniel's day job is organizing and participating in triathlons. In the kink community and among friends, he is referred to lovingly as Moose.

"Tina, over here!" Moose shouts and we muscle our way through people milling aimlessly in passenger pickup. I guess I was recognizable despite my "nerdy exhausted mama" disguise.

I quickly walk up to the gentleman, Emma bouncing up and down in my arms. She wants to get down and play, but she will have to wait.

"Hi there. Only my mother calls me Tina. I'm Madison, this is little Emma, and James Mogul," I motion to James.

"Oh, sorry about that. It's a pleasure to meet you, Madison. I'm kind of new to this whole thing so I'm still figuring out how this alternative name thing works. But folks like to call me Moose."

"Pleasure to meet you, Moose," James extends his hand and we follow Moose out to his black SUV in the parking garage.

"I picked up a little something for Emma." Moose hands us a plush toy moose clothed in a red sweatshirt with a white maple leaf decal. Emma squeezes the moose tight in her hands and brings its face to hers to give it a loud kiss, "Muah!"

"How sweet!" I say, with a smile, and snap some photographs of Emma and her new friend.

We stop at the community center, where the conference is being held. We've been up since 4:00 A.M. and our evening probably won't come to a conclusion before midnight. More coffee is definitely necessary. I cross my fingers that Emma will not need to nurse from my soon-to-be-caffeine-laden breasts. Emma has been self-weaning, but still needs the comfort of her mother's milk throughout our daily transitions. She taps at my chest, pulling my shirt aside and seeking closeness as she asks for "nurse nurse." Her mouth latches onto my breast and suckles, soothing life's little disturbances and pains—an overly tired body, painful teething gums, aching growing bones, and bruises from her toddling body toppling to the ground while playing a game of chase with the stray cat that we have adopted and named Bukowski. Life's little bumps and bruises are a regular occurrence for our adventurous child.

We pull up to the community center and Moose begins unloading supplies: bottles of water, badge tags, gift bags of promotional materials, wooden paint stirrers printed with the name of a local BDSM store, condoms from STI testing facilities, and pamphlets on BDSM safety spilling out of the trunk of his car. While Moose is unloading, James takes Emma to a park across the street. After being confined to a seated position for so long she needs to run. I grab a coffee at the café next to the community center and check out the space in which we will be teaching.

As I sip my coffee, I wander through the halls of the community center, a bustle of activity. Volunteers fill the space in a race against time to set up for the weekend-long conference. I find a chair and sit down in the corner to watch the community come together. It's a preconference hustle that I am very familiar with after ten years of organizing LGBTQ programming at my own nonprofit arts organization, Femina Potens. I watch the various supplies and literature for the conference being distributed. Dental dams, gloves, and condoms fill clear plastic containers on a display table. Three women behind the table unload boxes of badges and begin printing nametags to slip into each plastic case. The next morning, those badges will dangle from attendees' necks as the rooms fill with a diverse crowd seeking connection, community and education to better their relationships.

During the conference the attendees might not exhibit much fanfare, with the exception of the presentations. The attendees and presenters could be mistaken for those attending a technology conference: average in appearance, perhaps with brightly colored hair, but often simple enough not to draw the attention of coworkers at their day jobs. The presentations could incorporate kinky, feminist porn projections or demonstrations in which a nude woman suspended by rope is pierced with needles or whipped while she releases high-pitched screams. There will be first-timers, young women who parade into the conference in a corset-inspired top from Hot Topic or a naughty schoolgirl uniform; there would be the elders of the leather community, dressed in leather vests, leather pants, or leather corsets and decorated with pins and badges from past events. For the most part, BDSM is not about pageantry or plumage. It's about action, interaction, and experience.

I thumb through the conference catalog of the weekend's events, workshops, and roundtable discussions. "Rope Torture as Spiritual Cleansing" by Boss Bondage—his picture is a blue-collar hefty gentleman wearing a trucker hat, focused on complex knot work that he is using to rig his female submissive. Another class, taught by a butch woman in a denim jacket, is enticing people with the title, "Care and Feeding of the Top: Now that You've Caught One, How Do You Keep It?" A sexy silver-haired transgender man named Mac offers a class on "Tenderness and Discipline: How to Balance Them as a Daddy." Our good friend and colleague Lochai has photo and class offerings staring at me from the opposite page that make me smile as I recall the shoot that Lochai's presenter's photo was taken from. You can partially see my naked and bound body bowed in the child's pose position in the picture. Lochai is wearing a nice blue button-up shirt with his favorite kilt and looking straight into the camera, rope falling from his hands and looping toward the lens. He is honest and solid, an unwavering rock of support.

Lochai, James, and I were all educators and artists before we became performers and directors. In our porn work we had tried to gracefully bring the authenticity of the BDSM community forth for the masses.

"I've been making toys for the leather community for the past fifteen years. I do it all by hand. This is naturally dyed leather." I watch as a local leather maker sets out her wares on the table: hand crafted strap-on harnesses, paddles, and floggers. She picks up a reddish-orange leather paddle, "This one is what I call the real Canadian experience. It's dyed with red maple leaves." She beams with pride in her craftsmanship. I'm impressed. It reminds me of the difference between this community-focused BDSM conference and the industry-focused fetish conventions that I frequented in the years before I became a mother, when I was still searching for my career path.

At a fetish convention, the main attraction is the stars of BDSM and fetish-related erotic DVDs and sites. They sit at booths and take photos with huge numbers of fans, sign autographed photos of themselves where they appear bound in advanced-level yoga positions that look like a dirty adult circus—contortionist meets aerialist. Attendees circulate in lavish costumes that

include leather chaps and vests, superhero outfits of
latex and rubber, Bettie Page look-alikes wielding whips,
and, of course, Bernie the pink bondage bunny. Bernie
is a furry, an individual with a kink for dressing up in
fursuits. In Bernie's case his fursuit of choice is a giant
pink Easter Bunny in a red rubber ball gag, leather
collar, and wrist restraints. He annually attends fetish
conventions and poses in candid photographs with his
favorite fetish performers and kinky porn stars.

In the chaos of commercial fetish conventions, I
was always the exception to the rule. I make feminist
pornography. I listen to women and couples and they
tell me their fantasies and I create a safe space for
them to play out those fantasies. My focus on genuine
pleasure, empowered performance, and positive
relationships made me an advocate for authenticity
in a world made of plastic; in that world, I was an
organic farmer among McDonald's cheeseburgers. I
always felt tired at those commercial conventions. I
would inhale the stale smell of the convention hall air
and look around at the familiar sights: booth babes,
fanatics, people running from one table to another,
giddy as schoolchildren to show off autographed
photos of their favorite stars.

Thank goodness that's over. Now I feel at home
among a community of familiar faces that facilitate
pleasurable and healthy relationships within BDSM. I'm
not the only organic farmer at this market, and that feels
pretty damn good. Moose puts his hand on my shoulder
breaking me from my reverie, and I look up.

"All ready. Let's get you and your family back to the hotel for an hour of rest before the presenter's dinner."

Moose sweeps me up and leads me out to the car where we find James buckling Emma into her car seat while she nibbles on half of his grilled cheese sandwich. She opens her mouth wide to sink it into the toasty wheat bread and gooey cheese, then rubs her tummy, making a monster sound.

RAINY NIGHT FALLS ON the city, and James and I are standing in the hotel suite with Emma and the babysitter. Emma is running around the suite exploring every crevice, opening every drawer. James pulls some rope out of his kink bag and ties the drawers closed before Emma can smash her little fingers rolling the dresser drawers open and closed, open and closed. Daddy ties them closed. No more open.

James gives Elizabeth, our sitter, the run down. We have to explain the details of Emma's dinner, bottle, bedtime, and books ritual. Emma, freshly bathed and in her pajamas, is clearly excited by the new environment.

"Make sure to keep the bathroom door closed. The bathroom can be dangerous," I say, nervous. On the television, Canadian children's program, *Max and Ruby*, is playing.

I quickly slip into a black Marilyn Monroe-style cocktail dress and black patent leather high heels, which I'd kept after a shoot for *Shoe Sex*, an erotic film for the true high heel fetishist.

I perform my five minute makeover: pull my hair back, apply classic red lipstick, a quick dab of concealer under the eyes, a puff of talc-free powder foundation, a smudge of pink crème blush on my cheek bones, a whisk of the waterproof mascara wand and presto chango, Mama's ready for a night on the town. "How do I look?"

"Beautiful. Are we ready to go?"

"Let me give Em a kiss goodnight. Mama loves you, Emma. We will be back in a little bit," and we're out the door. It's the first time we've had an evening to ourselves in six months. With a baby, an arts organization, and a brutal economy, we needed to cut our expenses when Emma arrived. Date nights were put on hold and we moved from urban life in San Francisco to live with James' brother in a large suburban house in Southern California. We know our move is a temporary one, but the lack of privacy is frustrating. It isn't really possible to receive a nice hard flogging or loving lashing with James' brother in the other room zoning out to *Dancing with the Stars*. We had been looking forward to this conference not only as a re-entry into the kink scene after our parental hiatus, but also as a moment to get lost in each other and reconnect, in an effort to release some of the tension that's built up over recent months. We love Emma with all of our hearts, but Mommy and Daddy need playtime, too.

Andie, the coordinator of the BDSM conference, is driving us to the VIP Meet the Presenters dinner. A sweet woman in her mid-twenties with dyed red hair and glasses, Andie is short, round, and anxious.

The wet cobblestone streets make Vancouver feel both exotic and quaint, with humility quintessential to Canada. After Andie circles nervously around the downtown streets several times, she pulls up to a little alleyway with a discreet restaurant sign. Linked arm in arm, wearing clothing that we hadn't worn since our pre-child days, James and I walk under the cover of an umbrella into the warm, glowing light of the restaurant. In four-inch heels, I have to navigate carefully while we make our way downstairs to the room where the party is being held. Daddy holds my hand to help me balance. Vibrant music and amber lights warm the space where fifty people are sitting around a large table engaged in conversation. Several of them get up from their seats to greet us before we can sit down, welcoming us with a chorus of compliments. As a couple, we are rarely sighted, celebrated icons of dominance and submission that have primarily been in hiding since the birth of Emma.

"We're so happy that you could make it!"—"I'm such a huge fan!"—"Your work on *Training of O* opened my eyes to the world of dominance and submission!"—"Wow! I can't believe it's Mr. Mogul and Madison Young!" It was strange to hear fans refer to James as Mr. Mogul. It originated as my pet name for him, and only after we began performing on camera together did fans and other models started calling him Mr. Mogul. The name still felt intimate between me and my dominant—Mr. Mogul and Slut: names that used to be used in private. I still winced when I heard them in public, part of me resented that strangers had appropriated our private experience into their own fantasies. But I had to come to terms with slices of our private lives becoming public consumables. After all, being integrated into others' fantasies is part of my job.

We took seats positioned next to Lochai and his Little Girl Amy, a twenty-five year old psychology major. Amy had a kink for age play and winning her Daddy's nod of approval. We hadn't seen Lochai since he was fired from KINK over a year ago. Leaving KINK is never easy, whether it's your choice or the company's. KINK is a Disneyland of adult BDSM debauchery housed in an old armory modeled after a Moorish castle. The surreal workplace and production studio is a world of its own, a bubble of myopic disillusions located in the gritty hipster-laden Mission District of San Francisco. Once you've adapted to the all-encompassing work-life of KINK, it's challenging to re-enter the world outside of those walls. Lochai had taken some time to adjust to life outside of KINK, first as a substitute teacher for special needs classes, then in a more permanent position with an insurance company. It was good to see him. Lochai might be an insurance salesman by day, but in Vancouver he was a superstar of the bondage world. James and I, too, had handed over our work-at-home mom and stay-at-home dad badges at the door. We were allowing ourselves a moment to bask in the gratitude and fandom that we earned through years of trying to bring authentic moments to the once void adult industry.

Our waiter circled around to take our drink order. The restaurant was primarily meat, cheese, and wine—a challenge for a sober couple, and for my vegan diet. I settled on a fizzy, sugary drink, a mocktail with pomegranate juice and soda water. The table of kinksters was buzzing with excitement. Most of the attendees were local to Vancouver, but some had traveled from other parts of Canada or driven in from Seattle for the weekend-long event. Many of the submissives wore collars, a symbol of commitment and service. Earned leather fastened around a submissive's neck, leather full of charge and meaning, leather that the submissive had worked for—not just bought with money, but earned through devotion. Some flagged their sexual and kinky preferences through handkerchiefs that were tucked into their right or left back pocket (left signifies a top, right signifies a bottom). The 'hanky code' is complex, with over forty colors and preferences to flag: gray for bondage, green for Daddy; it's a whole language. Green is my favorite color, though there is no longer any need for me to flag for anything or anyone. My Daddy is here, sitting beside me, his hand up my dress.

The woman across from me looks young and shy, but still listens intently to the conversations buzzing around the table, waiting for the right moment. Below her dark brown hair lays a simple, silver locked collar and a low-cut black party dress that looked like it came from Forever 21. Her push-up bra presents plentiful breasts and draws my attention when she timidly opens her mouth to speak.

Her name is Abbey. A young college student majoring in gender and sexuality, Abbey has taken up moonlighting as a fetish model to help pay for her college education and to explore her fetishes onscreen.

"Can I ask you a question? How did you come out to your parents? You know...as kinky...and as being a fetish performer? I just don't think my parents will understand."

I take a sip from my cold drink and slip into the mode of sex educator. This is what I love: coaching individuals toward better communication around sexuality. I am familiar with the situation that Abbey is in; I've been there myself.

"They might not be supportive at first. That's a risk we take. I come from a pretty conservative family so it was challenging at first to talk with my parents about my sexuality and my choice of work. But I didn't feel like I could hide it from them either." In truth, I had left home and was 3,000 miles away in California before I felt courageous enough to start a dialogue with my parents about my identity as a queer kinky woman and my choice to pursue a career in sexuality, a career that didn't just involve talking about sex but also performing in front of the camera.

"You've been in the industry a long time now, though?" Abbey asks. I detect a hint of self-doubt in her questioning.

"I've been in the industry for ten years, so my family has had a long time to digest and become used to my way of life. My mom was furious when I first told her. I think her mind just raced to the worst possible scenario, a fictitious world of guns, drugs, and illicit crime that she thought her daughter was immersed in."

To my mother, performing in porn was an act of desperation and not a position she ever wanted to imagine her daughter in, but she was coming around, slowly but surely.

"You know Abbey, it's not always easy, but I just keep talking with my mom about why I chose to step in front of the camera. I tell her that, you know, what I do is a different kind of pornography."

"Yeah, I think it's so much more powerful when I watch porn with real couples. Like your *Training of O* series with Mr. Mogul...wow! It was like a romance novel come to life. It's a love story." Abbey adjusts her strapless party dress, which has slid down to reveal a peek at her large areola. She tucks her dark brown hair behind her ears, a little embarrassed by her outward display of excitement, and quickly changes the subject: "So what about kink? How did your mom take that?"

"Well, when I came out to my mom as kinky, I faced a lot of the same obstacles." I took a sip of my mocktail and placed my hand over Daddy's hand. I love the look of our hands coupled, and I looked admiringly at my gold and diamond rope ring, remembering the special meaning behind it. I am his; the jewelry is a constant reminder of my service and dedication to our relationship.

"Did she stop speaking to you?" Abbey asks, digging for more information. I'm exhausted and want to bring my attention back to my Daddy.

"No, no. Nothing like that. I guess my mom was concerned primarily with my safety. We all want to know that our kids are safe, physically and emotionally."

After eighteen hours without sleep, I am no longer able to compute or articulate my theories, or solve the problems of the world. It is time for someone else to take charge, to take care of me. My Little Girl wants to play with Daddy.

"But you know my mom and dad probably won't even find the movies that I perform in," she says. "It's not like they are into BDSM." She laughs at the thought of her parents hiding handcuffs and paddles under their bed.

I lean away from my Daddy for one final bit of advice, "Abbey, everything is accessible on the Internet. If you're going to do it, be committed enough to talk to your parents. I have a motto: *Reveal all, fear nothing.* Just know your true voice and follow that in everything that you do, and you'll be fine."

AT 9:30 P.M., DINNER is coming to a close. The presenters, conference organizers, and VIP attendees gather their belongings. Some people are headed home to rest for the next day's full schedule of workshops, and some are going to a private bondage play party to celebrate the kickoff

of the weekend-long conference. Elizabeth, our sitter, is only scheduled to watch Emma until 11:00 P.M. so James and I have about an hour to play before we turn back into pumpkins. The bondage party is only five blocks from the restaurant, so we decide to walk in the rain together. I take off my high heels and chase after Daddy, skipping and running through the wet cobblestone streets.

"Wait for me, Daddy. Wait, Daddy. You're going too fast!"

Daddy turns around, runs back to me and, swooping me up in his arms, kisses me deeply.

"How is my Little Girl?" he asks, looking into my eyes and grabbing my hair, pulling me along the cobblestones.

I gasp with pleasure, "Ah...very good, Daddy. I'm very wet! But I'm a happy Little Girl. I'm excited to play."

"Is that right, Slut?" Daddy shoves a bag of ropes into my arms and whispers into my ear. "I want you to go into that party, find us a place to set up and play, and disrobe. I want you to stretch, have two cups of water nearby, and be waiting in slave position by the time I'm out of the restroom. Do you understand?"

"Yes, Sir."

With a smile I walk purposefully into the recreational hall where the party is being hosted. It's a multipurpose building with a large room that reminds me of a junior high gymnasium.

I quickly spot an open corner with a freestanding suspension stand. I navigate, dripping, through the leather and latex clad dominants using whips, floggers, canes, and paddles on one or more submissives who are bent over furniture, nude or in lingerie, asses exposed for pleasure and pain. Throughout the room pulses a current I love: the deep exchange of power, sensation, and energy that exposes vulnerability, trust, and fearless presence in the moment.

I have just a few minutes to get ready. I place Daddy's rope bag on the outer parameter of the suspension rig, untie my dress, allowing the silky fabric to fall to my feet, and fold it and place it beside the rope bag alongside my heels. It is all a part of the scene. My service and psychological submission to Daddy has begun before he is even present in the room. I kneel down, legs spread, and expose a tuft of red pubic hair and pink, glistening wet cunt, then fold my arms behind my back. Face forward, eyes twinkling, staring past a sea of onlookers, a childlike grin on my face I wait with great anticipation for my Daddy.

Daddy approaches me from behind and slams his hands down hard against my back, nearly taking my breath away. I let out a deep moan, surrendering to his touch, and exhale in pleasure. Daddy steps in front of me and grinds my face into his pants; I can feel his cock harden. Then he gently kicks my cunt with his bare foot, "Up, Slut."

I stand up and to attention, though I am weak in the knees from a long day.

"We only have twenty minutes left to play so I'm gonna make this quick and dirty. Is that alright with you, Little Girl?"

"Yes, Daddy. That sounds perfect. Thank you, Daddy." I close my eyes and smile with sheer joy at having twenty minutes of play all to ourselves. He quickly wraps his ropes around me, like an extension of his body, holding me close. His hands and ropes grasping my breasts, pushing into my ribs, squeezing the air from my body as Daddy tightens the ropes and hoists me off of the ground. He secures the ropes around my thighs to the overhead point in the suspension structure, relieving some of the pressure from my ribs, and I am able to move around in the ropes, in the air, exploring the spots of greatest tension and shifting my weight to those spots until the tension is released. I take in a breath and exhale when the touch of Daddy's hand comes down strong on my ass and thighs.

Breathe, in and out, breathe. I trust my Daddy. He is here to guide me to my physical limits and will take care of me when he brings me back down to solid footing. Daddy lets go of the rope and steps away, allowing my suspended body to spin a compact aerial pirouette. I relax, releasing the building tension in my body and surrendering to the volition of the dance. The momentum propels my body forward, and I feel completely in the moment and connected to Daddy.

Once the ropes and my body come to a stop, Daddy swings me toward him, pulling me into him by my nipples. I smile in ecstasy.

"Push me higher Daddy, higher!" I exclaim, melting into James.

◇◇◇

WE WALK BACK TO the hotel in the crisp cold night, just before 11:00 P.M. The rain has stopped, and as we walk I catch a scent of tree leaves on the wet wind. The smell conjures a blissful memory: my father and I raking leaves when I was a child in Ohio. Orange, yellow, golden, and brown by autumn, the leaves would pile up in and around the tree swing that my dad built for me, a sturdy piece of two-by-four suspended from the tree by thick, scratchy ropes, to hang onto as dad pushed me higher and higher. Dad would rake the fallen leaves around my swing and around the tree, then we would dive into the enormous pile of crunch and color.

3

I'M NOT SURE IF I started off kinky or not, but I always knew I didn't want what other girls wanted. My mother wasn't always open to conversation about sexual identity and feminist pornography. A devoutly religious and traditional mother, the idea that sex is shameful was planted in my head at an early age. It's hard to say what came first: the desire or the realization that my fantasies were forbidden. Either way, the pressure I felt to be good, to be clean, to be chaste, wound up compounding the excitement I felt imagining an alternative. As a young girl, I did what I thought I was supposed to do: I avoided confusing relationships with boys and took refuge in the safety of female playmates. As a preteen this cycle of shame and subversion led me to want one of the most alternative lifestyles I thought a young woman could want: other women.

I thought sex was rooted in evil and would lead a young girl down a path of destruction and desperation, ultimately severing all ties to family. It was a choice: sex or family; sex or a career; sex or respect; sex or education; sex or success. Sex didn't go with anything, and I was terrified of it. I wouldn't even say the word out loud. "It" had the same fear attached to it as "Satan" or "fuck." In the safety of my own bed, with the door closed, buried under covers I would privately explore my sexuality, and slip away into fantasies. It felt like it made everything better.

Sometimes I would fight the urges, but eventually they overcame me and I had to let go. I would dream of kissing the girls on the cheerleading squad—the girls who laughed at me in the hallways as they passed. They felt so perfect and so unattainable. I embraced the discomfort I felt in their presence; I reveled in the humility that became eroticized in my shame. I thought, perhaps, if my lips met hers and my hands found their way along the small of her back, I, too, could grasp perfection.

Then there was a golden-haired goddess who ditched classes and smoked clove cigarettes, hung out at coffee houses past curfew, and rejected perfection and sameness. We would lie under the covers in her bedroom, and I would inhale the smell of her hair—a subtle perfume of jasmine—and she seemed perfect and safe. She was a friend, a close friend, with whom I could share stories, awkward moments, and feel comfortable mutually discovering our morphing bodies. Back in my own bed, when I closed my eyes, she became more than a friend, and I explored the feelings of ecstasy I could bring by touching my own body. When I imagined fulfilling fantasies with my peers, I could feel their skin rubbing up against mine, soft and juicy like a peach, and I thought I could almost taste them.

My dad didn't fit into that colorless world either: white picket fence, two and a half children, nagging wife. He sought illicit one-night flings and after-work rendezvous with escorts. He found his escape with Cilla, a young prostitute with whom he fell in love. As a young married man, my dad had dreams of going to college and traveling the world, but they were extinguished by domestic hopelessness. He felt he had to escape if he was going to find belonging, happiness, and pleasure. I had only just begun to understand his choices years after he left and set out on his journey, when I began exploring my life as a teen. I came to respect and even admire him for his choices. I wasn't sure exactly what my journey in life would be, but my father's lifestyle gave me hope that alternatives to nontraditional family dynamics and atypical relationships did exist.

AT 6:00 A.M. MY alarm clock went off in Loveland, Ohio. I fumbled to halt the annoying loud beeping; my eyes heavy and not yet open. The beeping was a reminder that it was time to go to school and, in an act of defiance, I slammed my hand down on the snooze button. Pink roses sprawled up the wallpaper in my perfect princess bedroom. Dorothy and her friends from Oz looked down on me from a framed, limited edition print, and my Cabbage Patch Kids and My Little Ponies stood guard as I slept. My bedroom was a holy space, anointed with the purest of intentions.

I tried to think clean thoughts, but I was just entering junior high school and already having wet dreams.

I rolled over in bed, smashed my face into the mattress, and pressed a pillow down on my head to block out the sounds and lights of reality. My favorite stuffed animal, a gray bunny that my father gave me for Easter when I was nine and had the chicken pox, was stuffed between my legs. I rubbed my clitoris on the hard plastic bunny nose and face, closed my eyes and disappeared into a then misunderstood world of pleasure.

Beep Beep Beep Beep.

"Ughhhh!" I groaned, emerging from my cocoon to the ear-stabbing sounds of my alarm clock. I quieted the obnoxious beeping and removed my stuffed bunny rabbit from between my legs. My mouth had fallen open, drooling, interrupted mid-orgasm. This is a word I did not yet know, but a sensation I was familiar with all the same. I was always petrified that my mother would walk into my room while I was "cuddling" with my bunny, and that I would be kicked out of the house for the thoughts that ran through my head.

I opened my closet and pulled out my Girl Scouts uniform: white button-up shirt with green vertical stripes and the GSUSA logo, khakis, and a royal blue sash full of badges and pins that I earned. I had recently graduated to Cadet, the second highest-ranking placement girls can achieve in Girl Scouts. I felt a sense of belonging in the Girl Scouts that was missing at school. They accepted me and made me less fearful of the adult I was becoming. It was a Wednesday, which meant I went to my Girl Scouts meeting directly after class, and then Dad would pick me up with my brother and take us to dinner. I always looked forward to Wednesday dinners with my Dad: big bowls of chili spaghetti from Frisch's Big Boy or chili coneys from Gold Star Chili Parlor. It still felt special to sit down with him and talk about our days at work and school. I felt like Daddy's little princess when he tucked me into bed before heading back to his apartment in Madisonville—the dicey area of Cincinnati that Madison Tree Service called home—an area that Mom preferred we not visit.

I can still hear my mom running up and down the stairs of our two-story farmhouse as I buttoned my shirt and slipped into my fifties-style saddle shoes. I found them at a thrift store a few weeks before and used some of the money I earned working landscaping with Dad to purchase them. Mom was buzzing about the house, collecting my brother's homework and ensuring that it was packed away in his backpack, when I walked out the door. He had developmental challenges and required more time and attention from my mother. She packed our lunches in the kitchen, while I watched her from the stairwell. Grabbing the kitchen phone in a flurry of manic energy, she aggressively dialed Dad's number.

My curiosity got the best of me so I quietly slipped up the stairs to pick up the phone in her bedroom and listen in. The first couple rings went unanswered.

"Damn it, Richard, pick up!"

"Helloooo," a voice sounded in my ear, and a stab of jealousy and unease raked across my body like hot coals. The voice on the line was not my father's. It was a woman's voice. Someone I had never met. I knew that my dad had another life outside of the days he shared with us, but since my brother and I weren't part of that life, I blocked out its existence. This crossover between our lives was confusing. The secrecy—we had only once met any of my dad's girlfriends and only once visited his apartment—made his life outside of our family unit seem shameful and dirty and brought uncomfortable feelings that turned my stomach and filled me with fear and anxiety. I didn't want my father to change; I wanted to keep the dad of childhood nostalgia alive in my mind.

My mother barked into the receiver in emotional hysteria, "Who the hell is this? Is this another one of Richard's whores!? Put Richard on the phone now!"

The woman barked back, "Bitch!"—then faded into the distance. "Richard, I'm going to put on some coffee. Do you want some, Daddy? I'll make it sweet and dark. I know you like it like you like your women. Oh, and your bitch of an ex-wife is on the phone."

As I listened to my dad's morning unfolding I wished he were a part of my morning ritual, that his laughter filled our house. I wanted to laugh with my dad, too.

Finally, my dad's strong, comforting voice became audible, "Yes, Gail, what is it? What do you want?" He sounded annoyed and exasperated.

"Very cute, Richard. Is that a new whore that you have answering your phone?"

"What is it, Gail? I need to get ready for work. Are the kids okay?"

"Well, Richard, I just wanted to call and remind you that today is Wednesday. Tina has Girl Scouts after school and you will need to pick her up from her leader's house. Do you remember where Trish lives? Do you have that address? Fourteen-hundred Maple Drive, it's off of Guinea Pike. Reo will be at the house after school and he has tutoring and therapy so you will have to see him another night." Mom spoke in an emotional staccato that made me visualize my father listening to her berating tone from his messy bachelor pad apartment, clothes strewn about on cheap, sparse furniture, fridge full of Coca-Cola and ketchup packets.

"Okay, Gail. I've got it. Anything else?" he mumbled. I pictured Dad sitting at the kitchen table while a woman in a robe cheerfully made coffee and kissed him on the cheek lovingly. Maybe she had a closet full of wigs, some with caramel colored hair, pixie cuts and bouncy curls, and maybe she had the complexion of rich ebony.

"No, Richard. That's it. I'd just really appreciate not hearing your little slut's voice when I call you about the kids." My mom was still emotional and tender, eight years after their separation.

"Just call me on my cell phone next time. I've got to go." Dad's voice disappeared, leaving a single note ringing in my ear.

◇◇◇

A NERVOUS AND UNPOPULAR kid at school, I used my fantasies as an escape. When I was in situations where I found myself unable to breathe, I disassociated and transported myself to another world in my imagination, a place where I felt safe. I avoided the lunchroom. Instead, I hid in a corner in "the commons," an area of our junior high school between the crowded hallways and the lunchrooms that was usually occupied by misfits, losers, and geeks. I sat alone, in an attempt at making myself invisible, and recalculated my grades in each of my courses on a daily basis. Classwork was the only way I could find logic and direction in a life that felt very out of control.

Keeping my eyes cast down, I used to watch the shoes of my fellow classmates pass by. Girls in their first pairs of heels—training heels—clicking by echoed the sound of seconds passing on the clock. These girls and the neat, clipped sound of their shoes on gray vinyl stirred reckless desires in my adolescent brain. To me, those shoes represented control and power. As they clicked through the hall I ignored the girls' nasal, snide remarks by listening to their feet marking time—a comforting rhythm that drowned out the sounds that caused my unhappiness.

◇◇◇

ON THE SCHOOL BUS, on my way to my Girl Scouts meeting from junior high school, I stared out the window at the suburban, cookie-cutter vista. I already knew I didn't belong, that I needed to escape. Wads of crumpled paper, paper airplanes, and spit wads constantly flew in my direction, coupled with profanities. The cacophony of words and voices echoed in my ears, and left me with a blank expression and practiced stoicism. I never looked at their faces, but their voices melded together in a barrage of squeaky teenaged boy snickers that attempted to permeate my consciousness.

"Hey. Hey you, fat ass! I know you hear me ass face! What do you think you are, better than us? Can't talk ass face? She probably shoves Twinkies up her ass."

"I'll shove my Twinkie up her ass."

"Gross! I wouldn't rape her if someone paid me."

"I know you hear us, fuckin' dork."

A text book flew by my head but my eyes stayed vacant, removed. My mind found a safe space somewhere beyond where I physically was in that moment. I was a natural target: a bookish, introverted redhead with braces on my teeth and a face full of freckles, blemished with acne.

"Why would you touch her with your book? This fuckin' book's infected now."

"Yeah. It's probably all stinky and smelly. Dude, she got grease AIDS all over it."

"What's your address, ass face, so I can fucking piss all over your front door?"

"Check out her uniform! What are you, eight years old or something?"

"Is she a retard? A retarded whore! Ha ha yeah!"

I inhaled deeply and exhaled a fogged up circle onto the cold bus window. I imagined myself older and beautiful, with long, flowing, fiery hair, and a body that got attention from the boys and girls that I desired. I dreamed of groups of uniformed boys at boarding school fighting for my affection, make out sessions with girls with golden locks who wrote poetry, and latex-clad women returning 'home' to me, so I could bathe their bodies with my tongue: sweet blood, salty flesh, bitter cunt.

The bus arrived at Trish's home, only a few miles from my school. A friendly, upbeat honest woman, Trish was our Girl Scouts leader and her daughter, Amanda, was in our GSUSA troop. To me, Trish seemed fearless. She was always exposing us to new adventures and activities. We learned how to sculpt and use a kiln, ate fresh coconut, and went on nature walks where we identified plants, birds, and trees behind Trish's home. I had been in the GSUSA since my dad left. The girls in the troop made me feel safe, an early version of chosen family. Trish had a big, beautiful home on a large plot of land and a pool that had a diving board and slide. The property was covered in trees and blackberry bushes, and we would often pick berries from the bushes for a snack. This afternoon we were learning knots; I was working toward an outdoor skills badge to add to my sash. The lesson was also intended to prepare us for our upcoming overnight camping excursion, where we would be required to secure a line of rope for laundry, suspend our clean dishes from mesh bags, and secure tarps to protect our exposed belongings from morning dew or rain.

Each girl had a skein of rope in her hands. The bristly fibers felt comforting between my fingers, prickly perfection that made me think of working with my dad on the weekends at Madison Tree Service. I couldn't wait to show my dad my newly acquired knot tying skills. I smiled, thinking about how proud he would be, paying close attention to Trish as she lead us step by step through the basic square knot.

"Listen up, girls. A basic knowledge of how to tie a few knots is an essential outdoor skill, just like learning how to cook over an open fire or finding food in the wilderness—and I'm not talking about Jungle Jim's Wild Market here, you know what I mean?"

Trish was a boisterous woman, bold and assertive. She wore pants, not dresses, and her shamelessly loud personality and individuality made me feel at home when she was around.

"Okay, so what you have here is a three-foot length of sisal rope or sometimes this very thin variety is referred to as twine. This is your basic rope that you'll find at the local hardware store. Now does everyone have their rope?" Trish surveyed the room, ensuring that the eight girls in the group had the necessary materials.

"We've got it, Mom. What next?" Amanda yelped out from the group of girls impatiently toying with their strands of rope.

"Alright there, Amanda. Thanks for the check-in. Now we're going to start with the square knot. You can use this when you are in a pinch and need to secure a bandage or a sling, or if you need to secure something to your backpack or belt, like your water bottle." Trish picked up her backpack, which had a Nalgene bottle dangling from one strap by a knotted piece of rope.

I continued to run the rope through my loosely closed fist and nodded in acknowledgment of the knot's useful qualities. The friction of the rope against the palm of my hand felt calming, like petting a cat. The texture of the rope felt good to my touch. I was still emotionally shaken from the bus ride, and it felt like the rope was purring, a quiet whisper, *It's okay, everything is going to be okay.*

"Now, this is going to be easiest if you pair up with someone. Can everyone pair up with a neighbor? We are going to practice securing a bandage with the rope. I have some gauze here in this first aid box. Everyone grab some gauze for your bandage," Trish said, while passing out precut portions of gauze to the coupled girls after we settled into place.

I listened to Trish and focused on her fingers and how they interacted with and manipulated the rope with such ease. I was paired up with Amanda, who I found beautiful and strong. She had sandy blonde hair and beautiful brown eyes.

I cuffed Amanda's pants, and, exposing her sun-kissed skin, placed the bandage on her calf. I followed her mother's instructions for securing the bandage in place with a square knot, and then wrapped the rope around her leg and the bandage. I could sense her body close to mine, and I held her leg in my hands as I circled the rope around it. I avoided looking up at her eyes, afraid I would get lost and keep staring, but I felt her gazing down at me. I braved a peek and found her smiling at me. Her mother's robust voice dimmed to a faint whisper when the soft-spoken words of Amanda reached my ears.

"Is this your first time using rope?" She met my eyes. "You seem pretty natural with it." She looked at me the way I imagined a girl looking at me in my fantasies, but in person I was terrified. Instinctively, I knew those urges and desires weren't safe to live out in the real world.

"Now the rope that is on top stays on top and makes the second part of the knot by tying another overhand knot. Everyone got that? Good, good," her mother's voice interrupted my reverie. "We're going to pull the ends tightly to secure the knot. Great job, girls!"

"Thanks. Does it feel secure?" I smiled up at Amanda, overwhelmed by her body and her smile.

"Yeah, it feels perfect." Amanda laughed and her hand grazed over mine as she fingered the rope work. I earned my outdoor skills badge.

Later, I waited in a euphoric bliss at the end of Trish and Amanda's driveway for my dad. I couldn't wait to share with him what I'd learned. None of the crap that the kids on the bus had to say mattered anymore. I did something that would please my daddy and made Amanda happy. Parents' cars came and went as night fell and the street became dark except for a single carriage light at the edge of the long driveway. I sat on my backpack, practicing my square knot over and over with a length of sisal rope that Trish let me keep. I focused in on the knot, a full hour passing by without much notice. Finally, Dad's truck pulled into the drive and I jumped into the cab, silent.

"I'm so sorry, my princess. I ran late at work and I thought your mother was picking you up." His words were apologetic and convincing. I wasn't sure if he was trying to convince me, or if he was trying to believe the words himself.

"It's okay, Dad. I understand." I focused on my length of rope, repeating the knot over and over.

"Really, I'm sorry, Tina. Can I make it up to you? How does Outback Steakhouse sound? You can order whatever you'd like." His voice was low with bravado, hiding something.

"Really? Oh Daddy, I love you!" I couldn't resist an award of adoration or gift of a steak dinner. "Guess what I learned? I learned how to make a square knot," I continued with excitement, hungry for further approval from my dad.

"Woohoo! Really? Watch out, world, my princess has got her hands on some rope!" He yelped and howled with pride in his little girl, and pride in his own victory of winning back my affection after yet another failure.

   We drove down the winding road with the windows down and the night air flooding through the car, laughing and howling at the moon all the way to the steak house. I wanted to believe that Dad really was working, that he really thought that mom was picking me up, but somewhere in the center of my being I felt disbelief in the words that he was saying, but I missed him and I needed to laugh, so this night I continued to believe in Daddy.

4

MY MOTHER'S FATHER LEFT when she was five years old. She doesn't remember him, but a picture of him in a Marine Corps uniform sat on our china cabinet while I was growing up. Ten years after he left my grandmother, he died in a car accident. My mom raised her four brothers—three younger and one older—in their tiny, two-room apartment while my grandmother worked. My grandma worked into her seventies when cancer started consuming her body and prevented her from washing dishes at the Westin Hotel. She had a strong and honest work ethic: everything my grandmother bought had been saved for and earned over time. If she gave something to you, you knew that it was important to her for you to have it.

There was a story my grandmother used to tell us about going to buy my mom's wedding dress. She had the money in her purse and had picked up a bucket of fried chicken for the kids before heading to the consignment shop to collect my mom's gown. Outside of the consignment shop she was mugged. The man tackled my grandma, but she held on tight to the purse strap. The culprit dragged her for a full city block before the strap broke and he got away. She never let go; she returned home with a bucket of chicken and the remnant strap.

My mother was as stubborn as her mother; blonde, beautiful, and smart. As a child I used to wish that I would grow up to be as beautiful as she was. She was a powerful force who commanded attention and, at times, instilled fear in those around her. My mother was a raw circuit of emotions—love and fear and anger sparked out in unpredictable, electric zaps.

Perhaps my dad, or rather, the other women that he coupled with, provided the greatest catalyst for my mother's tantrums. One weekend afternoon, the summer after my parents separated, my brother and I sat sparsely clothed next to the fan in my bedroom licking melting cherry and grape popsicles and trying to keep cool in the non-air conditioned house in the middle of a scorching hundred-and-three degree heat wave. My mom became aggravated easily in the heat. She was soaking in cool water in our lime-green porcelain claw-footed tub when the phone rang.

"Can you get the phone, Tina? I'm in the tub," she yelled from the bathroom.

I ran to Mom's bedroom to pick it up. "Hello, Butcher residence. This is Tina speaking." My mom had explained to me how she answered phones at the doctor's office where she worked as a secretary and I wanted to answer the phone like a secretary, too.

"Hi, Tina. Is your mommy there? I have a very important message for her."

"Who is this?" I didn't recognize the voice on the telephone.

"This is a friend of your mommy's. Her dad is very sick and I need to talk to her right away." the woman's voice was soft and snickering.

I ran to get my mother. "Mom, some woman on the phone says she is your friend and that your dad is sick."

My mom, instantly furious, jumped out of the tub and wrapped a robe around her still dripping wet body. Since her dad had passed away twenty years prior, my mom knew that something was wrong. She grabbed the phone off her bed, "Who is this?"

"Hello, Gail. I just wanted to fuck with you! I'm bored and hot and was just thinking, *Who would be fun to fuck with?* You were the first person to come to mind. I'm fucking with you, just like I'm fucking with your husband."

"Ex-husband, you bitch."

"Whatever. I know you still care about him. I'm going to suck him off and then I'm going to suck him dry so you don't get a penny for your pathetic kids or your pretty little house."

"You whore! I will kill you! You are dead." And with that my mom threw on a T-shirt and jeans and stuck my brother and I in the car, still wearing our underwear. I had never seen my mother so angry. She sped down the winding country road and merged onto the highway, her teeth grinding and her eyes glaring, piercing at anything that crossed her path. My brother and I sat still and quiet, trying to disappear. I huddled close to my brother, feeling the urge to protect him from mental shrapnel or flying curse words that were guaranteed to propel from the cyclone that was brewing inside of my mother.

We pulled into an apartment complex and Mom grabbed the crowbar from the trunk of the car. With speed and purpose she stormed the door while I trailed a safe distance behind with my brother. We followed her up a staircase to the third floor of the complex. Could this be where my dad was living?

My mom swung the heavy iron object into the apartment door, "You fucking bastard! Come out here, you coward! I'm going to fucking kill you and your whore. You won't fuck with this family ever again!" Tears were streaming down her face, which was red and consumed with hate; her anger was palpable and the dent in the door was getting big.

My dad opened the door in a red silk embroidered robe. He nearly received a crow bar to the head.

"What the hell are you doing, Gail?" He grabbed her arms, trying to control her tantrum. His lover peeked her head around the doorframe; she was wearing an identical robe. I could only faintly make out a sliver of a feminine silhouette, with long legs extending from the dark shadow of the doorway. I thought I saw her smile. My mother looked as if she was looking at Satan herself. "Whore! Demon! You want to fight, bitch, I will fight!"

Despite only nearly avoiding injury at the hands of my mother's fiery temper, my dad was still the only person I knew that was capable of calming her down. He held my mother close in his strong arms, and ordered Cilla to go back inside the apartment and give him some time alone with his family. I saw my mother's body crumple into my dad's arms, melting in a fit of hysterical sobbing, snot running down her face and breathing heavily as she nuzzled her face into my father's chest. My dad continued to hold her close, "It's okay, Gail. It's going to be okay."

AFTER THE DIVORCE, AND gossip that his newest girlfriend was actually a prostitute, my dad became the black sheep of the Butcher family. Their perspective of him changed and, in turn, they looked at my brother and I differently, too. We were invited to major holiday functions, but we were conveniently passed over for intimate family brunches and weekend gatherings. Our broken family seemed to fit better with the dysfunctional McPenney's (my mother's side of the family) and, perhaps because of this, I romanticized Christmases with the Butchers. Living with my mother was about survival, but being with my dad came to represent being coddled, taken care of, and treated like a princess living in a world far away from my daily reality.

5

IN OHIO, SUNDAYS WERE important for two reasons: God and Dad. Sunday mornings were spent with my mother at Goshen United Methodist Church, and Sunday afternoons were spent with my dad. In the small town where I grew up, the church was right next to the school and the minister's house; it was our community center, where our larger Girl Scouts functions and ceremonies were held and where I went to bible school in the summer during my preteen years. I liked to sneak sugary, crème-filled cookies and Kool-Aid from the nursery when I helped watch the toddlers and infants. When I got too old for bible school, I was brought out to sit with my mom in the pews to listen to the sermon.

My dad didn't attend church. While my parents were married he may have, but I was too young to remember. For my dad, Sunday mornings were made for hunting. He said he felt closest to God and was at one with nature when he was in the woods. It made sense to me; I didn't see why getting dressed up in our best clothes and going to church somehow put us in touch with the Lord. I have

always connected with the idea of there being a guiding
force, but somewhere around the age of twelve I began
to question whether that force was God, and why God
would impose so many rules, and why God had a book
of rules written by men. I had a lot of questions. My
time at church was spent deep in thought: *Why am I here?*
Where am I meant to go? What am I meant to do?

I began to dream of building connections and
relationships between people and community. I felt
isolated. I wanted to know what it might be like to make
a space sort of like a church, where people would gather
but break all the rules. In my imaginary community,
people would feel free to express themselves, to be
themselves, to cultivate individuality and develop human
connections. During the minister's sermon I would
make notes in my journal and occasionally look up and
nod my head, trying my best to be attentive.

ONE HOT SUMMER MORNING in Ohio, the summer before
eighth grade, I wore a sundress that my dad bought for
me the weekend before. Sweat ran down my neck and my
thighs were wet, sticking to each other and sliding on the
wooden pew. The church was full, and rows of women
and men added to the heat and absorbed any little bit
of breeze the window fans generated. Our minister
was preaching about traditional family structures, and
how the sins of nonconformity in our community
were rearing their ugly heads in the form of adultery,
prostitution, and homosexuality.

"I pray for these sinners. Let us pray for these sinners," Reverend Thomas pled with his audience. "Ladies and gentlemen, we are being faced with a major crisis. Homosexuals are now petitioning in the state courts to make marriage between homosexuals legal. This is a precious union blessed by the sanctity of the Lord, and although I will pray that these souls be steered to the path of the righteous, we cannot condone their blasphemous relations in the house of God."

I was only twelve years old, but something in the tone of Reverend Thomas' voice sent chills up and down my spine. I had a growing awareness that everyone deserved the same treatment, regardless of how different they seemed; that awareness would soon turn into a deep passion.

Reverend Thomas passed around a petition in support of the church's objection to gay marriage. I leaned in and subtlety whispered to my mother, "Mom, if two people love each other it shouldn't matter if they are men or women. They just want to pledge their love to one another in front of God. Because God loves everyone. Right, Mom?"

The petition came down down our aisle.

"Mom please, don't sign that petition. Please, Mom, for me?" I looked up at her, my eyes starting to water. It felt like my mother's signature could change the entire world. It felt like she had the power to erase me. I knew that if she signed that petition she would be confirming that my secrets could never be shared with her.

She took the pen, and I saw in her face a loyal, dedicated single mother who would do the right thing. She loved me. She would listen to me. *Right?*

"Tina, everyone is watching," she whispered, "I have to sign it." And she did. For the first time in my life I watched my mother back down in the face of peer pressure rather than stand up for what she believed. Actually, I could see that she wasn't standing up for what I believed—and this was the first time I realized that there was a difference between my life and my mother's.

I refused to return to church after that. I spent my Sunday mornings at home reading library books, especially Shakespeare and Hemingway, and anxiously waiting for Sunday afternoons when I could see my dad.

6

AFTER MY DAD LEFT, my mom had set frugal guidelines, which were necessary for the survival of our single-income family. Sunday afternoons and Wednesday evenings were a break from the ordinary coupon cutting and beef stroganoff routine.

Anything seemed possible in the world when I was with my dad: he took us ice skating, rollerblading, bicycling on trails, to matinee movies at the cinema down the street, and dinners out at restaurants. And sometimes our family bonded while gathered around the television together, an activity I would normally forego in favor of a trip to the public library or a family outing on the bike trail.

Sometimes, caught up in homework or in the middle of a really great book, I wanted to read one more chapter. But when Dad came to visit, bookmarks were stuck in place and textbooks were slammed shut. I thought it was funny that my family put television time above reading, but it was our thing—it was something special that we shared. We bonded over sitcoms and melodramas and horror films.

O<small>NE</small> W<small>EDNESDAY</small> <small>NIGHT</small>, <small>THE</small> doorbell rang and I bolted from my seated position in front of the television to the front door, where I found a teenaged boy of about seventeen wearing a moss green Nirvana T-shirt that featured a disembodied alien holding a red rose in its severed hand. He held out a steaming hot cardboard box from Angelo's Pizza.

"That will be eleven dollars...uh, little girl," he said, looking a little confused. I handed him a ten and a five-dollar bill that Dad had given me to pay for dinner and scooped up the large cheese pizza.

At thirteen years old, I had just entered my second year of junior high school. I wasn't a woman but I didn't much feel like a little girl, either. I felt awkward and displaced, but I was able to forget all that when my dad was home. My mom and dad fought viciously, but they seemed to have passion together and love for one another. Their quarrels never lasted long and at the moment, my dad was focused on rebuilding closer ties with his family, including my brother Reo and me.

On Wednesday evenings my mom worked late, so on Wednesdays Dad would come to our house after he finished working. We would order pizza and gather around the television to watch one of our favorite programs, *The Wonder Years*.

We piled pillows on the floor and our two dogs, Chester and Velvet, ran circles around us, panting and jumping, bouncing off of the couch, begging for a bite of warm, gooey, cheese pizza. Mom liked to keep the dogs in their kennels, but when Dad was around he set them free. Dad didn't have any rules.

The program's theme song (Joe Cocker's cover of The Beatles' "With a Little Help from My Friends") came on and we starting singing along together, swaying with our pizza in the air back and forth and watching the opening sequence of super-8 home movie footage.

My nine-year-old brother got up and started jumping on the couch, singing: "What would you do if I sang out of tune? Would you stand there or walk out on me? Lend me your ear and I'll sing along."

I picked up our smallest dog and started waltzing around the living room holding his paws in my hands and belting out the familiar tune that we knew so well.

My dad coiled up a magazine, knelt onto one knee and started singing into the magazine as if it were a microphone. "I will try not to sing out of key! I get by with a little help from my friends."

Hanging out with dad felt like we were hanging out with a friend. We watched Fred Savage go through puberty, deeply involved in his high school traumas: pimples and first dates, crushes, breakups, school dances, and the period of mourning following a death in the family. Watching these fictional stories on TV, stories that—though fiction—rang very true, I both felt empathy for the characters and a voyeuristic charge from watching how a "normal" family functions.

On the television, a family was bickering. The oldest brother had just decided to enroll in the army rather than have to take his SATs. His family completely terrified that he would be shipped off to the Vietnam War. I understood; I knew what it was like to be separated from the ones that I love. Dad may have not been shipped overseas, but sometimes it felt that way. Every time he left, we were terrified that he would never come back. *What if he just never comes back?* I knew Reo, too, felt that fear.

"You want another slice, Reo?" I asked, and handed him another piece of pizza.

"Thanks, sis." He took the slice and sunk his teeth in, then washed it down with a big gulp of soda. The ice cubes had melted in our drinks, and we knew it was getting closer to dad's scheduled departure.

I looked over at Dad, surrounded by the dogs, eyes glued to the television, barely touching his food. He stared at the television watching as the parents sat down with their son. Their anger dissipated, exposing fear and vulnerability when they realized their son might be taken from them. My dad's eyes started to get watery and he quickly wiped a few tears away with the sleeve of his shirt.

I took a seat next to my father and the dogs and patted him on the shoulder. "It's going to be okay, Dad. It's just a TV show."

The Wonder Years was the closest thing that we had to home videos, and I lived for those moments huddled around the television like it was a campfire. It was my fantasy of a family life we didn't have that I could escape into and live vicariously through, one episode at a time. The stories were not our own, but the emotions rang true. Scrolling credits meant our family moment was over. I had to return to our fractured world, with my absent father and bitter mother.

The ending credits started to roll and I heard Mom unlocking the front door, home from work.

"I think that's my cue, you guys. I need to get going. It's getting late." Dad took the dogs by the collar and led them back their kennels.

"Just stay ten more minutes. Pleeeease, Dad?" I whined and took his truck keys from the coffee table to hold them hostage.

"No, Tina, I need to go. Give me my keys. I'll see you guys on Sunday after church. How does Castle Skate Rink sound?" Dad held out his hand and I reluctantly tossed them into his palm.

"Cool. Can we get licorice rope?" My brother joined in with a bargaining plea: *If you are going to be absent from our lives for days then we want candy and family fun time in return.*

"You bet. Alright, give your old dad a hug." Dad was happy to meet our demands: part-time dad, full-time fun. We rushed to him and gave Dad a tight squeeze, an affectionate bear hug.

My mom was in the foyer hanging up her coat in the closet. "Hello, Richard. Did you and the kids have a nice time? Didn't leave a mess for me, did you?"

"Life is a little messy, Gail. If you don't have messes it means you aren't living."

"Why is it that you're always the one livin' while I'm the one stuck with the mess to clean up after?" Mom's eyes looked a little watery, she was speaking under her breath and seemed about to loose her cool.

"I'm doing the best I can. We've got some great kids," Dad peeked over his shoulder and caught a glimpse of two little heads, watching.

"Yeah...yeah we do," my mom sighed in exhaustion. Dad nodded his head in respect like a Western cowboy and headed off into the dark night.

Reo and I, noses pressed to the family room window, watched Dad's pickup pull out of the driveway and drive off toward a home that was his, and his alone.

Part 2

7

"ONE ORDER OF FRIES, two cherry sodas, one veggie burger, hold the onions, hold the pickles, and one cheeseburger, no bun, with the works." The waiter at Orphan Andy's Diner in San Francisco's Castro District slung our order down in front of us as we drunkenly pawed at one another. Blake and I had been pawing all night. She was hot, a petite five-foot-two queer gender-fucker with strong, masculine arms and legs that had been decorated with delicate flowering cherry trees. She was also twenty-one years old and a Japanese-American art school student, sexual deviant, and MMA fighter-in-training. Fucking badass. We started our night in San Francisco's official dyke bar, the Lexington Club, a little hole-in-the-wall, maybe eight-hundred square feet, including multipurpose bathrooms that had seen more sexual play than a men's bathhouse. On a busy night you might find up to a hundred and fifty women flooding the small bar. Blake had texted me to meet her after her grappling lesson.

As soon as I walked through the doors a sexy femme bartender with dyed jet-black hair, a septum piercing, and bangs asked to see my ID. Thumbing through my wallet I found my laminated proof of age, twenty-two, an Ohio state ID. I'd arrived in San Francisco nearly a year ago in 2001, but I hadn't yet gotten a California license. I had more important things to do than stand in line at the DMV. I ordered a whiskey and cranberry juice and surveyed the room. It was still early and the bar was pretty empty. In the middle of the room, two stone butches about thirty years old, one with a short buzz cut and the other with a long mop of hair and bangs sweeping over her eyes, dressed in a football jersey, were playing pool. In the corner there was a party of three enjoying the jukebox. A curvy, short femme, breasts spilling out of her vintage bustier and donning a fifties-style dress, a cigarette in hand, crossed the room. She whistled as if calling for her dog, "Heel, Blaire! You're not going to let me smoke out front all alone are you? "

Blaire, it must have been, possibly her lover, scampered after her like a scared puppy in checkered Vans sneakers and cuffed jeans. She was wearing a florescent green trucker hat with *Suck It* on the front, and fumbled through her pockets for a lighter.

They seemed to have abandoned their third party, a young transgender man in his early twenties with piercing blue eyes and light blonde waves of hair peaking out from behind a black AK Press hoodie. He pulled a book out of his messenger bag, which was decorated with buttons from assorted punk bands, and adjusted large black Buddy Holly glasses, sliding them back up the bridge of his nose.

The door to the bathroom swung open and Blake appeared. She had a grin from ear to ear and I could tell she was up to something. She was mischievous. When Blake set her eyes on me, I became putty in her hands. She approached and slammed a tumbler full of ice and liquid onto the bar. I stepped off of the bar stool and she slowly pushed me up against the wall. We were right under a fabulous painting and I was vaguely wondering who the artist was, thinking their work deserved to be showing at my gallery rather than this low-lit dive bar. There was no time to think about work right now. Blake already had one of her hands on my chest and the other pushed hard against my cunt. She inched her hand up from my sternum to my neck, where she applied just enough pressure to make me weak in the knees and wet in my cunt. She then grabbed the tumbler off of the bar and replaced the hand that was on my cunt with her knee, pressing, thumping, and grinding her thick, fibrous thigh between my legs. She leaned in close to my ear, and whispered, "I made you a little something. It's a Blake special—orange juice, pineapple, vodka, and piss."

I opened my mouth in distaste and then something stopped me.

"Chug this down and I'm going to take you into the bathroom and fuck you so hard you bleed." Blake smiled, and brought the glass to my lips.

Sweet tastes of pineapple and orange hit my tongue as I chugged the strange, icy mixture. It mingled with the salty sweat-like taste of urine and the astringent sting of vodka. It was not nearly as bad as I thought it was going to be. Blake's delicate left hand reached through the pocket of my paint-splattered jeans, serving as a welcome distraction while her right hand tilted the cold, dewy glass into my mouth. My eyes remained tightly closed, and I couldn't help but smile at the taboo pleasure I felt from obeying Blake's bizarre orders.

When the glass was emptied I opened my eyes, mouth still agape, as Blake's lips met mine. She kissed me hard and dragged me across the bar through the bathroom doorway, then pushed me into the stall and locked the door. The small, low-lit red room had only a filthy toilet and walls covered in graffiti and fliers for queer and lesbian club nights and film festivals.

Blake removed my T-shirt and pinned my arms above my head, exposing my small breasts and tossing my shirt onto the wet floor.

"Take off your pants, I want to fuck you right here," she moved down my body, her mouth surrounding my nipple and biting hard.

"Ahh, not quite so hard, Blake, please," I pleaded, turned on but unsure. I was still pretty new to San Francisco, and to sex. Though open to trying everything, I was still terrified and didn't know what to expect.

"Ha, is that too much for you, Tina? Don't worry; you don't have to worry at all right now. Just relax and enjoy the ride. Every dyke needs an initiation in the Lex bathroom—a nice, hard fuck."

I looked into Blake's eyes and suddenly believed every word she said. Her lips returned to mine and she pressed hard against me in every way. There was nothing gentle or delicate about Blake, or the way she fucked; it was raw and primal. There was no fear, no façade, and I felt like she could tear me open and expose me whole to the city of San Francisco, to the cold night air full of drunken hipsters wandering aimlessly down Valencia Street. Queers, artists and outsiders who had moved here to seek refuge; people like me. This was a place that would accept us for who we were; a place that would love us and celebrate our differences and flaws. In this hilly city between the bay and the ocean, I had a chance to discover my humanity and let go of shame. It was terrifying and beautiful at the same time.

It was hot in the bar and sweat was running down Blake's face as her wet mouth trailed down my body, past my navel, toward my cunt. I arched my back and thrust my hips forward toward her, aching to be devoured. I ran my fingers through my own hair, pulling at the roots, unsure how to react in the face of the building intensity that Blake was generating between my legs, her nose nuzzling my clit like the nose of my stuffed bunny rabbit once did. She opened her mouth wide and sucked my entire cunt, her tongue roving vigorously in different patterns—up and down, running circles around my labia and clitoris—that made my body tingle. My legs splayed open wide, one foot propped onto the toilet, I balanced with pointed feet as my excitement continued to build. Her tongue reached deep into my cunt and I felt myself approaching orgasm.

"Oh my God, oh God...so fucking good. Please, please!" I didn't know what I was begging for but I knew that I wanted to beg for it.

"Not yet, Puppy. So eager, in such a rush to get to the finish line. Turn around and stick your ass out to me." Blake rose from her knees and her hands came down onto my ass with a thunderous clap. Her paws clawed down my now red and sensitive ass cheeks. She placed one hand on the arch of my back and with the other reached around for my wet cunt. Her hand zeroed in on my pulsing clit before slipping into me, wet, sloppy, and unapologetic. She vigorously filled me up with her fingers, and I yelped in pleasure with each rotation of her hand.

"Ah. Ah. Ah. Ah. Ah!" A wave of warmth came over my body and I collapsed onto the wet, grimy, beer-scented floor, my body sticky with a mix of sweat, come, urine, and saliva. I felt both completely undone and whole at the same time, a feeling that I had never experienced until that moment. Blake squatted down next to my disheveled body, kissed me on the mouth, and looked me in the eyes. "Are you okay?"

Naked, next to a filthy porcelain toilet, and covered in assorted bodily fluids, in the middle of San Francisco at a dyke bar, I was more than okay. I felt a complete sense of belonging. Tears streamed down my face and I laughed, surprised by my own lack of self-control. Embarrassed, I hobbled to my feet, still weak in the knees, and I awkwardly maneuvered my way back into my damp and foul-smelling clothes.

"Yeah, I'm okay. I've just never quite had sex exactly like that before," I said. "I'm good. I feel really good." My hair was damp and knotted. It looked like I had just come in from a winter storm, and it kind of felt like that, too. I was open and vulnerable and it felt like it was time to seek shelter.

"Let's go grab some food. I know just the place." Blake took my hand and helped me to my feet. We exited the bathroom, where a small line of women had started to form.

The butch girls playing pool nodded and smiled at us as Blake and I passed them on the way out the door into the chilly San Francisco night. It was March and in the evenings the temperature dropped to the forties with a chilling wet mist that blanketed pockets of the city. We were only a few blocks from the gallery that I had just signed a lease for on 16th Street and South Van Ness. Femina Potens was a DIY feminist art space that I had started nearly two years earlier. After begging and pleading with my father, I had convinced him to give me a $5,000 loan so I could lease our first official space in San Francisco. The first two fledgling years, we held pop-up gallery shows in alternative exhibition spaces, warehouses and lofts in San Francisco's SOMA district. The $5,000 loan was a start on permanence, but it wouldn't last us long in San Francisco. After first and last month's rent and deposit, I only had enough money to get the gallery through three months.

We walked up Dolores, a palm tree lined street, and crossed onto Market Street I smiled at the view, walking hand in hand with Blake, staring up at the huge rainbow gay pride flags, colorful beacons shining and leading us down our yellow brick road to the country's gay Mecca.

"It's beautiful," I said, shivering and staring up at one of the pride flags at Sanchez and Market. We were standing in front of Image Leather. I peeked inside, able to see through the window, as a man in jeans and an A-frame T-shirt cut a large sheet of leather and placed it under the needle of a sewing machine. It was 11:00 P.M. and this man was still hard at work, serving the queer community and paying the bills. His handlebar mustache reminded me of a Tom of Finland drawing. Every night in front of the leather shop, a homeless gentleman named Barry set up camp for the night. His long white beard was reminiscent of Walt Whitman. As I stood watching the leather man at work, Barry pulled out a pen and sketchpad from one of numerous bags stuffed in his shopping cart. I stared through the window, mesmerized by the leather floggers, belts, pants, shiny boots, and vests. Leather hide is tough and resilient, able to take a lashing, a beating, and still persevere. Barry began to draw and I patted my pockets looking for a dollar or change. There was none. I crossed my fingers that Blake was picking up the check.

I felt comfortable enough to allow Blake not only full access to my body, but also to my psyche. I wanted to toy around with dominance and submission. I was ready to go further.

The way the man in the window was illuminated in the dark night of the Castro emphasized his strong masculine figure, a pillar of strength, protection, and control. He was a leather man, a Daddy.

In a moment of clarity I realized I wanted that, an iconic embodiment of masculinity. I wanted someone who could take control, someone who could look after this Little Girl and protect her from all the hurt in the world. *Is Blake that person? Could she be my Daddy?* It was too early to tell, but I thought her unpredictability and wild streak probably weighed against her reliability as a Daddy. Besides, Blake had many lovers, including a wife, two girlfriends, and a boyfriend. Blake and I were lovers and I was satisfied with that; I was buzzing with anticipation of uncovering our next adventure together and trying not to subject our relationship to too many expectations. I had just fought my way out of a very controlled childhood; I wasn't about to go bounding into a whole new rigid relationship.

Blake placed her black wool scarf around my neck and held me close, rubbing my arms and warming my body. "We're almost there." I smiled and we continued on our journey another two blocks. We arrived at

Orphan Andy's at Castro and Market and took a seat at
one of the available booths.

I FELL IN LOVE with the Castro's vibrancy and flamboyance
when I was seventeen, after visiting San Francisco for
a post-graduation getaway with my high school friends.
A group of sheltered Ohio kids looking for something
new, our entire vacation was spent getting kicked out
of bars and people-watching at all-night diners. At this
time I discovered there was a culture that I fit into and I
started to really embrace my sexual deviancy.

In Ohio, it was dangerous to be open about your
sexuality and there were few places to safely meet other
people who also had alternative sexual orientations. It
seemed like it was impossible to meet someone and fall
in love, but in the Castro I could sit at Orphan Andy's
and chow on fries and milkshakes while drooling over
plenty of eye candy. I saw leather Daddies, armored
in chaps and leather caps or vests, bears with rough
exteriors and wooly faces, pretty boys who looked like
Calvin Klein underwear models, butch lesbians, softball
dykes, art school lesbians, and beautiful punk rockers
decked in leg warmers, short skirts, fishnets, high heels,
and pushed up breasts that I couldn't stop noticing.

I could gaze at them for hours, and I did. I sat and
daydreamed about what our lives would be like when we
moved to San Francisco. I imagined packed nightclubs,
makeout sessions in dark corners, waking up entangled

with our fictional lovers then having breakfast in bed with the sun shining into the bay windows of our Victorian apartments. I watched couples holding hands and kissing tenderly in public, and didn't see any fear in their eyes. I felt like I could be safe here; I knew this city was my home.

In late 2000, when I received an acceptance letter from Antioch College for a credited internship in San Francisco, I felt like I had just opened a formal invitation to join my new family at a fabulously gay dinner table. I had proposed to the liberal, anarchist-run university an ambitious set of goals for a twenty year old, as-of-yet-inexperienced community organizer and artist. I would embark on an internship, four semesters long, working to build the infrastructure for a feminist nonprofit art and performance space. I would learn marketing, event coordination, curatorial design of visual art, and how to staff a volunteer run organization. There were no teachers to guide me to success or failure. I would have to gain the experience on my own. Fundraising was perhaps the most challenging of my many tasks. As an artist and as woman, asking for money for a worthy project can be a challenge. I come from a line of women who worked hard for every penny that they earned. As the fourth semester of my internship was coming to an end, I was still struggling to find a way to build my own community space. I had carved out a space in the world for Femina Potens to exist and thrive, but we still lacked stable funding for our programs. I didn't have all the answers, but I did know I would not be returning to college after my internship concluded. I couldn't abandon Femina Potens in its infancy. It needed me and I needed it. I needed San Francisco. I was driven and impassioned by a desire to create space for a new family of punks and artists, queers, and allies. It all seemed possible while I was sitting in the diner, sipping on cherry sodas with Blake, reeking of sex and alcohol and come, decimating a steaming plate of fries.

8

THE GALLERY WAS LITTERED with plastic cups holding remnants of cheap wine and empty bowls that once held guacamole, salsa, and hummus. A single fly landed on the chip bowl, considering its options of post-party leftovers.

Hardware store clamp lights were strapped tightly to the exposed water pipes that ran across the ceiling of Femina Potens, providing the makeshift lighting for the exhibition space. Below, bold reds, traces of deep blue, and spirals of cold steel gray caught my eye on the illuminated canvases and abstract images hanging from the walls. On one thickly painted canvas, an aerial view from a thousand feet over Los Angeles' maze-like loops revealed highways that tangled into one another, the bright colors beating down on the viewer with the intensity of the Southern California sun. The knots of pavement created a walled-in anxiety, a concrete bubble around those that live within this play land.

An L.A.-based artist, Kathy Brady, was exhibiting her newest body of work at our gallery alongside the portrait photography of Ace Morgan. Ace was part of the "it" crowd in San Francisco. Artist by day and Lexington Club bartender by night, he lived in San Francisco with his wife who was an artist, professor and founder of the feminist independent record label Mr. Lady Records. The San Francisco-based record label had developed a reputation as the most influential label among the queercore movement with releases like Le Tigre's *Feminist Sweepstakes*. The couple attracted a crowd of brilliant theorists, artists, and academics, as well as popular feminist riot grrrl and punk-rock legends.

This evening was no different. Wynne Greenwood of Tracy + the Plastics and JD Samson of Le Tigre stood in the corner of the gallery with Tammy Rae Carland drinking Two-Buck Chuck, laughing, and listening to Ace comment on his portrait series, "Boys of the Lex." Larger-than-life photographs of transgender men looked down at the audience, their bodies maps of scars, piercings, branding, and tattoos; physical manifestations of their journeys altering and shifting their bodies to better match their internal identities.

Kathy's young daughter, who was about four years old, was running around the gallery while Kathy and her girlfriend trailed after her. The young girl's blonde curls bounced up and down as she raced around, landing in front of one of Ace's images of a man on a San Francisco rooftop burying his face in a colorful frosted birthday cake.

The little girl pointed up at the photograph, "I like this, Mama."

Kathy took Parker's hand and put it down at her side, swaying back and forth with her daughter in a rocking motion meant to calm the excitable child. "Don't touch, sweetie. I like this one too. Why do you like it?" she asked, smiling, as her daughter squinted hard at the photograph.

"That boy is messy. He's got cake face, Mama!" Parker looked up at Kathy, a bit of confusion in her features, as she pondered how this boy could make such a mess all over his face. Earlier that evening her mother had been chasing after her with a damp handkerchief. Hummus and avocado remnants still clung to her tangles.

"I'd be shy with cake face, Mommy." Parker smiled "He's not shy." She didn't fully understand why this boy lacked embarrassment with his overt defiance in following the social precepts of cleanliness, but Parker beamed a little as she stared at the picture. "Yeah. I like it. Is there cake, Mama?"

"Does that photograph make you hungry, Parker?" Her mother laughed and kissed her on the forehead. "Let's go look."

Kathleen Hanna took a swig from a bottle of Red Stripe and turned to the little girl. "Psst...I think I saw a couple of cupcakes next to the chips. You wanna go check it out?" Parker ran to the table excitedly and Kathleen handed her a cupcake, grabbing another for herself.

"Okay, ready? On the count of three." Kathleen and Parker stood next to the table full of food, armed with pink frosted cupcakes and bubbling with laughter and delight. They counted off together, "One...two...three!" then smashed their faces into the pink cupcakes, soft cake crumbles falling everywhere and icing sticking to their cheeks.

"That was good, huh?" Kathleen took a napkin from the table and began to wipe off the little girl's face.

"Yeah! Like the picture!" Parker licked her lips, trying to get every trace of sugar with her tongue.

The party was dying down. Guests started to thin out, heading on to late night dinners or the after-party at the Lexington Club. I had larger problems to solve than which late-night party I planned to attend. The rent for Femina Potens was due in a week. I had seven days to come up with $750 if I was going to keep the doors of the gallery open. Although over a hundred people had circulated through the gallery that evening, not one piece of art sold. Our gallery was flooded with hipsters, queers, students, and artists who were all impacted by the unemployment crisis and San Francisco's exorbitant prices. It made living as an artist nearly impossible. I had to find a way to get the gallery funded, and quickly.

The gallery was beautiful and at night, once everyone had left. The walls echoed with voices, radiating with a warmth and energy. I felt like I was finally carving out a nook in the world where artists of my own tribe could gather and display outward, unapologetic reflections of their lives. Though there were many places for queers and feminists to indulge in inebriated hook-ups at bars and eighties club nights, Femina Potens provided the only all-ages art gallery and performance space where our lives, our politics, our art, and our identities could be discussed openly. This was a place where on-lookers could see something of themselves, an empathic connection through experiencing our differences.

I sat down at my desk, located in the back corner of the gallery. I had rescued a beaten-up office chair from the dumpster across the street and scavenged a small wooden desk from the sidewalk. Blake received a new computer from her father for her birthday and generously gifted me with her old one; it was slow but it worked. On the wall next to my desk, taped up with black duct tape, was a neon green paper that read:

Goals
Build a space for queer family to gather
Actively seek mentor (Daddy? Leader in the community?)
Fund Gathering space
Document (Don't want to get lost now, do we?)

I chewed on my nails, my mind buzzing, trying to find a solution to ever-growing financial obligations. I opened Craigslist to scour through listings for odd jobs and temp work.

Scrolling down the page I was looking for anything I might be qualified for. With an unfinished theater degree and minimal work experience on my résumé, I had a difficult time standing a chance at any positions other than those waiting tables or working at nonprofit organizations that offered substandard living wages. Besides, I needed a job with a flexible enough schedule that I could keep regular gallery hours and be available for evening events and openings.

Then I spotted Craigslist Erotic. The link directed me to lists of job postings, everything from posts asking for someone to come over and provide them with a golden shower to asking for the full-on GFE (Girlfriend Experience). Though I found these requests fascinating, I wasn't really interested in fulfilling them on an up close and personal level.

After scrolling through a few pages I found a posting that sounded interesting, "Local Kink Porn Company Now Hiring Models":

We will do all we can to make your modeling experience as enjoyable as possible. We want to find models who enjoy the activities our sites portray. You can expect us to be respectful and to work strictly within your limits. For any kind of bondage activity you will have a safe word. Word travels fast in the Internet age. If we were to abuse your trust in us, we would quickly find fresh models hard to find.

It listed the sites it was casting for:

Whipped Ass: Domination by a dominatrix. Model Rate: $700

Hogtied: Tight rope Bondage, Male Dominant, gags, hoods, vaginal dildo and finger penetration, flogging, forced orgasms with vibrators. Model Rate: $800

Water Bondage: Tight rope bondage, gags, floggers, breath play and water submersion. Model Rate: $800

Please inquire for an interview by emailing our talent director, Mackie.

I had already modeled for Blake and some of her friends doing pin-up and nude modeling and found it exhilarating. I loved interacting with the camera, collaborating with other artists and further documenting my blooming sexual identity. These were freedoms that, growing up in the heartland, I just didn't have.

The sound of the door opening startled me out of an intense state of concentration. Blake appeared, wearing her bike helmet and rolling her single-speed bike into the gallery.

"Knock, knock. How did the opening go? These paintings are hot. Nice job, T." Blake's eyes were wide and approving. She nodded her head, circling the gallery with her bike.

"Huh? Oh yeah, the exhibit. It's great, isn't it?" I was still staring, dazed, at the computer, considering whether I should apply for the modeling position at KINK. I considered my choices; performing in front of the camera in BDSM pornography really didn't seem so different from posing nude or in lingerie for Blake. In fact, some of the imagery on their site reminded me of some of my favorite performance artists. Jenni Lee may have been pulling a butt plug from her anus instead of a yam, but like the performance artist Karen Finely, she used her body as material to say something to the world. I knew I had something to say. Anyway, did it really make a difference if I was being spanked and fucked by a beautiful woman in front of the camera if I was doing the same thing when I went on a date? *Won't I be playing a key role in the documentation of a woman's sexual pleasure?* I had just read feminist sexologist and former sex worker Carol Queen's *Real Live Nude Girl: Chronicles of a Sex-Positive Culture* and the concepts behind sex positive feminism in relation to sex work were fresh in my curious young psyche. Besides, packing my bags and heading back to Ohio wasn't even a consideration. I would rather live on the streets, or on Blake's couch. Closing down the gallery wasn't an option, either. It was just starting to gain momentum and recognition. If I had to close the gallery doors, I would have felt like I had failed my community and family for squandering the loan they gave me on an unsuccessful dream.

"What's up with you, T? Why don't you put your work down for a minute and relax? You pulled it off! Femina Potens is open and alive. I heard Kathleen Hanna stopped by."

"Yeah. Where did you hear that?"

"I stopped by the Lex on the way here. Everyone was talking about the new gallery space. You're on the map, baby! And it's only been, what? Four months?"

"Three months," I corrected her, my voice expressionless, my mind preoccupied.

"Three months, that's amazing!" Blake pulled two beers out of her messenger bag, twisted the cap off of one and handed it to me. "Relax and have a drink."

I got out of my chair and took a big gulp. Blake collapsed into the office chair and patted her thighs. "Come have a seat on Daddy Blake's lap and tell me all about it."

I curled up in Blake's lap, nursing my beer and peeling nervously at its label, my shoulders tense and high. I was a young girl in Daddy's lap looking for answers. I wished I could pull my head back into my shell to wait until the world made sense again.

Blake looked at the model application and casting call open on my desktop. "Are you thinking about doing porn, Tina?"

"Yeah...maybe. I've gotta figure out how I'm going to pay rent on the gallery. I don't know. What do you think?"

"I think you should do it! Sex work is probably responsible for funding more marginalized artists than the National Endowment for the Arts. If you ask me, they should offer a class in art school called Baristas or Brothels: How to fund Art on the Fringe. I know the woman who works in the talent office, in casting. She comes into the Lex all the time. I could give her a call for you."

I lifted my head in surprise, I felt like I had just received a surprise treat. "Really? Wow! Okay, yeah. Yeah! I could do this, right? We have kinky sex, it couldn't be that different, right?"

"It's different. But I think you can handle it, T. You're a pretty tough chick."

I liked the thought of being a tough chick. Invincible. Blake's fingers, meanwhile, were making their way under my dress and into my panties.

I surfed through the free section of hogtied.com, looking at beautiful curvy women with names like Sasha Monet and Jewelle Marceau. *What will my name be? A literary reference perhaps? Zooey Salinger or Sylvia Bell?*

Blake slapped her hand down on my thigh, hard, and I exhaled with enjoyment as the heat washed over my body. My ass still in her lap, I began to undulate my hips, pressing closer to her as her hand came down on my other thigh. Again, I inhaled and exhaled in an erotic moan on impact. Wetness was dripping down her hand.

"Can we go back to your place?" Blake breathlessly moaned in my ear, in a heightened state of arousal. "Marie has a date tonight and asked to bring them back to the house, so I could use a place to crash." Marie was Blake's wife. They had been dating since college and had been married for two years. Their communication with each other was incredible and was something I really admired about Blake. I had to run through my date book myself to be assured that no other lovers would be at my doorstep when I got home. It appeared I was available, and so was my bed.

I snapped the browser closed and the pictures disappeared. They seemed far away, somehow not real. Big hair, big breasts, heavy makeup and curves. They looked like women—I was merely a girl. My small 5'2" frame, A-cup breasts, punk hair cut, and numerous piercings didn't equate to the beauty that was on the kink site. *But I am a tough chick*, I thought.

9

A FEW DAYS LATER I walked into the KINK talent office. I expected an office interview with Mackie, Blake's contact at the talent office, so I arrived makeup-free in moss green cargo pants, flip-flops, and a white A-frame tank top.

I buzzed the intercom at the Howard Street location on a lively block in the SOMA district. The receptionist asked for my name, and I nervously responded to the intercom, worried maybe Mackie hadn't put me on the calendar.

"Tina Butcher. I'm here to see Mackie. I have an eleven A.M. appointment."

I entered the air-conditioned lobby and took the elevator up to the third floor office. Around thirty employees sat at cubicles in front of computer screens looking at kinky pornographic imagery. One woman was retouching photos of a woman who was bound and arched back like a seal, her wrists tied to her ankles and a long strand of drool collecting around a red ball gag. She reminded me of a stuffed pig served with a mouth full of apple. A woman with long, golden Rapunzel hair and a thick Australian accent quickly crossed the room holding an electric cattle prod. Her assistant, a young twentysomething wearing glasses and dressed in black, followed closely behind with a plastic container of dildos.

She shouted out to the office at large, "I need someone to try out this new toy. Any takers?" She looked in my direction. The foreign environment overwhelmed me. It was a bustling hub of bondage, a Grand Central Station of intense pornographic experiences. This was much different from the one-on-one kinky sex that I had experienced with Blake, and I found myself wishing Blake was here to navigate me through.

The woman shouted in my direction, "Are you a model? You look lost?"

"Um yes. I mean I'm here to meet with Mackie, about modeling." I was terrified that the woman was going to zap me with the frightening-looking electrical instrument she held in her hand.

She smiled and pointed to Mackie's office, "Good luck, sweetheart."

I knocked on Mackie's door and walked in. She looked frazzled, shuffling through papers on her desk with the phone up to her ear. She pointed at the couch and I sat down patiently, waiting for her to finish her conversation. I stuffed my hands in my pockets and gazed up at framed photographs on the walls depicting women in different states of vulnerability; tied and collared, their faces set permanently in orgasmic pleasure, perseverance, and strength while mascara dripped down their cheeks. It seemed genuine and uncontrived, like a documentary photography exhibit on sex and emotional vulnerability.

Mackie hung up the phone and breathed a deep sigh of relief. She picked up a mug and took a sip of coffee, then picked up a file on her desk and scanned through the information before addressing me. "Hi, sorry about all of the chaos. It gets a little crazy here sometimes. You're Blake's friend, right?"

"Yeah. Tina. Nice to meet you." I bit my lip, nervous about what an interview for a BDSM adult site might entail. I didn't have that much experience with kink and was completely oblivious about how to discuss my sexual desires. I knew I wanted a Daddy. I knew I liked rough sex and relinquishing control, but I had never been tied up or had a ball gag in my mouth. *What if my mouth doesn't open that wide?*

"Is that your stage name? Tina? Mind if I take a picture?"

"Um, sure. No, no I don't have a stage name yet. I'm still thinking about that." I tucked my hair behind my ears and tried to look seductively at the camera, pouting my lips and opening my mouth.

The flash was bright and startling. An unfinished photograph popped out and Mackie fanned it back and forth a few times before clipping it to the file that sat on her desk. "Well, I'm sure you'll figure it out. Blake tells me you run a gallery?"

"Yes, I just opened a new location a few months ago. It's our first storefront space." My voice was raspy, and my throat dry and scratchy with nervousness. Mackie handed me a bottle of water with a smile and I nodded in gratitude. She sat down next to me on the couch and adjusted her glasses, nodding her head, listening. "That's great, just great. Now listen, Tina. I know this is fast, but one of our models canceled on us last-minute and we're in a bit of a jam. Would you be willing to shoot today? It would be with our CEO, Peter Acworth. Very basic, some bondage, maybe some dildos and vibrators. Pay is $800." Mackie took another sip of her coffee and looked at me, waiting for a response that I wasn't yet willing to give. *I'm not prepared!* My mind screamed. I didn't even know if there is a way to prepare for this kind of thing?

I considered leaving or saying, "No"—or "I'd love to do this another time." Then I remembered that rent that was due. I took a swig of water and found the courage to respond: "Um...I didn't bring anything to wear or any makeup or anything."

Mackie handed me a model release to sign and assured me that "It's okay. Peter likes girls to be natural for his shoots, anyway. You look like the ideal girl next door."

PETER, THE MASTERMIND BEHIND the KINK empire, looked as if he had just come off a plane from a vacation in

Bermuda. He was wearing surfer shorts and flip-flops with a white T-shirt and he talked with a thick but pleasant British accent. He had a gentle and polite disposition; his youthful face complimented by twinkling eyes. He looked like a little boy at Christmas, all the toys under the tree that he could ever imagine. I could picture him tying up his sister's Barbie dolls with the same twinkle in his eye.

After twenty minutes under studio production lights, I felt sweat run down my face, plastering my damp hair to the side of my head. Peter slapped my flushed face and I smiled wide. My eyes came alive. I wanted more.

"Oh, I see you like that, do you?" Peter began to lead me in a circle, and I hobbled along in the shackles.

"Let's see how you behave with a little more rope and a nice lashing." Peter grabbed several bundles of almond-colored rope lying nearby in tight coils. I watched the rope as he grasped the familiar material, wrapping and cinching it tightly around my body. It felt like an embrace from a familiar lover. The rope held tension around my breasts and ribs, and I sighed and purred like a kitten. I dipped my face toward the rope to feel the fibers against my cheek and lips and between my teeth. I bowed my head in reverence and inhaled the deep scent of natural jute fibers. I became lost in the euphoric release as endorphins raced through my overly aroused and stimulated body.

I was in love. My entire body quivered with anticipation for the next touch. I needed more.

Something was unleashed in me when the rope bit into my flesh; I became free. Free of anxiety, feeling deeply aware of and completely removed from myself at the same time. My body fell into the fibers of the rope, pushing against it and finding the spots of greatest tension and greatest weakness, rolling around in bliss. I felt the sting of a whip wrap its way around my thighs. My body felt like warm butter, the whip cutting through me like a knife. I cooed with every slice, dancing from the sharp bites, not knowing how to respond, or if I was supposed to move into or fight against this punishment. It didn't seem like punishment, it felt like ecstasy, like all of the stars in the sky were flying down one by one to touch me. I felt blessed and whole, and my entire body opened up to the experience.

Just when I thought I had reached a peak, Peter brought out a Hitachi Magic Wand. The white tennis ball-shaped head of the vibrator landed directly onto my clit. When I took a breath I felt waves of orgasm ripple through my body while the erotic scents of rope and sweat wafted through the air, making me swoon and shake violently, contorting until all was released.

"Alright then, that's a wrap. Simone can you get... what did you say your name was?"

"Madison," slipped from my mouth. It felt natural and true, stirred from a memory of my first encounter with rope. The scent of rope had brought me comfort at Madison Tree Service long before I had developed any sense of my sexual self.

"Right, right. Madison. Could you get Madison some water? Matt why don't you untie Madison and bundle the ropes for me? How do you feel, my dear girl?"

I felt light-headed, euphoric, and completely unblocked. Like the way I felt after a nice long sit in a sauna or really deep meditation, coupled with the buzzing pleasure-drenched glow of an orgasm. I inhaled deeply, my body as limp as a noodle. It took me a moment to gather my thoughts, to form a sentence.

"I feel blissful. Thank you, Sir."

Peter smiled and gave me a pat on the shoulder, "Good. Good. That's what we like to hear. You're a natural, a natural! Madison, was it? When you head back upstairs let Mackie know I'd like to book you for our other sites, Water Bondage and Whipped Ass. Are you free next month? We're shooting in Cabo, Mexico, and I'd love to book you for the trip."

I nodded my head in affirmation, taking in the information and watching Peter's mouth move. Just a few hours ago I wasn't even sure if I was going to follow through, and now my next two months were booking up before the day was even over. I folded up the $800 check and headed straight to the bank to cash it and drop the rent money in my landlord's mailbox.

When I stepped into the California sunshine I saw an open road in front of me. If I'd looked up and seen cartoon birds following me, I wouldn't have been surprised. I had to fight the urge to float off into the blue sky. Was Peter my Glinda the Good Witch, offering me rope in place of ruby slippers? As I walked back to the gallery, I bounced through the city feeling one step closer to home, to safety. If rope didn't lead me to my Daddy, I didn't know what would.

10

I THINK I FELL in love with Gauge on our first meeting, an unintentional date at a dive bar in the Lower Haight called Noc Noc. It was small and the stone walls were covered with cave paintings while faux stalactites clung to the ceiling. DJs crammed into a closet-sized space by the bathroom to mix the evening's auditory cocktail, combining experimental electronic soundscapes with obscure British post punk bands like The Raincoats and Siouxsie and the Banshees. Noc Noc was decorated with disassembled car seat cushions for seating and only served sake, wine, and beer.

Gauge was in one of Blake's new genre art classes at San Francisco Art Institute. She was shy but intrigued by the gallery, and by me, so she had invited me out for a drink and brought along her artist's portfolio. Beautiful and intriguing, she was a complex swirl of masculine and feminine energy bottled into a petite Croatian package with olive skin, warm brown eyes, and short dark brown hair. As we discussed her work and artistic influences, I hung on her every word. One of her greatest inspirations was performance artist Hannah Wilke, whose exhibition of vulval terra-cotta sculptures was some of the most inspiring artistic work that rose from the women's liberation movement in the sixties.

I was thumbing through Gauge's portfolio, black and white photographs of her nude body covered in vulva-shaped sculptures made from chewing gum. "Beautiful. Really powerful." I was confused. Was this a work meeting or a date?

After the bar, she kissed me outside of my second-floor walk-up in the Castro, and I knew she was interested in more than just discourse on feminist performance art. She was a few years younger than me, and she touched my cheek and looked into my eyes and said, "I really like you, Tina. I'd like to get to know you better."

I laced my thumbs through her belt loops and pulled her body closer to mine, "I'd like to get to know you better, too." But she pulled away, looking awkwardly at the ground in the hallway outside my apartment and shuffling her feet back and forth for a moment before slowly looking up, her body shaking.

"I really have to let you know now that I can't really do the open polyamory thing. I just can't. I'm totally cool with the work you do. You know, the porn stuff. But if we are going to explore...this...at all...then I know myself enough to know that...you know, I need monogamy."

Gauge looked like a lost, terrified kitten in need of reassurance and love. I was a little taken aback, but at the same time impressed with her direct and honest approach. I felt like I needed to be close to her, to explore what that relationship might be like.

And if I needed to try out monogamy for size, well...I could do that. I pulled her body close to mine once again and promised, on our first date, "Just you and me."

After only a few weeks of dating, Gauge started to grow uneasy with my work in the adult industry. In theory, she supported my right to explore my sexuality on film and to bring feminist and sex-positive ideology to a traditionally misogynistic industry. The day-to-day jealousy, and her insecurity with my intimate encounters with total strangers, posed a greater challenge than she was expecting. In efforts to ease her discomfort I would make grand romantic gestures, like appearing with roses or daisies, scooping her up in my arms and pulling her close to me, hoping that she would finally realize how much I loved her. She responded by bombarding me with questions about my workday, "How many orgasms did you have?" and "Did you want to fuck the producer?" I thought that if I held her tight enough, maybe she'd understand.

GAUGE AND I HAD been dating for a year and six months. I was in Los Angeles, shoved in a taxi with my purse and a large backpack full of dildos, vibrators, and assorted bra and panty sets.

"Hi, there. Yeah I'm going to five-o-six South Grand Street. Do you know where that is?"

"Yes, Miss."

I sighed in relief and buckled my seatbelt as the cab took off for Downtown L.A. By now I had been working in the adult industry, primarily in the kink and fetish genre of pornography, for about two years. My schedule involved traveling to new cities once a month, for about a week. It was Los Angeles this week, and I was going to be working with one of my favorite rope artists and directors, James Mogul.

My cell phone rang, and I fumbled around in my purse. I fished out my phone and answered to the welcome sound of Gauge's voice.

"Hi, Baby. I miss you." She was sweet and lonely and cooed in my ear like a needy child. My heart cringed with guilt for not being home with her, cuddling in our bed, under the covers, wrapped up in one another.

"I miss you too, sweetheart. Is everything okay? How are the cats?" Gauge had moved into my apartment about a month before, and we had quickly fallen into a life of domesticity.

"Yeah, everything's fine, they're fine. I just wanted to hear your voice. I'm working on finishing my video piece for the exhibition at school that I was telling you about. Remember?" The taxi pulled up to the hotel and I fumbled through my wallet for a twenty-dollar bill.

"Baby, I've got to go. I love you. I'll call you after the shoot."

I stood in the lobby of the Millennium Biltmore Hotel watching the bustling crowds filter in and out of the door. There was a technology convention this weekend at the hotel that was occupying the majority of the rooms.

I looked down at my sheet of paper, where Room 402 was written alongside many scribbles in blue ink that had seen me through the last six months of travels. I pressed the elevator call button and ripped the page from my journal, stuffing it into my back pocket. The elevator doors opened onto the 4th floor. I was looking forward to seeing James. I was swept away with James' photography. His work was intimate, soft, and beautiful. There was an element of innocence and raw tenderness in each frame. I wanted to be one of his women, I wanted to be part of his collection.

James Mogul's site was a portal to galleries of his bondage photography, with the occasional video clip of a woman in bondage. He started this site after years of working construction and carpentry. James' journey into the adult industry began with a personal interest in Shibari, a Japanese style of bondage. When James wasn't remodeling kitchens in Seattle, he found himself leading skillshares and instructional rope bondage workshops. He studied photography and lighting, and would experiment with documenting his girlfriends in exquisite bondage that he rigged himself. James used his site as a platform to share the beauty that he found in bondage and in women. Soon the site grew large enough to be a full-time venture for him, and he had local and traveling models coming to him because they wanted to be part of his world.

THE FIRST TIME I met James, he was late and I was early. I was waiting for him in a circus of a warehouse that housed large theatrical props and bondage furniture in Seattle. Gauge had come along with me for that work trip, and I promised to meet her after the shoot at Pike Place where we would find a romantic Italian restaurant to share a bowl of pasta and watch the sunset. Waiting in the warehouse, I was startled by the sound of the doorbell and looked up to find James and his partner, Bren, carrying in photo gear and a cooler. James is over six feet tall; he towers above me. Short, dark, boyish curls sprinkled with gray spring from his head, and a goatee circles his mouth. I watched his lips move as he said the words, "You must be Madison. I'm James and that is Bren. I'm sorry we're late."

A familiar presence radiated off him. I felt so comfortable, like I'd known him before, *but where?* I had never been to Seattle and I couldn't imagine that we would find ourselves in any of the same circles in San Francisco.

He was wearing blue jeans and a black T-shirt. I looked down at his boots as he took my hand to help me up off the chair. As I felt his callused hands take hold of me, it hit me: I had met my Daddy. A comforting, blue-collar worker with good manners who looked at me like I was a princess, James was armed with rope, leather boots, and a pickup truck. Suspended off the ground, I cooed, hanging upside down and purring with every touch from this stranger. I felt safe. I tried to compartmentalize: this was work, and I was paid to enjoy myself. I was an activist, revolutionizing porn by being a woman enjoying herself in bondage. *This is just work*, I told myself as I signed the paperwork and asked James for a recommendation on where to take my girlfriend for a romantic Italian dinner.

THE LAST TIME I had seen James had ended in disappointment. James' hands and ropes never approached me. He stood by snapping photographs as his dominatrix friend, Catrina, paddled me and fucked me with her strap-on cock. I kept waiting for him to step in with his bag of sweet-smelling hemp rope and rig me in a position that contorted and stretched my body, but instead Catrina's partner stepped into the scene. A very nice gentleman with a thick gray beard and spectacles, he was well spoken and articulate, but he was concerned with making my bondage as comfortable as possible and he used white cotton rope. It didn't make sense to me. I need the complete sensory experience. I need the rope to tear me open passionately and hold me tight and safe in its tangled web. It was frustrating, but I recognized that these people were not my personal playmates or dominants. I was only here for my job. If James didn't want to tie me up, I couldn't ask him to. Still, after the shoot I found myself sulking on the ride back to my hotel. I had never reached my bondage high and was irrationally disappointed. James looked into the rear-view mirror and caught a glimpse of me curled close to the car door, nose pressed against the window, watching the other cars drive by as we maneuvered through the gray city of Seattle. "Is something wrong, Madison?"

"No." I hesitated before I opened up, afraid that my personal desires would cost me future work with James. *If I don't tell James, who can I tell? Certainly not Gauge.* "I was just expecting to get tied up by you, that's all. It just wasn't what I was expecting. I was looking forward to having you tie me up." I knew that it would be at least three months before I had the chance to work with James again. I was mourning the waiting period, trying to think of other producers that made me feel the same way as James. There were plenty of rope artists at KINK that hired me on a regular basis and were satisfactory, but none of them tied as tight as James. James handled his rope with care. There was a romantic intimacy that James brought to the scene, a beautiful marriage of tenderness and sadism that turned me on.

"You know, I can still tie you up even if we aren't working."

His response was shocking; my psychological circuitry was blown. *You mean this happens when a camera isn't rolling? You mean this could happen to me when a camera isn't rolling?* The camera had become a safe container for me, a place for my fantasies to exist without interfering with the domestic home life I had built with Gauge. The very mention of James tying me up without camera seemed dangerous. Tight rope pressed against my flesh, his body so close to mine. What might happen if a camera wasn't there to dictate our roles as "model" and "photographer"? Although James and Bren had arrangements for sexual situations outside of their relationship, Gauge and I did not. I couldn't take him up on his offer, but I couldn't get it out of my mind.

Los Angeles. Room 402. Back to work. I opened the door into a small, charming hotel room already set up with a video camera on a tripod and a photo camera lying on the bed. James and Bren hugged me, exchanging pleasantries before reviewing their ideas for the evening's shoot. After digging through my small selection of wardrobe choices, which weren't appealing to James or Bren, we decided I should shoot naked: pure and simple, natural, the kinky girl next door. I sat cross-legged as James tied my legs and Bren operated the video camera. James directed my hands behind my back and pulled my arms into the shape of a box. Soon James' tightly cinched ropes transported me.

The fibrous natural jute rope cut into my skin sending my mind off into space. James' hands cupped my small breasts and dug into my ivory skin, feeling incredible against my flesh. I had been waiting a very long time for this. Bren clicked away, taking photos while James brought the Hitachi up to my cunt and I thrust my hips forward, begging for more. My voice filled the hotel room and drifted down the hallway, "More, Daddy! Please, Daddy! I want more, fill me up, fuck me, please..." James snapped on a latex glove and squirted some lube onto my already wet pussy. The Hitachi was back on my engorged clit when his hand entered me for the first time.

He looked up at me, "Is this ok?"

"Mmmm...yes, please" is all I could mutter.

James teased me with the wand, holding it close then taking it away while his three fingers pumped in and out. I could smell the rope and feel it bite at my arms and legs. The ropes that made my chest harness pulled at my breasts with every breath and my orgasms kept peaking and crashing in intense oceanic waves. I could feel his latex covered hand in my cunt, pumping with pleasure, grasping for my g-spot, fucking my eager, wet pussy. I collapsed, bound, and in his arms while Bren was still taking photos.

"Wow, I think that's a wrap!" he said, barely keeping composure.

James undid his ropes with great care and tenderness. I was sad to see the ropes being packed away, I felt lonely in their absence.

When I regained my sea legs I stood up and made my way to the bathroom to shower and dress. As I stood, splashing my face with water, I listened to James and Bren softly bickering, the sounds falling like rain against the glass in a delicate percussion.

"I'd like to ask her, Bren. What if she sleeps on the floor? She can be our submissive for the evening."

This wasn't what Bren wanted to hear, and was actually quite a surprise to me. I closed my eyes and pictured myself lying on the floor; maybe with a pillow and blanket. *Maybe I'll fetch tea in the morning? Or make breakfast.* It wasn't the first time I had fantasized about James, but it was the first time that I had heard about James' desire for me. He wanted me to fill a role in his life, a life that continued when the cameras stopped rolling.

My cell phone went off. It was Gauge, she wanted to make sure I was okay. It was getting late and I hadn't called. I explained to her that we were just wrapping up and that I'd be going out with some friends afterward.

That night, instead of staying in the hotel room with James and Bren, he invited me to attend a fetish party in Hollywood. I had never gone out in L.A., and I'd never been to an event with a photographer or producer before. In my life I kept work very separate from non-work, but I felt those lines blurring as the night went on.

11

FIREWORKS EXPLODED IN THE sky in bursts of red, green, and blue lights as the plane landed at Sea-Tac International Airport on the Fourth of July. A small six-year-old girl with white-blonde hair pulled into two braids sat with her father, staring out the airplane window and pointed in wonder.

"Whoa! Did you see that one, Dad?" The girl's face was inches from the thick glass, watching the shower of brilliant colors shoot into the air and past the descending airplanes.

I watched as the landing gear lowered and the plane gently landed on the tarmac. The seat belt light turned off. "Welcome to Seattle, where the time is currently eight-thirty P.M. It is eighty-five degrees and partly cloudy. If you checked luggage with us today you can pick your bags up at carousel five. Thank you for flying with Jet Blue and we hope you consider flying with us for all of your future travel."

Passengers unbuckled their belts and bounced out of their seats, anxious to grab their bags and personal items and deplane as quickly as possible. I sat still and allowed the rest of the passengers to create their own chaos. I would not participate in the mad race to the luggage carousel that day. Instead, I rooted around for my phone.

One voicemail. Gauge. Telling me that she would be moving out and that her belongings would be gone from our apartment when I returned to San Francisco. Gauge and I had a series of volatile arguments the week before, which came to a climactic finale with my departure to Seattle for work. My constant travel schedule and my work continued to create a huge fissure between us. When I introduced to her the idea of trying out polyamory earlier in the week, she fumed. We each had a different idea of our ideal relationship, and were aware of it. No matter how much I loved her, it wasn't working out.

It had been six months since I last saw James Mogul, but I never stopped thinking about him: *I can tie you up when we aren't shooting.* I was in search of a Daddy, and from our last encounter in Los Angeles I determined that James was in search of a Little Girl. I stood at carousel number five watching the baggage rotating around in circles, heartbroken over Gauge, but the deep pain that I felt over the loss only made me want a Daddy even more, someone to hold me and make it all better. I spotted my large navy blue rolling suitcase and heaved it off of the conveyer belt.

James was going to pick me up from the airport. Outside, I watched the hands on my watch tick by while families piled into minivans, lovers reunited after long business trips, and college buddies embraced and heaved suitcases into open trunks. James pulled up in an old beaten-up pickup.

"Welcome to Seattle, Madison! How was your flight?" He tossed my luggage into the bed of the truck and I climbed into the cab.

"It was okay. Are we headed back to the model apartment?" Last time I visited, James kept an apartment next to the one he resided in. It was an apartment in which he shot domestic scenes, as well as a place for models to stay and a place for James and Bren to conduct love affairs outside of their relationship.

"No, we're headed to the studio in Pioneer Square. It's been a hard couple of weeks. Bren and I are separating. It's not looking so good. Anyway, Bren is taking both of the apartments and has left me with the studio. We...I mean, I, have an air mattress set up for you there and I'll be taking the couch, if that's cool with you."

It hurt to think of Gauge packing her belongings, sweaters that I sometimes wore, artwork off the walls, picture albums, but in the pit of aching nausea that churned in my gut I felt a small seed of warmth and hope. I was empathic for James' pain and his loss, but I welcomed our shared experience mourning lost loves.

When we arrived at the industrial warehouse studio, I followed him up the two flights of steep stairs and into the colorful loft. The studio was full of creative, vibrant energy. A graffiti mural of lush, juicy orange and candy-colored blue filled one wall and his sanded and finished hardwood floors retained painted break dance circles from the previous tenants. James poured me a glass of sparkling water and proceeded to pull out sheets, blankets, and pillows for the air mattress that lay by the large night-filled windows. Without words, I awkwardly changed into my pajamas and burrowed in under the covers.

"Good night, Madison," James called from the other side of the room divider.

"Good night, Mr. Mogul." I never called him that before, but it seemed to fit. I respected him and admired the way he seemed to retain control, even while experiencing a move and a breakup. I didn't handle transitions as gracefully.

I woke up to James making breakfast and the scent of chocolate. He toasted bagels and set out small dishes of hummus and soy butter. He heated soy milk on the burner and added rich cocoa to the warm milk, which filled the room with a sweet scent that made me salivate. He remembered that I was vegan and bought some of my favorite foods to have around the studio. I rose from the slowly deflating air mattress and tiptoed to the other side of the divider, which separated the living space from the workspace in his studio. A pot of coffee was brewing and James was mid-bite in an onion bagel topped with lox, cream cheese, and capers when he spotted me. I was wearing pajama pants that my mom sent me the previous Christmas (navy blue with little snowmen dancing in a wintery blizzard), mismatched argyle socks, and a purple cotton camisole, which clung to my breasts and torso. I rubbed my eyes with my fists, reaching around for my glasses.

"Good morning. How did you sleep? Was the air mattress okay?" He asked, while pouring steaming hot chocolate into a tall glass and pulling out a bar stool for me in the small kitchenette.

"Yes, it was perfect. I love all the sunlight that floods this studio. Your windows are amazing! You're lucky, it must be wonderful to work with so much natural light... as a photographer."

"The sun did decide to come out this morning. Not always the case here in Seattle. You want to talk about the shoot?"

"Sure. What do you have in mind?" I took a sip of my cocoa, beaming with excitement.

Working with James is always different than working with other producers. He's an artist. It's always collaboration between us. Working with him, I feel like we are making beautiful images that challenge the way that people perceive bondage. There isn't anything pornographic about the complex sculptural work and intimate photography that James produces. Rather, there is an element of pure, natural beauty and subtle eroticism in his gaze, which he brilliantly captures on film.

"I was up all night making sketches. I couldn't sleep. Here, take a look at these." James picked up a file folder full of papers and laid them out on the folding table in the middle of the room alongside other necessities for the afternoon: neatly coiled bundles of rope, several ball gags, and safety shears.

A series of sketches lay in front of me, pencil on paper, of a female figure bound in rope with one foot on a tower of precariously placed apple boxes that were ready to tumble. One of the figure's arms was bound tightly behind her back, the other, tied around the wrist, reached longingly upward and outward toward an object of desire just out of reach.

"So, what do you think? It's all about yearning. Obtaining the unobtainable." He pointed to the drawing and the woman's upward gaze. I smiled and nodded, excited to slip into this role.

"I figured I would do something a bit more conceptual with you since you are an artist. What do you think?" James was giddy with his concept and the opportunity with a willing model.

"I love it!" I beamed and headed to the model's dressing room to slip out of my pajama bottoms and into the black négligée that I had packed in my suitcase for the shoot. It was a Valentine's Day present from Gauge and it was the only piece of actual lingerie that I owned. After a dab of foundation and a light coating of lip-gloss, I was ready. Lights and props were set, so I stepped out directly into the warm spotlight. Mr. Mogul picked up a coil of rope and approached.

"Wow, you look beautiful. You look different. I think your hair is longer than the first time we met? Mmmm, okay, well are you ready Ms. Young?" he asked, holding the first coil of rope to my skin and whispering teasingly into my ear. I felt nervous and shaky, like I was being asked to dance for the first time at homecoming.

"Yes, Mr. Mogul. I'm ready." As I looked up at my Daddy, I knew I was ready for our dance to begin. He circled my body and pulled me close as he cinched the braided jute fibers tightly around my ribs, taking my breath away. His hands wandered up and down my body, as if sculpting my clay form into the vision he imagined. I purred with each coil, each cinch, and each touch, pacing my breathing, in and out, the ropes cutting hard. He began to adjust the ropes, adding greater tension, heaving at the ropes that connected the chest harness to the overhead points bolted to the ceiling above, like a sailor attempting to control billowing sails. My body weight was suspended from the ground with my toes pointing and reaching for the tower of toppling apple boxes and my hand, the hand of a marionette, extended futilely toward the object of my desire.

"You look amazing, Madison. Just keep doing what you're doing. This is beautiful. This is just what we wanted." The camera fired off shot after shot as I gazed into the distance, visualizing my Daddy, visualizing Mr. Mogul's face and body, near tears from the growing pain and intensity of the bondage position and the emotional turmoil from having Mr. Mogul so close, yet not being able to look him in the eyes and say, "I want you, Daddy."

As tears welled in my eyes, he lifted my body up, relieving the tension in my muscles and nerves, which had taken all of the pressure that they could stand.

"It's okay, Maddie, I've got you." He held my body in his arms like one of the lifts in ballet that always enchanted me as a little girl. James gazed up at me as I stared down at him, tears gently streaming down my cheeks, still wanting what was just out of reach. Still holding me in his arms he pressed me close to his body and bowed his head, his lips finding my flesh, starting at my navel and working his way up to my breasts, my neck, and eventually my lips. He slowly brought me down to the ground, caressing me as he unwrapped my limbs, his mouth tracing the red marks that were left behind. I was liquid, a confused mess of desire and need, laughter and sobs, moaning with pleasure. He scooped me up off of the ground, ropes dangling from my arms and torso, and placed me on the air mattress, where he unzipped his jeans and removed his white T-shirt and underwear. His chest, strong and defined, was covered in hair. He was the first man I had been with in two years, and the only man with chest hair that I had ever felt up against my skin. His hands and mouth toyed with my breasts, then he gently slid his condom-covered cock into my tight, dripping cunt. I nuzzled my face against Daddy's furry chest while he held me close, pumping his cock into me, both of us insatiable and hungry with desire. Daddy came hard, as I clenched around his cock, then he curled up next to me, my limbs were still twined in rope.

"Thank you, Daddy," I whispered in his ear.

"You're a good girl, Maddie."

◇◇◇

FROM THAT DAY FORWARD, we couldn't get enough of one another. He flew to San Francisco for my birthday and we fucked on my rooftop while watching the sunset over the foggy city. I flew to Seattle for Thanksgiving, where we prepared a vegan feast of Tofurkey, artichokes, and mashed potatoes. He spent an hour creating the perfect lighting for our dinner and dressing the table with autumn leaves he found on the sidewalk pooled under cement-bound oak saplings that lined the streets and avenues of his Pioneer Square studio. We ran around playfully, inspired by overcast Seattle afternoons, me dressed in head-to-toe latex with James' ropes clenched firmly around my body, accentuating and hugging my curves, binding my ass into one tight package.

The seasons passed by with haste and I felt like my life was split between Seattle and San Francisco. My queer activist life immersed in the arts remained in San Francisco, but work and stress melted away once I handed over the keys to the gallery intern and boarded a flight to Seattle, where I would be welcomed into the arms of Daddy. When I was with Daddy, computers were turned off and books were shut, and it would just be us.

Christmas came, and I flew to Seattle to be with Daddy. We sat around the loft sipping cheap champagne out of licorice straws, feeding one another artichokes dipped in melted butter, and huddling around the television watching *Scrooged*. At home in Ohio it was our tradition to watch this movie every year, my brother and I laughing hysterically as my dad mimicked the high-pitched voice of the air-headed Ghost of Christmas Present in her large pink taffeta princess dress. "Sometimes you have to *slap* them in the face to get their attention," my dad would shout in a falsetto voice.

12

I SAT IN MY Castro studio apartment at my kitchen table, answering emails while my cats rubbed up against my legs. Bouncing back and forth from my Femina Potens emails to my Madison Young emails. Travel for work still kept me couch surfing and in and out of airports around two weeks out of the month.

In contrast to my relationship with Gauge, travel actually created closeness and trust in my relationship with James. We were two independent people, madly in love, and we supported one another in our individual wellness and careers. James didn't have the streak of jealousy that I was accustomed to with Gauge.

James and I celebrated our one-year anniversary over that summer. He had moved to the Bay Area four months earlier to be closer to me and the freelance directing gigs he had developed at KINK, which had taken a liking to James when he was guest director of their female dominant/male submissive porn site. He was hesitant, at first, to direct for KINK, since his work is much more artistic than pornographic, and he expressed mixed feelings around the pornification and appropriation of the BDSM community for mass consumption and commercial gain. But his trips to San Francisco to visit me became so frequent that he needed a way to pay for all the travel involved. KINK became the solution. James' eye for visual beauty and strong narratives won him an offer of full-time employment and to be able to live a life with a financial cushion, a savings, a retirement, seemed like the responsible thing for Daddy to do. Just like that, our lives were swept away by KINK, but I was holding Daddy's hand in mine.

THAT SEPTEMBER DADDY WAS immersed in preparations for the launch of his new site with KINK, *The Training of O*. Engulfed in his new work life, his calls started to become infrequent, texts often went days unanswered, and I had begun to fear that my Daddy was leaving again. *Had I done something to upset him?*

The doorbell rang and the cats scurried to the door. "Who is it?" I asked into the intercom.

"It's James." I buzzed him into the building. It was the day of the Folsom Street Fair, the world's largest leather event that celebrates everything kink. Once a year, the fair takes over approximately thirteen blocks in San Francisco's SoMa District, attracting over 400,000 people and hundreds of BDSM-oriented vendors from around the globe.

Mr. Mogul and I descended on the enormous crowd at Folsom Street Fair. The sidewalks and streets were filled with naked, hairy men that spanned in age from mid-twenties to sixties or older, some wearing nothing but big leather boots, leather chest harnesses, and leather cock rings. Women and men in British riding jackets rode in carriages pulled along by teams of human ponies who neigh from under their bridled mouths as their drivers whipped them with riding crops and ordered them to giddy up. A thick parade of debauchery, exhibitionism, and voyeurism, all sandwiched between city sidewalks. Young women hung, suspended by rope, from lampposts, and men standing in windows above the fair made out with gay lovers, some jacked one another off as the crowd cheered for orgasms. Two men paraded down the street with butt plugs protruding from their anuses, the toys molded in black silicone and sculpted to look like a curled puppy tail. Each human puppy was collared and on leash, heeling at the high-heeled boots of their latex-clad, whip-wielding mistresses, whose sweat dripped from their faces and necks, falling into their corseted cleavage.

James and I followed behind two human puppies, their tales bobbing up and down with each forward scamper, making our way to the KINK stage that was set up around 8th and Folsom. Lorelei Lee, a bombshell bondage model, sat smiling and sipping on a diet soda at the KINK booth beside the stage. She was wearing a white latex nurse's outfit and signing autographs on black and white fetish photographs of herself stamped with the KINK logo. Peter Acworth beckoned to us over crowds of people: "James, Madison, this way!"

We waded through nearly nude, sweaty bodies, slippery latex bottoms, ball-gagged submissives, and drooling creatures of every persuasion. A leggy brunette onstage—who was being pummeled erratically by a piston-powered dildo machine—captivated me. Her screams of pleasure echoed through the crowd as on-lookers cheered and applauded. Peter ushered James and I into the roped-off area designated for performers.

I kissed James and took a seat next to Lorelei, where a stack of my photos sat in a tall pile, waiting to be autographed for eager fans. After four years of consistent work in the adult industry, I was becoming a familiar face to many viewers, and as a member of the KINK family, had developed a loyal fan base. Peter ushered James onto the KINK stage, and one of the production assistants on duty escorted a new model onto the elevated platform, Bobbi Starr. She was tall, with long chestnut-colored hair, a warm, beautiful smile, and optimistic, sunny eyes that seemed not yet jaded from working in the industry. She had a look of wonderment on her face as she gazed out at the sea of people and looked up at James, expectant and giggly.

I felt an unexpected jolt of jealousy as his hands touched her hands and ran up and down her body, entwining her limbs in his rope and hoisting her off the ground. A secure chest harness compressed and accentuated her breasts, and James toyed with them, pinching her nipples and spinning her around in dizzying circles as the audience watched, captivated. They were flirting, I realized. *There's nothing wrong with flirting, we are in an open relationship, we can flirt or fuck whomever we want. Right?* Suddenly the lines of polyamory felt blurry, confused by the complications of sex work.

I sat at the booth next to Lorelei, trying not to pay attention to or care about what was going on with James and Bobbi on the stage. *This is work.* I flirted with the riggers that tied me up as well. It was innocent and compartmentalized...just work.

I looked up to see who was standing next in line: a round man in leather pants a couple sizes too small and a leather vest that exposed snow-white chest hair grinned down at me.

"Can you make this out to George?" he asked. "It's my birthday! Can you put on there happy birthday?" He handed me a photograph he had printed from a site I modeled for called House of Gord. In the photo I am corseted, hooded, and stuffed with a stainless steel anal hook while I dangle, suspended from the ceiling, twenty feet in the air in a foyer, like a chandelier.

"Of course, George! Happy birthday!" I signed the photograph with a silver marker and gave the photo a kiss, leaving a red lipstick mark.

I grabbed a cold energy drink from the cooler and took a gulp of the sweet beverage. I needed the caffeine if I was going to put up with this amount of public interaction and still project the energetic, positive personality that the public expected from Madison Young.

Lorelei is more than a kinky porn star, she's a writer, and I often find myself in healthy competition with her. We are artists of different mediums—she is a quiet and humble star in the San Francisco literary community with a compelling luminescent energy that shines from her. When she speaks, she makes you want to listen. She would show up at Femina Potens open mics and for our monthly writers series to divulge sweet, subtle intimacies in a breathless voice. It felt romantic, and she seemed vulnerable in a brave and enticing way.

Lorelei had leapt feet-first into the depressing landscape of the San Fernando Valley's mainstream porn industry where she didn't just get tied up or vibrated to orgasm, but where real pulsing condom-less cocks pounded in and out of her under bad lighting and cheesy narratives played out in come-stained porno mansions. I admired her for being able to bounce in and out of the sand-trap that was L.A. with such grace and ease and still fit snugly back into her San Francisco lifestyle, her pockets full of L.A. porn money. I had started to consider the possibility of shooting in L.A. myself. After all, I was now having sex with men, and James and I were in an open relationship. If I was shooting in L.A., rather than globe-trotting around the world chasing fetish producers, my life might be more streamlined and give me more time to spend at home with Daddy. Now that I had a Daddy, I didn't want to lose him.

"Hey Lorelei, who is your agent in L.A.?" I asked, smiling while a topless-except-for-rope woman flashed a camera in my face.

"Oh, I'm with Speigler. He's pretty good. Are you thinking about doing some work in L.A.? You don't do boy/girl scenes, do you?" She said, taking a quick sip of diet cola and signing a photograph for a human puppy who stood on his hind legs panting on the table. The puppy playfully swatted at Lorelei's hand as she drew on the photograph. "Behave, Puppy," she scolded, shaking her finger and returned the autographed photo to the puppy's mouth.

"I haven't done any sex scenes with guys yet, but I'm open to it. I think it would be nice to not have to travel around so much for work. Just jet down to L.A., in and out, right?" Two other models relieved us from our duties and we walked over to the backstage area, where James was just finishing up.

Lorelei unzipped her sweaty latex dress, "Well, I'd recommend Speigler. He'll get you work. Some of the girls will tell you that he's a bit controlling and has a Daddy complex, but I think he's sweet. Good luck!" She toweled off and slipped on a simple blue sundress, pinning up her peroxide-blonde Monroe-like locks of hair, while I did the same, peeling off the latex panties and pearlescent top and toweling off my sticky flesh before slipping on a vintage silk green dress that looks like something an amorous June Cleaver might wear after tucking Beaver into bed.

James took my hand in his and we broke through the crowd of perversion. "How's my Little Girl?" Papa asked as we rode BART back to his Oakland penthouse apartment, his hand running up and down my thigh.

"I'm good, Papa. Are you fucking Bobbi?"

"What? No, I'm not fucking anyone but you right now, Maddie. What makes you say that?"

"I saw the way you looked at her, Daddy."

"I was tying her up, baby. Bobbi was the girl I shot for *Training of O* last week. She's just a model, that's all. Understand? I'm your Daddy and only your Daddy. Got it?" I smiled, nodding my head in approval.

We arrived home, a sixth floor penthouse loft with a back door that opened onto the rooftop overlooking downtown Oakland. We were the only residents in the building. During the day it was home to law offices, accountants, bookkeepers, and insurance companies. At night, after the offices emptied out and the nine-to-five office staff went home to make dinner for their families, my screams and moans couldn't be heard by anyone but Daddy. That night it would be a cane—Mr. Mogul had a new toy, a rattan cane he would use like a switch against my bare bottom. I quickly shed the green dress.

"Ass in the air my beautiful, beautiful slut." He grabbed my ass and pulled it upward, smashing my face into the carpeted living room floor. Tendrils of strawberry blonde hair fell into my eyes, the cane came down hard on round mounds of flesh.

"Thank you, Daddy." I exhaled in gratitude, digging my fingernails into the carpet.

The strike of the cane against my body stung, but it was a welcome sting, the sting of affection, like a bold, beautiful kiss from my lover. When the cane made impact with my body I winced for a moment as waves of pain melted into buttery pleasure and spread over me. Soon I stopped wincing, as my body relaxed, feeling fluid and welcoming to each loving stroke that I graciously received.

Daddy teased me with multiple sweet light taps on my thighs that built anticipation for stronger impact. The thin reed cut through the air with a whistle before landing with a delicious, precise sting that felt not unlike the burn of jalapeños on my tongue. Daddy's hands traced over raised, reddening welts, his mouth licking my flesh, kissing the fiery stripes that marked my thighs and ass. I inhaled deeply, opening my eyes and wondering if that was my kiss goodnight. No, of course not. That would be too tender. Daddy's mouth opened and he spit on me before raining a thunderous storm of percussive beats in rapid succession on my eager ass. I was overwhelmed with intense sensation, and I squirmed both away from and toward the rainfall of strikes while screeching like a giddy schoolgirl, pleasure and pain releasing in one confusing, emotional purge. Daddy exhaled and tossed the cane aside, then pulled my naked body close to his. I was raw, red, and emotionally cleansed. I felt whole in his arms, and safe. Daddy pulled me into his bed and wrapped his arms and legs around me, and I feel his warm furry chest rise and fall with every breath. I was home.

13

A HOT, DRY SUMMER was in full effect on the Friday before Memorial Day weekend in L.A. I opened the door to the Bank of America and the arctic cold from the blasting air-conditioning was a welcome contrast to the stale, arid heat. I walked the two miles to the bank from my agent Mark Speigler's apartment in Canoga Park.

I was one of several girls staying at Speigler's apartment that week being carted around by a driver to multiple shoots in "porn valley." At Speigler's, there were several options for places to sleep: a sectional couch in the living room that fit two girls, or two bedrooms, which Speigler rented out for a minimal price. There were girls constantly coming and going, either represented by Speigler or wanting to be represented by Speigler. I had been represented by Speigler for three months and was going on my second week on the sectional. Lorelei, who was also in town that week shooting, was my bunkmate.

Speigler is short, unshaven, and grisly. His blemished, squinty eyes, and sloth-like unkempt round body give him the appearance of a rodent. His apartment perfectly reflected its caretaker, with random clutter piled up in every corner. The carpet smelled of cat litter, and framed photographs of different incarnations of the infamous Speigler Girls hung on the walls in cheap wooden frames. Models' urine samples—Spiegler tested the girls for drugs—sat next to a defunct PC computer that had remained untouched nearly ten years. Stacks of unopened mail cluttered the dining table, buried under magazines like *Hustler* and *Penthouse,* which featured girls that he had represented. A copy of *Los Angeles Magazine* sat on the table, featuring an article on the newest starlet on his roster—a barely eighteen-year-old lithe and inquisitive girl, fascinated by architecture and the avant-garde—Sasha Grey. Dirty dishes often piled up in the kitchen and attracted bugs, reminding me of neglected university housing of my youth. The bathroom was always cluttered with trash of the trade: discarded enema bottles, cheap red lipstick, used disposable razors, douche bottles, and half-empty fruit-scented body wash.

After working for two weeks without a day off, I finally had a reprieve. I walked to the bank to deposit my checks: $8,400 from seven companies with names like GF Films, DP Productions, JM Studios, and Mile High, Inc. I approached the counter and prepared to sign my real name, a name I hadn't heard out loud in weeks. "Tina Butcher," I mumbled, while filling out the deposit slip. It felt foreign, like a lie. *Madison Young earned these checks, not Tina Butcher. She had no part in this.* Regardless, it felt good to finally have money of my own. I knew as soon as the checks cleared, I would be able to pay for the remodel work on our new Castro gallery space.

I signed a lease on the new gallery in my dream location only a month before. When I saw that the Image Leather storefront was empty and available for lease, I knew it would be a perfect home for Femina Potens.

I felt like an impostor holding so much money all at once. It made me nervous. I held the checks close, nervously, I didn't want anyone to see the names of the companies written on them. What if the tellers or patrons recognized these names? It felt like dirty whore money and the sooner it was out of my hands and used for something good, the better. I approached the teller, shaking and slightly afraid they wouldn't believe a twenty-six-year-old girl was depositing $8,400. I was afraid if they asked me my name I might respond with Madison, instead of Tina. I felt like a sexual outlaw in a corporate system.

A day off was a rare and appreciated gift, when you were a Speigler girl. Speigler wanted his girls to be available 24/7. Always available and willing to do anything, Speigler girls were a special breed. Many of us were into BDSM and rough sex, and Speigler liked to play Daddy (though I never thought of him that way). For me, it was more comfortable to be surrounded by other kinky women. The Speigler girls tended to be smarter than other industry girls, more self reliant, responsible, and less likely to have the canned porn star look with fake tits, fake tan, and fake nails. Many of us were fair-skinned, natural, and curvy, and Speigler wasn't afraid to represent women over the age of twenty-three. Other agencies hosted a continually rotating bevy of eighteen to twenty-one year olds who were in and out of the business before anyone ever knew their names. I was happy to be a Speigler girl, aligned with other women who shared my passions.

IN THIS INDUSTRY, A day off can mean one of several things: it's the holidays, you are "over shot" and the big companies want fresh faces, you have a bad reputation for being late or showing up too fucked up on drugs or liquor to perform, or you've contracted an STD. That day, I just happened to not have a booking. Earlier that month however, I had been forced to take what the girls refer to as an STD vacation. It's a roll of the dice every time you step in front of the camera. Los Angeles porn companies, at that time, didn't subscribe to the practice of using condoms on their cocks or their toys. Instead, we relied on a monthly STD screening for chlamydia and gonorrhea, and HIV tests were administered and kept on record at AIM, the Adult Industry Medical clinic and testing facility.

"It's the only time I ever get off work. Take advantage of it, you're lucky. Last time I had an STD vacation, I went to Disneyland with my sister," Adriana, another Speigler girl, said sardonically as we rode to the Burbank Airport in Speigler's Mercedes. If I couldn't work, I was flying home to be with Daddy. I didn't feel lucky and I didn't want an STD vacation. My private parts were swollen, itchy, red, and inflamed, and felt completely removed from the rest of my body.

Only an hour earlier I was at the Van Nuys Urgent Care lying on a table with my feet in stirrups for an examination, the doctor probing with cotton swabs and a speculum, I felt like I was going to vomit. I had been vomiting all morning and was running a high temperature that left me sweaty and red, with a complexion so bad makeup couldn't hide it.

Dr. Riggly, the doctor at the urgent care, was known as the porno doctor. He was a little sketchy—he asked for my stage name, which didn't seem relevant—but I was desperate and needed someone with a medical license to look at me and tell me what my body was doing. As a porn actress, every time you visit a doctor you risk judgment and bias. I'm sure Dr. Riggly had judgments of his own, but I found comfort in knowing that I wasn't his first sex worker patient.

He delivered the diagnosis, "Well, young lady, you have a couple things going on. You have a textbook case of herpes, for one. I mean, if I wanted to show a medical student a classic case of genital herpes, I would show him this outbreak. It's quite bad. You also have bacterial vaginosis and a urinary tract infection." The doctor scribbled something on his pad of paper, tore the paper from his pad and handed it to me. "Here's a prescription for some antibiotics and I'll write you a prescription for an antiviral for the herpes outbreak. Once you're all cleared up you should continue to take this antiviral prophylactically to suppress future outbreaks and to significantly decrease your risk of transmitting to any future partners. I'll give you some pamphlets to look over, okay?"

"When will I be able to work again?" I began to worry about the bills that were already piling up from the gallery, which I had yet to really be present at during the renovation of our new storefront.

"You should be able to be back at work in about seven to ten days, after a full seven days of treatment and after your outbreak is completely healed."

I felt so stupid, forever marked with a scarlet "H." *What will Daddy say? Will he still want to be with me now that I'd be living the rest of my life with herpes? Why did I decide to work in the porn industry again? This wasn't part of the plan, was it?*

When I told Speigler, he seemed unfazed. "Everyone in the adult industry has herpes. It's not a big deal. Go home, take your medicine, and let me know when I can start booking you again. Let me know as soon as it clears up."

While some girls took their STD vacations in Disneyland, I planned on dedicating mine to Femina Potens. Our gallery was reopening in four weeks and there was much preparation to be done. *Spread Magazine* was going to do a cover shoot and interview about the gallery and the way that I was funding the gallery—through sex work. I had coined a phrase through social media that I used to blog about my porno experiences—Anal for Art. Four anal scenes paid the gallery rent, another four paid the deposit, and ten anal scenes paid for the remodel. It was simple math, and it meant that anything in life was within my grasp; I just needed enough anal scenes to get there.

Once my outbreak cleared up, it was back to the math, and back to L.A. I had money in my pockets and a clean bill of health. I felt like a gladiator of sexual entertainment bravely facing the lions. I might lose a limb in the process, but I would hobble back into the arena with dignity; I was a dignified whore.

BACK AT SPEIGLER'S AFTER the bank, I go to the mall with Bobbi. I don't place a lot of value on shopping, but I have been getting in touch with my feminine side since dating Mr. Mogul. *Perhaps it's his hyper-masculinity that makes me feel I need to tip the balance on the scales?* I had begun exploring my femme identity with high heels and vintage dresses.

We strolled through Bloomingdale's, testing perfumes, and I wondered which one Daddy might like. I needed a signature scent, and he can be particular about smells. Once or twice I came home smelling like a new perfume that I tested at the mall and they all repelled him. I wanted a scent that would turn him on, a scent that would make him want to fuck me immediately. I wanted to find a scent that did for him what the scent of rope did for me.

"It's a rite of passage. Choosing a scent is something that a woman does before she, in turn, becomes that scent. I know it sounds corny but it's true," Bobbi shared. "It's part of how people will remember you, they will think of your face and then swear that they could smell lavender or spices or vanilla, whatever. It's an important decision, Madison." She picked up a bottle of Coco Chanel and spritzed it on her wrist. The scent was strong and vulnerable, a delicate blend of feminine flowers, warmed with wood and leather.

"This is my scent. Classic, isn't it? I remember the first time my mom bought me a bottle of this perfume. My mom uses Chanel Number Five." She grabbed her mother's perfume and inhaled deeply, closing her eyes, drifting off to some fond memory.

"I want to get something that James will like," I pondered, as we veered off to the neighboring shoe department where high heels of every color and style stood promptly at attention like so many pieces of fine art. Some were more expensive than the artwork at Femina Potens.

"Well, all men love vanilla. It's pretty much a given. Look for something sweet. How long have you two been dating?"

"Almost two years now. Yeah...two years in July. We just moved in together about a month ago. We've both been working a lot though, I miss him."

"Are you guys open? Or how do you handle the whole porn thing? My fiancé and I are open. It works for us." She fingered the small solitary diamond on her right hand.

"Right now, it's just us," I said. "I'm open to us being with other people and I know he is supportive of that, I'm just not comfortable with him fucking other models, you know? It's...I don't know. It gets complicated. I don't want him fucking my coworkers. I just can't deal with that."

My phone rang, and it was Daddy. "It's James, I'm going to get this. I'll be in the perfume department. Vanilla, right?"

"Daddy! I missed you so much," I was hungry for the sound of Papa's voice.

"Hi, sweetheart. I got your voicemail. I miss you, too. How is my Little Girl?" I could hear hammering and nail guns going off in the background.

"I'm good, Daddy. I was just talking about you. Oh, did the volunteers show up to help you with building the wall?" I picked up a bottle of La Vanilla Laboratories Vanilla and Grapefruit blend and sprayed it on my wrist. I inhaled a bright, cheerful bouquet that had a sexy, rich sweetness. *This is it, my scent!*

"Yeah, they showed up, but they basically helped sweep and hand me tools. They didn't really have any experience. They were sweet, though. Who were you talking to about me?" Daddy shouted over the phone to be heard over the loud clamoring of hammers and nails. I was so proud that my Daddy is helping me build and launch the new Femina Potens. We were doing it together.

"Oh, Bobbi. She's staying at Speigler's right now, too." I handed the woman behind the counter my debit card. She handed it back to me and pointed to the digital read-out that said declined. Puzzled, I reached for my wallet and paid in cash.

The phone began beeping with a call from Speigler, "Daddy, Speigler is calling. I gotta go. I'll call you tonight. I love you."

Daddy's voice came through and I smiled, "Love you too, Maddie."

I picked up Speigler's incoming call and he got straight to the point. "I have a shoot for you."

"When?"

"Now. You need to be there in an hour. Where are you?" His voice was gruff and unappealing, he sounded like a troll.

"I'm across the street with Bobbi at the mall."

"Well, get your ass over here and grab your things so we can make it to the shoot on time." Speigler barked into the phone.

I rushed back to the apartment and rifled through my backpack for my anal prep kit. Whether or not we are booked for an anal sex scene, we are always prepared for one. An anal scene pays $1,200 (as opposed to $1,000), which means more money in the girls' pockets as well as in Speigler's. I fashioned a preparation kit of baby wipes, a douche bottle, an enema bottle, a small bottle of lube, and a lucite dildo.

In two hours, I was on set, spritzed with new vanilla perfume, asshole clean, and ready to be pummeled by a huge cock. Don began throwing me around like a rag doll while Ashley Blue masturbated and ran commentary, "I think that slut likes it. She's a filthy whore. Fuck that dirty whore, Don!" He stuck his huge cock into my ass and then into her ass and then into my mouth and then into her mouth. Ashley stuck her hand down her throat, gagged herself, then spit huge gobs of saliva into my mouth and I spit more saliva back into her mouth. It was a relay race of pornographic proportions, a theatrical ballet of vulgarity.

Don was Ashley's agent, and he also worked as a performer in adult films. I had met and performed with Don multiple times but he never remembered my name, and he always acted superior to all the other talent on set. As much as I despised him, I still loved having his huge cock in me, deep and fast. Don maneuvered my body into a pile driver position and plunged, fucking me hard. I was only moments away from coming, I began screaming, panting, and barking like a dog. Don pulled his cock out and looked down, horrified. *Did I not cleanse enough? Is there shit on his cock? But it isn't poop, it's blood!*

"Go to the bathroom and clean up, it's probably just a little tear. Does it hurt?" Ashley asked, taking a closer look.

"No, I feel fine." I felt unhurt, but I was scared and embarrassed and I just wanted to go home. I ran off to the bathroom with bloody baby wipes up against my butt. My ass was bleeding badly, and I couldn't get it to stop. After a few frantic minutes, all of the blood seemed to be gone and, like a good gladiator, I fixed my makeup and hopped back in the arena.

Don re-entered, but I started to bleed again. *Damn it, I can do this!* Don cleaned off his dick and we decided that he should just fuck my pussy for a bit and then pummel Ashley more. Ashley and I knelt at Don's waist, taking his come in our mouths and swapping it back and forth.

"Cut," the director shouted. "That's a wrap." An assistant handed me a towel and some water and asked if there was anything that I need.

"Uh...I have to go to the bathroom." I ran to the toilet and sat down. There was an uncontrollable urge building, a pressure that felt like I was about to shit everywhere, but what came out wasn't shit—it was blood. A *lot* of blood. At least a cup poured out as I sat on the toilet, crying in horror. I called Speigler and begged him to pick me up.

"Yeah. What is it?" Speigler answered, curtly.

"I'm done. I need someone to pick me up. I'm going to the airport," I sobbed into the phone. My voice was hoarse from crying, screaming, and moaning for hours.

"What happened? We have you booked on Tuesday. Are you coming back Tuesday?" I couldn't think about Tuesday, and I needed a little sympathy. I needed a moment to regroup outside of L.A. I needed my Daddy. *Where are the promises that everything is going to be okay?*

"Speigler, I just busted my ass. It's bleeding!" I cried, questioning my own sanity.

"That happens all the time. It's no big deal. This guy Tuesday has a really small dick. It will be easy." I grabbed more toilet paper to blot my bloody anus.

"Speigler! I'm sitting on the toilet and blood is gushing out of my asshole. Do you hear me?" It was the last bit of fight that I had in me. I wanted out, and back to the arms of Daddy.

"Okay, okay, I'll send someone over."

I called James. "Daddy?" I cried, still squatting on the toilet. One of my glued-on eyelashes had fallen off and mascara was running down my face.

"I'm coming home, Daddy. I need you to pick me up." I used my shirt to wipe the snot coming out of my nose, it seemed more comforting than toilet paper.

"Baby, I was planning on playing pool tonight. What's wrong?" I was so happy to hear Daddy's voice, but I didn't have energy to negotiate or explain the details of the situation.

"I need you, Daddy. I'm hurt. I'm catching the 8:00 P.M. flight so I'll be in Oakland at nine. I love you, Daddy. I just want to go home. My anus is bleeding." As we spoke, I slipped on a clean pair of panties and contemplated my puffy, sad eyes. Bondage modeling seemed so easy by comparison, so safe and secure. The sex being filmed in the San Fernando Valley always felt foreign to me, removed from everything honest and genuine that I believe in. Clearly, my body agreed.

"God, Maddie! Do you need to go to the hospital?" Mr. Mogul's concern sounded perfect to my ears.

"I just want to get home. Let's talk about it then." I felt reassured.

"Okay, Maddie. Come back in one piece."

On the trip, every twenty minutes like clockwork my ass filled with blood and I had to bolt to the restroom to expel it. I felt like I was dying. *Feminist porn star found dead on commuter flight to Oakland from Burbank from anal hemorrhage,* I imagined. It was not the headline I wanted to leave behind.

Daddy picked me up from the baggage carousel, escorted me to his pickup truck, and drove me straight to the hospital, all the while holding my hand.

The doctors immediately hooked me up to an IV. The constant enemas caused a dangerous level of dehydration, and my rectum was starting to prolapse. I'd heard of rectal prolapse: it happens when your rectal tissue basically hangs out of your anus like an outie belly button. It happens when your sphincter is severely weakened, one of the causes is extended anal penetration. Some people fetishize prolapse, endearingly referring to it as "rosebud." My tear was significant and deep (deep in your anus you have less nerve endings, which is why I didn't feel it), but it wasn't bad enough to need surgery. Still, the doctor put me on permanent anal rest. He advised me to "never stick anything up there again." This was not the advice that I wanted or needed.

Daddy climbed up into the hospital bed and I rested my head in his lap while the IV slowly dripped. "I've got to work, Papa."

Mr. Mogul ran his hands through my hair, "Shhhh... Daddy will take care of it. Right now we need to take care of you. Everything is going to be okay, Little Girl, Daddy is going to take good care of you."

14

Topsoil blanketed the rich forest floor. We were
standing in cool earth, and James helped me scoop
soil into two green ceramic flower pots. Coming from the
compact spaces and cement sidewalks of San Francisco, I
was used to performing this ritual with store-bought potting
soil that I poured out of plastic bags. I missed James.
I missed the way things used to be. I wanted to go back
to the night we first made love and live it all over again. I
wanted to wake up on some wet, Seattle morning to mugs
full of hot cocoa and watch the rain fall from an inflatable
mattress in his artist's loft in Pioneer Square. I yearned to
feel his warm body next to mine as we wrestled under the
covers, discovering mutual insatiability for each other's
touch. I felt my eyes start to well up with tears, and James
handed me a handkerchief. He was good at having one
nearby to wipe away the tears when something wasn't right.
He had become an expert at holding me and calling me his
kitten and letting me know that everything was going to
be okay. I blew my nose a little and handed him back the
handkerchief, a little dirtier from the earth on my fingers.

As soon as we got to Santa Cruz we set our iPhones to search for gardening stores, so I could buy dirt, but when we arrived at the wedding location, I felt a little foolish about bringing dirt into this beautiful natural space. Towering majestic redwood trees, moist earth, and hills of green grass surrounded us; it reminded me of home.

I was preparing for my performance in the wedding of the world's ultimate art couple, Annie Sprinkle and Beth Stephens. Annie and Beth had become family to me—not just artistic mentors but zany aunts who speak my language—and I was elated to share this day with them. Annie Sprinkle started her career working as a porn star in the seventies, and in the late eighties she began to make art about her sex work. Beth was a fellow artist; the two had been friends and collaborators for ten years, but it was only in the previous five years that they became lovers. Love radiated from them, filling whatever room they were in. They were the Yoko Ono and John Lennon of sex, and the Björk and Matthew Barney of love.

Their best performance pieces explored their connection. For "Extreme Kiss," they sat down in a gallery and kissed for three hours. For Cuddle Art they moved a bed into my gallery for a month and would come in on certain days and cuddle in the bed while gallery-goers who signed up for a cuddle appointment joined them in loving embrace. These projects seemed revolutionary to me; a lot of art is about purging negativity, but Annie and Beth were making work about celebrating love. To continue their love-themed art performances, they vowed to get married seven times in seven years, and for each wedding to be a performance—an event to gather, create, and give love and blessings to the community, the world, and each other.

This was their fourth wedding, and this year they were holding the event at the University of California, Santa Cruz, where Beth was the chair of the art department. There, beneath a towering cathedral of redwood trees in the Sinsheimer-Stanley Festival Glen, where every summer Shakespeare is performed in the damp woods, they would recite their vows to each other and to their third love, Earth. The entire wedding was environmentally sustainable and was as much about caring for our environment as about caring for each other. Everyone invited to Annie's and Beth's weddings had been asked to participate, and I offered to do a performance piece, which is how I came to find myself wrist-deep in the soil with James by my side.

Everyone was wearing green (it was the theme of the wedding, after all). In the art of feng shui, it is believed that the color green shouldn't be near a lovers' bed or it will make them sick with jealousy. There must be some truth to that; jealousy was eating me alive. I needed to reconnect with James. It felt like, though I glimpsed him occasionally, we were miles apart, even when he was right in front of me.

The wedding party and artists would be descending off of a hill to a stage that was nestled in the heart of the glen at the start of the ceremony. It could have been a scene out of *A Midsummer Night's Dream*, it was so magical and lush with eroticism and creativity. Sparsely dressed green fairies flitted about, artists in elaborate costumes of goddess-like creatures with flowing green garments that looked like nymphs were blowing bubbles. There was an opera singer in a lime bikini and a whip-wielding dominatrix—Sadie Lune, a dear friend—that sparkled in the sunshine, adorned in gems, sequins, and tulle. She was reminiscent of Madonna's VMA performance of "Like a Virgin," and she had her pet snake coiled around her neck. Annie's fellow veteran porn stars Veronica Vera and Sharon Mitchell were in attendance, along with well-known artist Linda Montano.

"I'd better line up," I said to James, and took my place with the magical misfits, artists, fairies, goddesses, and porn stars. This is my community, my family; we are a varied and visually astounding group of people. It was impossible not to be overcome with happiness standing on this hill, ready to descend and give our offerings to the elated couple whose blessed event made the front page of the local paper. I tried to keep my mind from wandering to what has been consuming my relationship with James: the Internet. Specifically, sites full of pornographic imagery. The images that once signified our positive relationships with our sexual selves and community now filled me with fear and distrust.

James moved to the Bay Area to be with me, but it was his site that really tied him down. KINK offered a comfortable, stable salary, but left me with a partner who was emotionally unavailable. He had been building the world of The Trainer for a long time, compiling it from notes and concepts gathered up and developed over years of experience as a bondage photographer in Seattle. Finally, a company with the resources to make his concept for a BDSM training site a reality had taken an interest in the idea, but something was missing from his initial vision: Sex.

There had to be sex, and sex with Daddy. There was suddenly a price tag on him. Girls he hired would have the experience of being his submissive for an entire week: including bondage, sex, and emotional intimacy. It was more than simply an exchange of bodily fluids and physical closeness. It was a built-in one week on-camera relationship with my Daddy and it was eating me alive. It even extended to my friends and fellow Speigler girls Bobbi Starr, Lorelei Lee, and Adrianna Nicole. They all became a part of the growing anxiety that I was developing around losing Daddy. Many of the girls had strong boundaries, they knew how to compartmentalize and return to their off-screen lives and daily routines, but some girls were in search of a Daddy themselves, some girls didn't care who gets hurt in their process of fulfillment. The experiences lingered on well past their on-screen training, and these girls yearned for something more with James. They called him while we were at dinner and clung onto him at company parties, greedily drawing his attention away from me. It was my job as his submissive, to stand by him always.

When we first discussed the site's development, James talked about male talent–stunt cocks–being brought in for the sex scenes. Six months went by before Mr. Mogul admitted to me his full job description at Kink. He was also working as a sexual performer.

"Why is it okay for you to have sex on film but not for me?" he would ask.

"Because you didn't even ask me!" I yelled. James waited until just days before the site went live to sit down and disclose this secret that he had been keeping.

That kind of a breakdown of communication was becoming typical for us. Mr. Mogul was worried about his future. He felt scared and vulnerable, like he'd been given the choice between a 401K plan and telling his girlfriend the truth. He was choosing the job, and I couldn't really blame him. His work was his security blanket, and he was mine. We tried to create boundaries and come to agreements when it came to work. We discussed what we were comfortable with each other doing on-camera with strangers and what was to be reserved for our home life. The weekly site updates taunted me with images of James breaking our agreements.

After a dramatic outburst about the site, James simply cut off all communication about it. It had become a forbidden subject. The site was an entity of its own. I felt like I could trust Daddy, but not the site. I caught up on gossip in makeup rooms and green rooms full of models that sent shivers up my spine before being called to the set of another production, my mind fully preoccupied by what was happening on Mr. Mogul's set. I never knew what to believe, or when it would stop.

What I didn't know is that we were equals in our isolation. James, terrified that he would lose me, had put up walls and created distance. He avoided conflict whenever possible, and that meant unanswered phone calls and a bed that was often inexplicably empty. I became subject to erratic fits of passion and child-like temper tantrums that would result in public scenes. I stormed out of a four-star restaurant after clawing at the man I loved and tossing both insults and high heels at him. Once, I stood paralyzed on O'Farrell Street as trolley cars full of tourists stared at us feuding. I was immobilized, shaking, on the street corner, unwilling to move forward with James beside me and unsure if I could get past a city block on my own.

I knew I wanted to move forward with him, but neither of us seemed able to make real progress in our relationship, much less create the kind of happiness I was witnessing in that magical glen.

THE GROUP STARTED DOWN the hill, looking a bit silly in platforms and stilettos trying not to tumble into a pile of glitzy broken ankles. With our heads held high we sank into the grove of trees, and something bigger than our group took hold and guided us—a parade of participants that look like a mixture of St. Patrick's Day, Mardi Gras, Gay Pride weekend, and Victoria's Secret at Fashion

Week—onto the stage. It was beautiful, vulnerable, and brave. It made you want to grab hold of the person next to you and give them a big kiss, embrace them with all the love that crackled in the air. We took our seats and watched as Annie and Beth climbed onstage, joined hands, and sat in their thrones.

Here they were royalty, and each of us had something to present to them: a gift, a blessing, a moment of brief entertainment, a breath to share. One man presented himself in a headstand with a ribbon tied around each of his big toes, his legs spread wide. Bells jingled as he wiggled his feet up and down and paper tags dangled from the ribbon with Annie and Beth's names along with words like "Love" and "Peace." A champion yogi presented a series of yoga positions, flowing with ease from one beautiful pose to the next, pushing her body to contortionist extremes.

When it was time for my performance, my gift to them, I handed them each a bowl of dirt and asked them to coat my body with the cool, blessed earth. They dipped their fingers into the ceramic pots of soil and smeared the black mud over my white flesh. Their touch was powerful, filled with love and erotic energy, and my body shivered and tingled as their warm hands traced my thighs, across my breasts, and tenderly around my face, leaving dusty tracks. I was covered with earth, buried standing up and breathing deeply. My toes sunk into a pile of remnant soil as my breath grew stronger, allowing their touch and my exhalations to fill my erotic self until I was overflowing with desire and love for the world and ready for the expulsion of my words. The words weren't going to just fall from my lips this time; I had a coiled scroll of paper with my blessings for the brides tucked into my cunt. My fingers dove between my moist lips and pulled out the soggy tribute to the couple as I moaned out in pleasure.

"Mmmmmm...I think I found it," I said, and the crowd laughed a little. I uncoiled the scroll and composed myself, looking at Annie and Beth. The three of us took a deep breath in and released on a slow exhale in a perfect connection.

"From the depths of my body, my heart and my soul, the radiating aura of love that Annie and Beth share has left permanent imprints on this dirty girl." My eyes welled up, I was so full of emotion. Annie and Beth cooed.

"We are forever planted in common soil," I read, then I kissed the loving couple, wished them all the love and happiness in the world, and headed back to my seat.

Before they exchanged their vows, Annie and Beth wanted us to get in touch with their lover Earth. They slipped off their shoes and stepped onto the soft, green grass.

"We would like to invite all of you to give the earth a massage with your feet," they welcomed, and I slipped off my shoes and watched as James slipped off his. Dress shoes, high heels, flip-flops, and sandals were all discarded as we sunk into the plush landscape, toes curling into green blades of grass while ladybugs maneuvered their way around our manicured nails and beaded ankle bracelets.

"Step right and left, a little to the right, a little to the left. Now a little more to the left. Put your consciousness in your feet." We were a marching army of lovers engaged in a simple dance, and the movement brought us closer together. Watching my mentors—my mothers—leading us forward into battle, connecting us with our lovers, our reality, our potential, I knew where this march would take me. I stared across the grass at James, seeking out his gaze.

"Massage the earth, because she is your sweetheart."

I smiled when our eyes finally met and he smiled back at me. *I am ready to do this. I can do this!*

"Breathe...feel all that love and support." Our feet shuffled back and forth, right and left, right and left. I could either face the demons of my past and move forward, or remain in that past and allow myself to be subject to its corrosion. Before I went anywhere, I needed to go deeper.

"Feel your heart. Open your heart." I needed to give up my weapons, my sword, even my rope, spelunking deeper with a clear head and a pure heart.

"Send that love to your lover Earth." My enemies were jealousy, fear, and shame—not James. James was subject to these emotions as much as I.

"She is starting to relax. Ahhhhhh." I shed these emotions like a snake coming into a new skin, a new life.

Like a Buddhist monk, I gave up all of my worldly possessions. As Daddy's submissive, I would be in service to my lover. I would seek enlightenment and freedom, learn his desires, and focus on the pleasure of someone other than myself.

"With these steps, let us reach your love. Through our senses, we will become your lover. Every day we promise to breathe in your fragrance and be opened by you." On this journey, I would find true contentment within myself, and I would reunite with my love, my Daddy, to create a union as powerful as the one I saw in Annie and Beth.

"Let us not be severed from your love." I knew it was time for training. I knew that it wouldn't be easy on James, or on me. We were both raw and exhausted from fighting, from the fear of losing each other and the anxiety of never getting past the past, but in that moment, I felt ready.

THE SUNRISE OVER THE Santa Cruz Mountains was breathtaking enough to pull me out of bed and toward the room service waiting outside of the soft, warm, compliant bed. James sat on the deck, facing the woods, reading the paper, and eating his morning pancakes and sausage. I splashed my face with cool water and prepared myself for a talk. As I watched him through the glass sliding door for a few minutes, I wondered if he could feel my eyes on him, and if he would turn around. I grabbed my camera from the small indoor dining table and stepped out. A squirrel with a big, bushy tail jumped from tree to tree.

The morning sun shined down on James, who was wearing the hotel's big white terrycloth robe and hiding behind movie-star sunglasses. I wanted to find him, to find us. I snapped a photo and he was disgruntled by the flash, but amused by my early-morning impishness. It made him smile; I wish I had caught the smile on film.

"Mr. Mogul?" I sat down on the white lawn chair next to him.

"Maddie," he said, looking my way.

My hands were antsy and quickly made their way to my mouth. Nervously, I chewed on my nails. I needed a manicure; my nails were a wreck—chipped and filthy with soil from the wedding.

"I was thinking..."

"Stop picking, Maddie." Daddy scooped my hands away from my mouth. "Do I need to put you in mittens?" I smiled at the thought of an anxiety-laden child with mittens belted onto her hands. I pulled my hands from my mouth and put them in my lap. "Yes, Daddy. I was thinking about us and...I'd really like to do submissive training on your site."

Mr. Mogul picked his napkin up from his lap and wiped syrup from the corner of his mouth. He sat the napkin on the table and took another sip of his coffee. His site was never an easy subject for us and I felt his hackle rising.

"I don't think it's a good idea, Maddie. This is my job. I can't take any chances here. If you flip out on set, what am I going to do? How is that going to look?"

"I won't flip out, I promise, Mr. Mogul. Remember what Dossie said?" Dossie was our therapist, a respected pillar of health in the queer and kink communities and an expert on open relationships. "If I'm ever going to get past this I have to face my fears. I want to do this, Daddy. I want to learn how to make you happy."

Daddy leaned over and brushed my hair out of my face, tucking a lock behind my ear. "Maddie, you already make me happy."

"I want to be a good submissive. I want to put our relationship first, and in order to do that I need to put all of my baggage aside and figure out what makes us tick." At this point tears were streaming down my face. I may not have been doing the best job of showing composure, but at least I was being honest.

I took Daddy's hand and slowly took off his sunglasses so I could look him in the eye, "I can do this."

He looked at me, stroked my hair, and waited a moment before giving in. "Okay. When we get back home I'll tell the talent office to put you on the schedule."

"Oh thank you, Papa!" I leaned in to give him a big, teary kiss. I wiped my eyes and slipped on his sunglasses to cover the mascara dripping from my tears.

Undertaking submission training was about more than me overcoming my jealousy of his other models. It was a personal journey that Daddy and I were committing to, to see if we could make it to the other end of the tunnel. We had to move forward, because we couldn't stay here. Here, there were only lies and deceit. We would use this week of work to construct not only entertainment, but also a set of protocols, a new type of bondage and erotic play, a new connection that would serve to deepen our devotion to each other.

"I want one by the tree, Daddy!" Trees and nature walks surrounded the resort where we stayed. It smelled of life, of things green and of growth. I knelt down and ran my fingers through the vibrant grass, digging my fingernails into the dirt. I breathed in its scent as Daddy's camera flashed. If I was going to find my connection with Mr. Mogul, I was going to need to strip myself of all of my armor. I was going to walk into this situation humbled and debased, and offer myself fully and wholly to him. This wasn't about rope anymore, this wasn't about looking good in bondage or being the top rope suspension model. I wouldn't be allowed rope there; we were going beyond the ropes.

Daddy took another sip of coffee and pat his lap. "Come be close to me." I smiled and curled up in the lawn chair. His flesh was warm and furry. I liked to pet it, it soothed my wandering mind.

"I love you," he said.

"I love you, too," I whispered.

ON THE DRIVE BACK up the coast to San Francisco, we spiraled up and down the mountains watching the waves crash on the coast. On the straight passes of Highway 1, I had a clear view of the Pacific; I became transfixed by the rhythm of the waves, which gained momentum and then reached the point of greatest tension before crashing into foamy waters and washing up onto the shore.

"I love the ocean," I said, nose pressed against the glass, fantasizing about being someone else, someone who wouldn't have to face the coming waves.

"Why is that, Maddie?" Daddy asked. His eyes on the road, he placed my hand on the crotch of his jeans.

"It soothes me to watch it, to listen to it. It's like you can hear the earth breathing, inhaling and exhaling with every wave."

Mr. Mogul laughed. "And that's why I love you, Maddie. Most girls would just say they loved the beach because it's the perfect place to get a tan. But not my Maddie."

"Most girls..." which meant most models, really. These were the women who made up our world and with whom I felt in constant competition. He was silent for a moment, the sound of the waves muffled by the car window.

"What do you know about submission, Maddie? About service?"

"Not much, Papa. I love rope and pain, though I don't really understand service. But I am drawn to it. I know that I can do a good job."

"I'm sure you can, Maddie." He was quiet for a moment. "When I first got into BDSM I had a mentor, a

Daddy. I was at a point in my life where I knew I needed to be broken in. I needed to go through an initiation, to enter into a new stanza of my manhood. In some Native American tribes, young men are taken out into the woods, pierced with animal bones, and suspended by their back flesh from a tree. Either their bones or their flesh must break for them to be released. They are left there and told to transcend the pain. This is how they become men. For me, it was my service to Drake. He didn't need me for sexual service—he had other boys for that—but I would accompany him to parties, talk with him, be his companion, take his coat for him, and occasionally take a beating from him. He taught me the pleasure of a job well done, the absolute satisfaction of providing for a leader in our community. It was my rite of passage. I needed to feel what it was like to be under the whip before I could give that to someone else. I needed to earn that right. You know, he's been gone for nearly ten years and I still think about him, I still want to make him proud. With this site, I want to put something intelligent out there, not just the same old porn. There are values that I'm trying to instill in this project, a history that a lot of these girls have never been exposed to."

This was the most open and communicative James had been in months. We hadn't talked like this since his move to San Francisco. I missed talking with him.

"I'm ready for that, too, Daddy." And I felt ready, ready to confront the site that had caused such a struggle between us. I wanted to believe that confronting this fear would end the pain that was consuming me. I wanted to be the submissive that Daddy desired. I wanted my own rite of passage, to take the journey with Mr. Mogul's hand in mine. I was ready to enter into an intense, week-long commitment with Daddy in order to uncover whether we had something worth salvaging. It had to take place on his turf, camera rolling to capture it all. I took a deep breath and watched as the waves crashed on the shore.

Part 3

15

Daddy and I woke up early, thrown from the comfort of sleep by our blaring alarm clock. Our bodies were damp with sweat and we separated slowly, peeling apart and becoming two individual entities by light of day. I groaned at the agony of getting up, and buried my head under the pillow. The smell of coffee and aftershave wafted through the loft. The digital clock's red LED display moved closer to the time of my training and I was concentrating on making myself invisible. I longed to disappear, to postpone, to avoid my impending responsibilities. Instead, I heard the sound of Mr. Mogul's voice.

"It's time to get up, Maddie. We have a long week ahead of us." Mr. Mogul was standing beside the bed and pulled the warm comforter from my body. The air was unusually cold on this summer morning, goosebumps sprung up along my limbs.

"Ugh...do I have to?" I kept the pillow pulled down over my head like a defiant young schoolgirl.

Mr. Mogul was quiet for a moment and things were frighteningly still. "No, you don't have to."

I peeked my head out from the soft pillow and looked up at him. He was neatly folding several pairs of jeans and T-shirts, placing them in his suitcase for the week-long shoot. We would be leaving the comfort of the Oakland loft for many long days of production at the Armory in San Francisco. It was all part of the site's training program: the girls taken out of their element, to have as little influence from the outside world as possible.

What am I doing? I tried so hard to get to this point, to embark on this journey, and now, when it came down to it, I was hiding under the covers like a child. This wasn't the way to show my dedication and appreciation for this opportunity; I needed to pull myself together and mentally prepared myself for battle.

"I want to, Daddy. I'm ready." I rubbed the sleep my eyes and stumbled into the shower.

I toweled my body dry and slipped into a sleeveless turquoise dress. I zipped on knee-high black leather boots and started to gather simple dresses and nightgowns for my suitcase. Mr. Mogul sat down on the leather couch and crossed his legs, contemplative, drinking his coffee, watching, as I scampered around the apartment fetching items for the journey. "Last night was your last night in our bed for a week, so I hope you enjoyed it. You're going to need to be strong this week, Maddie. This is going to be hard on both of us."

"Yes, Mr. Mogul," I said as I sorted through my pantyhose, slipping my hand into the stockings and checking for runs before stuffing them in my garment bag.

"I can't have our personal problems acting themselves out onscreen. This is my job. Your job, too. It's what pays the rent." I stopped and put down my stockings. James was serious, he was always very serious when it came to his work; I didn't want to mess that up. This week would require us both to show an immense amount of trust in each other. I needed to remember that this wasn't just about me; it was about us.

Mr. Mogul patted the couch and I joined him. "I'm going to be brave, Daddy," I said. "I promise."

James sat his mug down on the coffee table and ran his hand through my hair, "I know that you are brave. But I know you. Sometimes you let your emotions control you and you need to be the one in control this week."

I felt like a little girl looking up to her daddy for guidance, for a hint about how to face the challenge that lay before me. "Well what should I do if that starts to happen? If my emotions take control?"

"Let's make a safe word. Just say my first name and then I'll know something is wrong. If we need to hold or take you aside or give you a break or talk without the cameras on us, then we will. It will be our secret code, okay?"

Daddy handed me his white handkerchief without my asking for it. He knew before I did that my eyes were about to well up. "Thank you, Mr. Mogul. I love you."

Mr. Mogul leaned in and kissed me on the forehead. "I love you, too. Now grab your bags or we're going to be late." I tucked the damp handkerchief into my purse and, grabbing our luggage, we headed out the door.

WE WERE MOMENTS AWAY from starting the first day of shooting for *The Training of Madison Young*. The shoot was held at KINK's new home in the historical San Francisco Armory building, where the National Guard once trained their soldiers and housed their arsenal. After lying vacant for more than twenty years, the two hundred thousand square foot castle of a building seemed to have reclaimed its purpose. A new labyrinth of voices mingled with old memories as they echoed among the dusty walls and dirty floors.

I was locked in a cage that hung suspended from the ceiling by thick chain. The cage was a small metal box, aged by prop designers to be the color of rust. I sat in a compressed position,with my knees held to my chest, shackles and chain affixed snuggly around my wrists and ankles. Despite my butt being pressed up against the flat, checkerboard strips of metal, I felt entirely comfortable. It was reminiscent of squeezing myself into small spaces as a child—behind the couch, crawl spaces, and the cages my mom used to kennel our terriers. Outside the cage, the room was cold and lifeless: cement floors, cement walls, cement ceilings, metal suspension points, metal chains, metal cage. The Armory felt strong and unyielding; it conflicted with my love of all that is natural. Where was the soil, the rope, the leather?

I watched the crew run around set, gathering implements like whips and thin reeds, which would be used as switches that we referred to as canes. The production assistant, Lux, was a petite but spirited young woman in her mid-twenties with brown eyes and chestnut-brown hair that she kept pulling back in a ponytail. She was the kind of girl who didn't take shit from anyone but knew how to do her job, which was mainly to care for the models. She kept a knife that Daddy bought her in her back pocket. Lux laid tightly coiled pieces of rope out on a black, fluffy towel to keep them clean. My hands trembled as I grasped the metal cage, full of nervous energy but eager for full immersion. The anticipation was killing me—like watching a nurse preparing a needle.

The lighting crew—two stocky men, one silver-haired, and the other sporting a full beard and mustache—came in and adjusted the lights until they were warm on my skin. I started to perspire and took in a deep breath, patiently watching the production team finish setup. Daddy fastened a small microphone to his black button-up shirt and switched the microphone on.

"Testing, testing. Can you hear me?" Mr. Mogul glanced over at me and smiled.

"Seems to be working just fine, James." Carlos, the tech assistant's voice sprung up from behind the video camera.

I ran my fingers across the large, rusted chain collar that Daddy padlocked around my neck before placing me in the cage. It was heavy. Many collars could pass for stylish chokers or necklaces, like the ones you might buy at the mall or at a jewelry store, but this collar was a symbol of humility. A huge chain that looked like it came from a mechanic's garage. I thought about what Daddy said when he locked it around me, "You'll be wearing this all week. It's a training collar. Don't get emotionally attached to it. This collar is just a vehicle, a prop. It will be used on others after you and you will give it up at the end of the week. Is this understood?"

It was understood; this was a production. Though it was a personal journey for us, ultimately the goal was entertainment, and I knew that. I knew that, foremost, I was an entertainer, and our intertwined personal life had simply brought us to this public journey.

When performing with strangers or coworkers it was possible for me to have a pleasurable time, while also keeping things compartmentalized and emotionally safe. But this combination of Daddy, his work, and me, was an emotionally loaded triad and I felt incredibly vulnerable, sensitive, and terrified.

"Okay. Is everyone ready?" James asked Carlos, while looking over the notes on his clipboard.

"Looking good, boss," he yelled from behind the camera. Lux snapped a couple quick photos and Mr. Mogul stepped up to the cage. "I love you, Maddie. Whatever I say or do, don't take it too personally. This is meant to be fun. That's why we do this, right? Because it's something that makes us happy. You okay, Maddie?"

I nodded and kissed Mr. Mogul's hand through the cage.

"Action!" James called out to the crew.

Daddy circled the cage and took a step back, taking a good look at me. "Why are you here, Ms. Young?"

"To learn how to eroticize submission and how to be the submissive you would like me to be. How would you like me to address you? Mr. Mogul? Sir?" My voice was soft and unsure.

"Decide now, and that's the way it will be the rest of the week," Mr. Mogul said and looked down at his notes. I was used to following the dominant's lead, but Mr. Mogul seemed to be pushing me to make the first move. He asked for a declaration of my expectations, my desires—but wasn't this supposed to be all about serving someone else and not serving my own needs?

"I suppose...Sir?" I stared at James, looking for a clue as to whether I was on the right path.

"Good choice. You will be expected to follow certain protocol and specific rules this week while you are in training. You will be expected to follow these rules twenty-four hours a day and to report to me immediately upon any infraction. Is this clear?"

My eyes searched him as he paced back and forth in front of the cage. I listened attentively and tried to remember every word. I wouldn't fail. I could follow his rules. *How hard can this be?*

"Rule number one: You will refrain from masturbation unless I give you permission," he said. "Rule number two: You will ask for permission to orgasm. Rule number three: You will not use furniture this week. You will sit on the floor or stand, unless I give you permission to use the furniture. This includes the use of a bed, Ms. Young. Rule number four: You are to address me as Sir and only Sir for this week. Is this all clear to you, Slut?"

The camera panned across my body, zooming in on my face, then moved over to a tight shot of James' clipboard, where these rules were written. I imagined what my life would look like that week without vibrators—without orgasms—sleeping at the foot of the bed.

"Yes, Sir. Thank you, Sir." I maintained slave decorum, mindful of my physical position. I could look toward James, but never at him. Suddenly, I had to fight back a smile as a strange warmth spilled over me. It felt so good to shed the complex layers of daily life and exchange them for routine, absolute dedication and service to one person (if only for a week).

"You will have a curfew this week. You will be in your hotel room by ten P.M. every night. We will check up on you and if you are not in your hotel room by curfew you will be severely punished. You will need your rest and your strength to make it through this week. I don't need you slutting around town and coming in tired to our training sessions. I take this very seriously, Ms. Young, and I intend you to as well. Are we clear?" Mr. Mogul looked up at me for acknowledgment.

"Yes, Sir. Thank you, Sir." The camera focused tight on me from below, where I dangled in the cage. I usually felt a distinct awareness of the camera's presence, charging the scene with the energy of all those who would view this moment in the future, but naked and enclosed in this tiny box I focused. I was not sure what would be waiting for me at the end of the week, but I felt the experience itself solidifying.

"You will have homework that will be assigned every evening for you to work on in your quarters, and I expect you to have it completed and ready to hand in every morning. Is this clear?"

"Yes, Sir. Thank you, Sir." It was all in the details; it was in the way in which he spoke and the richness of intention in his words. It was verbal dominance, intended to gain my unfaltering attention. Maybe for the first time, I truly listened to what he said, observing what he liked, taking note of his specific desires. In our relationship, our trust had become fractured and communication had deteriorated, our voices muddled, muted, and stifled. Today, I was starting to hear him again, able to listen because it was being demanded of me and because I was stripped of distractions and resistance.

"Ms. Young?" Even the sound of his voice struck me differently; I instinctively trusted it.

"Yes, Sir?" My reply was more confident than the first "Yes, Sir" I mumbled only an hour ago. *How long has it been? An hour? Half an hour? How much time has passed listening to and watching this man?*

"Who do you belong to, Slut?" It felt like he was calling my name: *Slut*. It conjured an image of being ravaged and undone. It brought a sense of calm and well-being; it validated my sexual self. *Slut*. It was a word I owned proudly; it was sensuous, exciting, and full of life. Sluts deserved to be worshipped and adored, and at the same time to give themselves to others. Sluts filled chalices with their come, sweat, and blood; sluts blessed the town. I was empowered by my Slut self and now it was time for me to show my lover.

I looked Mr. Mogul in the eye and answered with complete confidence: "I belong to you, Sir."

I had never been more certain of anything in my life. Although this was just the beginning of our journey together, the distance between Mr. Mogul and I decreased every minute. I had never been so happy or so sad to see time pass.

"That's right. That's my good girl." He pulled the cage in close to his face and kissed me before he let the cage go and it spun in circles. I was like a little, captive bird: well fed and happy. I was ready for whatever he could give me.

16

I GAZED INTO A small video camera, set up on a tripod in a cheap motel in the Castro. I could see my gallery from the window. At the gallery, I was in charge, but this week had not been about coordinating events or writing grants for the next visual art exhibition. This week had been about delving deep within myself and reconstructing my relationship with Daddy, finding new avenues and building trust with each other. I set up for the training's required video journal, a reflection on the experiences of a submissive's week-long journey at *The Training of* O. James would meet me afterward and we would go out to sushi, Daddy wearing a tie and jacket and I donning lash marks and a large clunky chain with a three inch padlock around my neck—a training collar I would soon lose in exchange for a real collar. A collaring ceremony is the equivalent of a bondage wedding; it is a ritual, a commitment to one another bound by a dominant/submissive agreement and honored by a leather collar. I was tired and teary eyed, it had been a long and emotional journey.

In Catholicism, a couple wishing to exchange vows must go through several weeks of a guided spiritual journey in the form of premarital counseling and Pre-Cana classes that are designed to challenge, test, and question the couple's devotion while building their trust and challenging their ability to handle stress. Mr. Mogul and I were on a guided journey, but in a much different house of worship. The emotional stakes were high and the commitment was the same, but our journey looked different. We had just completed the third day of training, which means that the following day I would be free to collapse into my Daddy's arms, eyes full with tears of joy and exhaustion, and we would ride our human ponies off into the sunset.

I breathed a sigh of relief; we were almost there. I rested my heavy head in the palm of my hand and stared into the camera, trying to compose my thoughts. My fingers traced the red welts that striped my pale chest. I closed my eyes and I could smell the thick, dank, dusty air of the Armory. This training wasn't a competition between my will and Mr. Mogul's, it was a test: our relationship and our love versus the Armory, a place of power and wonder, an Emerald City in a dark forest riddled with flying monkeys. These rooms and their walls housed love and orgasms, lies and broken agreements, the pulp of my and my partner's sexual engagement with others. We were trying to rebuild trust in the very rooms in which our vows had been broken.

Overwhelming to most visitors, the Armory is jaw-dropping due to its sheer size; these old, beautiful walls hold the most decadent and open display of kink and BDSM in the country. More than just a landmark to us, the Armory is a massive, heavy, needy building. This was a complicated moment: our relationship—life, love, and drama, was playing out in front of a camera, and was also the source of a paycheck. I knew these were the terms when I started, but I still harbored some resentment.

I ran my fingers through my hair and opened my eyes. With a deep breath I pressed the red record button. I flipped the viewfinder around so I could see myself in the frame. I shifted uncomfortably and sat, legs folded in the chair, propping my small body up higher. I felt like a little child at the big kids' table.

"Hi, this is Madison Young on day three of my training. Hmm. Where to begin? Well, the first position that Mr. Mogul put me in was crawling. I do love being close to the ground and the Armory floor was really hard and painful..." Staring at my reflection, I told my story.

MR. MOGUL BOUND MY upper and lower arms, then bound my calves to my thighs, and positioned me on my elbows and knees on the filthy Armory floor. The floor was cold, hard, and damp, moist with emotion and history. He whipped my ass as I crawled back and forth, from one wall to the other, my elbows and knees screaming every time they made contact with the cement floors. A rubber bit gag muffled any sound coming from my mouth. I tried to contain my whimpers and work past the pain, wondering if my body might give out sooner than expected.

This was my place, where I belonged. I remembered something Pablo Picasso once said, "Every act of creation is first an act of destruction." We must tear down the walls of our identity, our relationship, everything comfortable that we thought we once knew, in order to rebuild. My bones ground into the cement with every step, but the rope was a welcome visitor. I knew Daddy was being mindful and considerate, binding me with rope rather than leather. Rope is my security, a familiar object of safety and love. The rope cinched tight around my arms and legs was a welcome pain, a hand for me to hold through this challenge. Daddy followed behind me as I crawled, periodically whipping my ass and my pussy. The leather whip fell, stinging against my cunt, an erotic delicacy that sent welcomed zigzags of pleasure through my body.

"Where is your place, Slut?" he barked like a drill sergeant as his whip came down with precision and artful technique, making contact with my labia.

"On the floor, Sir. I'm on the floor where I belong, Sir." I tried to articulate but the mumbled words fell from my mouth with viscous saliva that dripped from my chin to my chest in small, slippery puddles as I crawled back and forth, through a hazard of my own devices.

"Good girl. On your knees, Slut!" he barked again. I smiled through the gag, pleased with the praise for passing his first challenge. Daddy slipped on a black latex glove, and when it snapped against his hand it sent shivers through my body. I wanted him to enter me.

"Ok, Slut. Let's show everyone what we're working with," he grabbed hold of my cunt. "I need you thinking with your pretty head instead of your pretty cunt," he said and slipped his fingers into me. He smiled, looking at me, and I felt seduced by his gaze. I felt seduced as his lover, not as his submissive. *Was there even a difference?* It felt as if there was. We shared tender moments of care that informed the intense physical impact that we experienced together. With each lash of the whip I felt the warmth of memories and gifts we exchanged, like little books of poetry marked with notes on our favorite passages that we shared with one another. Those loving moments of intimacy and connection fueled the endurance and passage that we were in together as Daddy pumped his hand in and out of my red, swollen, and whipped cunt.

"This is the pussy I'm talking about. This is the pussy I want available at all times." Daddy pulled out and slapped my cunt again, hard. The sound echoed through the room.

As I SAT, RECOUNTING the experience for the camera, I felt my pussy throbbing from a week of being whipped, slapped, and filled with cock. I pulled my hair back and clipped it out of my face. I looked tired, thoroughly fucked, and rather bedraggled, but there was a glow about me, evident even in the cheap motel lamplight.

"The crawling was painful but I think I was still a little...cocky. I don't think I realized there would be anything physically, um...challenging. I'm usually pretty tough. I have a tough exterior, and there isn't usually any position that I can't do." I confessed on camera, to my reflection, to the world watching, to Daddy.

LEATHER CUFFS WERE FASTENED around my wrists and ankles, my sweaty palms pressed against the cold stone walls and I arched my back, accentuating the curve of my ass. Daddy ordered me to stand on the balls of my feet, legs spread. I'm familiar with this position, a perverted version of second position in ballet. I practiced ballet from elementary school through freshman year of college, and the art form instilled in me a love of discipline, of pushing my body to its utmost extreme. It seemed simple enough to hold the position for a moment or two, but what I didn't know was that this position was a military stress position, used to break the most hardened soldiers down to crying, whimpering babies. Could Mr. Mogul and I break each other down and rebuild?

My nipples were clamped with tight clover clamps, traditionally used for pulling material tight when sewing. The clamps were pulled even tighter by small, solid steel weights that hung from the chain of the clamps.

Mr. Mogul recorded notes, examining my position.

"How long do you think you can stay like this, Madison?"

"As long as you would like me like this, Sir?" I stared forward and found a spot on the wall to focus on. It had only been a few minutes, but already I felt my calves start to burn and my muscles strain to maintain the position.

There was a disturbing quiet for a moment and I heard Daddy set down his clipboard and grab his whip from the shelf. I knew I have answered incorrectly, but I didn't know what the right answer was. The whip stung my already burning thighs.

"When I ask you a question like that, I want an accurate and honest answer." He sounded annoyed, frustrated. I gave Daddy a canned answer, a performer's answer. I hid behind a fantasy rather than revealing my vulnerability and responding truthfully. I am a performer at heart, and a performative element still informs my responses. Mr. Mogul deserved more than a performance, and I wanted to give him more. I just didn't know how to do that.

"What you're giving me is bullshit." I stared forward, focusing my eyes on that same spot as he approached my quivering body, his hands finding their way back to my cunt. He whispered in my ear, "Now we wait."

Daddy pulled up a chair and sat down to watch, waiting for me to succumb to the exhaustion. Eventually, the lactic acid in my muscles would build to painful cramping and I would collapse. I would either have to disobey Daddy and move, breaking position, or wait for my body to give in, falling to the drool-splattered ground from which I have just risen. Carlos and Lux came in close, fascinated; as if watching a rare bird in an exotic environment, they studied my body's composition and form, documenting my physiology and emotional response. I trembled and stared at the chip in the concrete wall. Just a chip in the rock, a tiny flaw. I memorized it, dove into it, shrunk my body down to size so I could explore it like a crater. I filled it with water and went for a swim, my body floating effortlessly in the pool contained in that crater. Carlos panned up and down with his video camera, zooming in on my face, revealing my trembling body and cramping feet. Flashes from Lux's camera popped in my eyes, but I let it go. I guided myself through meditation, letting all thoughts, all people and actions in my periphery melt away. I acknowledged their presence and then let them float away. Determined that my body would be on the brink of utter collapse before I gave up, I meditated on the image of me and Daddy safe on the other side of this giant roadblock that laid in front of us. My body started to shake violently, but I held my eyesight, remaining focused. I visualized Daddy holding me tight, close, tighter, closer.

Daddy got up from his chair, surprised. His hand gently ran down the arch of my back as he smiled at me with pride, "You are a tough little thing, aren't you?" He laughed, amused by my perseverance.

I glared with determination, and a warm smile came over my face at the sound of Daddy's voice. More than ever, I was determined to prove my devotion. I gently whispered, full of love and honesty, "Yes, Sir."

"You will endure any amount of physical punishment, won't you?" I felt his eyes on me, but I wouldn't break my gaze. *Daddy is on the other side, don't lose focus.*

"Yes, Sir." My voice came out soft, honest, raw, vulnerable. It felt like we were practicing our vows to one another. My form shifted as different muscle groups tried to take over, my body's natural physical defense building, but there wasn't much give and take in this position. Daddy's voice was kind, gentle, and earnest. He was strong but not demanding, and he spoke softly. I knew he believed in the words as much as I did. I had a sense of pride, in holding the position, in pleasing Daddy. Daddy was proud of his little Slut.

"Please, Sir?" I begged, my legs convulsing as I grasped the solid cement wall. Daddy came up behind me and eased me to the ground, where he held me close in his arms. "You did good, Slut. You did really good."

After my legs stopped shaking and I had regained strength enough to stand upright on my own, Daddy walked me onto a large cement block that was basked in a warm spotlight. Lux handed me a black KINK water bottle and I sipped on the cool liquid. Water never tasted so good.

"I want you in standing slave position, Slut. Facing front, legs spread, arms folded behind your back, and I don't want to catch your eyes on me. Do you understand?" Daddy picked up his clipboard, thumbed through his notes, and scribbled onto the yellow lined paper.

I did as instructed, my arms folded behind my back as I stared forward, ready to receive the next challenge.

Mr. Mogul picked up his whip and leaned in with one foot on the slave block, close to me, asking earnestly, "Are you willing to let go of me as a lover in order to be my slave?" He smiled, staring at me, and my face was deadpan. Pausing before answering, I meekly replied with, "Yes, Sir," in an uncertain whisper.

Daddy stepped away from me and circled the room, contemplating his next move. He realized that there had been an emotional shift and we were walking a delicate balance between public and private, cameras rolling.

"Then get down on your knees and present yourself like a slave."

Daddy leaned in close. "You're a good girl. Hey, look at me." I abandoned the no eye contact rule, looking up at him with sadness. "You're a good girl," he repeated, grabbing my hair and leaning in to kiss me on the lips, while I retained my slave position. With a renewed sense of confidence I looked forward, arms folded, kneeling, legs spread.

"I think you have earned a reward," he shared, stepping onto the slave block. His hand scooped up my hair and directed my face downward to his black leather boot.

"Thank you, Sir."

◇◇◇

"IT WAS VERY HOT," I smiled like a giddy teenager divulging locker room kiss-and-tell moments. As I spoke, I wanted to touch myself, confessing erotic intimacies, but that would be breaking the rules and I knew better.

A glance at the clock told me it was 6:30 P.M. It was getting late and Daddy would be here soon to collect me and take me to sushi. I needed to wrap it up, but I was still processing. I fetched a sweater and turned down the air-conditioning, then resituated myself in front of the camera, film still rolling.

MY FACE WAS DEWY with sweat from the long day, and from the long week. My eyes closed and my legs splayed open to give Daddy access while maintaining the kneeling slave position that he has taught me. As his whip came down on me, I felt my edge. With each whipping I felt myself teetering on an emotional cliff, getting closer to falling. But what exactly would I be falling into? I opened myself to the energy that lay past the edge. I could feel the edge of my mind, a round, beautiful, safe feeling full of warm energy. This safe space of transcendence opened before me, and I knew if I went any closer I would cry. With release, with joy, with complete gratitude, it was better than any orgasm I have ever experienced. Daddy's hands touched my flesh and grabbed hold of my hair. The space we walked into was sacred, spiritual. I felt my body become weightless even though I still knelt on the ground, and each lashing brought my consciousness back to my body like an invisible lasso. I had fallen in love, and the world around me disappeared, all that remained was me and the person I loved. I was overwhelmed with gratitude for my very existence.

"Does it feel good?" Daddy's lashings fell on my skin, pink welts sprung up like wildflowers.

"It feels so good, thank you so much." I was riding waves of endorphins, my body mentally levitating, breathless and weightless.

"You want to cry? Go ahead and let it out." Daddy laughed as tears streamed from my face.

"Thank you, thank you so much, I love you so much! Thank you." I exhaled, overcome with joy.

17

T HE BRIGHT SUN PEEKED through orange fabric curtains, nudging me from a restful sleep. I was curled up on the floor at the foot of the bed in a nest I created out of a terra-cotta colored floral comforter and white plush pillows. My chain collar and padlock pulled heavily, leaving faint bruises from the four days that they had served around my neck as a reminder of the freedoms I was surrendering in order to attain true freedom. Daddy was in the middle of the bed; I heard faint snoring. The floor was my place. Daddy was enveloped in a white sheet, his feet hanging off the bed, sticking out from the thin layer of linens. I nuzzled my face against them, delicately kissing his toes. I was so hungry for him, I wanted to pounce on the bed and uncover his hard morning cock, wrap my lips around his member and fulfill my desire, but I knew that wasn't what this week was about.

One of my assignments this week was to learn my subject: Daddy. Although I knew that I desired him and that he had fulfilled my needs for the last two years,

I didn't know his routine. I couldn't tell someone what his favorite color was, or what he did first thing in the morning. I had never paid attention to those details, consumed with my world, my work, and my personal desires. Our relationship had been second to my efforts to provide community space, facilitate connection, and my own self-exploration through such community building. I saw my relationship as a personal need, and personal needs were put aside until after community and global needs were met. I used to reschedule date nights so I could attend community panels and meetings, but I was starting to see things differently.

BDSM isn't just about fulfilling kinky desires, it's about serving someone else on an individual level with care, focus, and intimacy. By serving my Daddy with complete dedication, I was participating in a larger community dynamic as a person engaged in service to my dominant. By caring for my own body, I nourish a tool. My body is an implement, a conduit for service to both my dominant and my community. If I disrespect or neglect my body, my mind, my spiritual, emotional, and psychological well being, then I am not only neglecting myself, I am a detriment to my dominant and my community.

In my time in San Francisco I had discovered my primal desires and figured out how to tap into those desires with self-love, but now I needed to focus on facilitating intimate exchange with my partner. What would Daddy need when he gets up? I looked around the small hotel room. Coffee. I had never made coffee, but I watched Daddy make it every morning. I poured in the premeasured packet of coffee and filled the small plastic device with water, and flipped the coffeemaker on. Soon, the coffee filled the room with an earthy, warm morning scent. Daddy's body stirred as I poured in instant creamer from a small, plastic packet and stirred until the liquid was the beautiful color of a Spanish girl's thighs.

I set the coffee cup on the bedside table next to him. Tangled in sheets, he had his face nuzzled into my green cardigan, with the faint scent of vanilla and perspiration. He requested it upon our return to the motel to keep the scent of me close by even while I was on the floor, far away.

I knelt in slave position, legs open, arms folded behind my back, eyes forward, waiting. His eyes slowly opened and he smiled lovingly. "Good girl, Maddie. Good girl."

DADDY'S HANDS COMBED THROUGH my long hair and he led me to my feet, bending me over the bed and placing the Hitachi Magic Wand vibrator in my hand. My face turned to one side, and I could see Daddy pick up a two-by-four from the corner of the room. I smiled in anticipation.

"Nicely done, Slut. You may turn on the vibrator now. That will feel good on that cunt. It must have been hard not touching yourself all week, wasn't that difficult, Slut?" Daddy paced back and forth, his eyes examining his target.

"No, Sir. It was my pleasure." I had a sensation of pleasure every time I abstained. All week long, the eroticism of obedience felt vigorous and fulfilling.

"Well, that's good to hear. I'm proud of you. You're a good girl. Now, when I beat you with this two-by-four it's not a correction. It's a reward. Do you understand?" The vibrator buzzed against my entire vulva. It was a welcome sensation: indulgent pleasure, vulgar in its obviousness but wonderful in its simplicity. My cunt needed some love and attention, a reward, after the service and beating it had taken throughout the week.

"I can already feel your muscles tensing. You're getting close, aren't you, hungry girl? Look at those feet curling. That's my little slut." The two-by-four came down hard on my body and I was overtaken and knocked off my feet by the strong wave. The thud on my ass enforced the jolts of pleasure radiating from my vibrating cunt.

"May I please come, Sir?" I begged, one hand grasping at the bed cover and the other clinging onto the vibrator as Daddy's industrial-size makeshift paddle fell hard. With a boyish pleasure, he laughed, "Come for me, Slut," and I did, loud and hard. With permission, I came for Daddy.

Thoroughly fucked and beaten, I knelt before my prince, my Daddy, my dominant. *We made it.* Daddy pulled a small key from his pocket and unlocked the heavy chain around my aching and bruised neck. "You've worn this training collar well. It's time for you to graduate."

"Thank you, Sir." I was humbled by his approval. When he fumbled with the key I knew Mr. Mogul must have been a little nervous, too. This was a milestone in our life together.

As the collar came off, I felt stripped naked. Unprotected without the symbolic temporal object I have held onto, I felt separated, even though I was warned not to get attached. Daddy drew a simple black leather collar from his pocket and I was caught breathless at the sight of it.

"You earned this," Daddy gazed down at this token with affection and respect, a gift that came with the promise of protection and safety, ownership and affection, and a bond of mutual respect.

"Thank you, Sir," I smiled, overcome with emotion. "Thank you." I closed my eyes and started to cry, an honest confession of the deepest gratitude when words failed to serve me.

"Kiss it." Daddy's eyes met mine, his hands touched my face and I surrendered to him completely. I leaned in to the leather collar, which he held close to my face, and kissed the leather and Daddy's fingertips and hands. He looked at me with tenderness, gazing earnestly into my tear-filled eyes and held the collar against my bare chest, "This is yours. Nobody can take this away from you."

I sobbed in reply, completely in love. I felt saved, rescued from the rest of life. Daddy clasped the collar around my neck while I held my long hair out of the way. He snapped the lock shut, and I was his.

As he pet my head, he looked at me with a love and tenderness that had gone absent since our first months together in Seattle. I composed myself and relaxed, contented, into a smile.

"Let's take a look at you, huh?" Daddy exhaled, taking a step back, admiring his freshly collared service submissive and trying to collect himself emotionally, cameras still rolling. Other women may have experienced Mr. Mogul as a trainer, but we were experiencing a journey between two lovers, between a Daddy and his Little Girl. The earning of a first piece of leather is sacred. A collaring ceremony is a commitment, a dedication, strong as a wedding, a ceremony we had just shared. I was not just another girl, I *belong* to this Daddy. For one week I had allowed the cameras to document it, but the life that has opened before us is ours.

"You earned your leather. This is a tradition handed down from others in our community and we try to keep it alive. I earned my leather, and now I'm handing that down to you. What are you feeling right now?" Daddy drew closer to my kneeling body and smiling face. He cradled my head as I gazed up at him, full of want and need, nuzzling my face, wet with tears, into his black slacks.

"I feel happy," I smiled, rubbing against his legs. I wanted our bodies coupled together. I was ready for our honeymoon.

"Yeah? You look happy." Daddy laughed and I wiped my eyes and stared up at him expectantly, ready for the camera crew to disappear. Together we built the infrastructure for our dominant and submissive roles, and now I was ready for our life to begin. Daddy's eyes met mine and we kissed.

He kissed me on the head and helped me up from the ground, and we walked off camera. Beyond the light stood the camera crew, he pulled me close to him, and I lost myself in him. "You're a good girl," he laughed, declaring: "Maddie, this is just the beginning."

"This is just the beginning," I repeated.

18

EVERY WEDNESDAY DADDY AND I practiced high protocol dominance and submission, whether or not Daddy and I were in the same room my focus returned to serving Daddy at 7:00 P.M. With ten minutes to spare I was seated on the floor, nude (except for my leather collar), my back pressed up against my desk and my shoulders hunched over my laptop in our penthouse apartment in downtown Oakland. My eyes focused on my computer screen as I tried to quickly move through the emails awaiting my attention. My assistant, Mev, a young vegan punk-rock queer artist from a small town in Texas, was returning the next morning to help me navigate through it all. Mev reminded me of myself when I was her age—young and determined, with a sense of honesty and integrity. She was a huge asset to both Femina Potens and my growing feminist erotic film production company.

I finally found a balance between Los Angeles and San Francisco that put less strain on my body and my psyche. I became less reliant on getting paid for scenes and supplemented my income teaching sexuality workshops at conferences and universities and directing films for Good Vibrations, the local women-owned sex toy store. When I worked in L.A., I used my own tools—just as I used to have a porno toolbox with baby wipes, lube and enemas, I had developed a toolbox of communication skills that helped me navigate porn scenes in a healthier way. I learned to guide my porn partners step by step through how my body worked, encouraging them with coos and moans and, in turn, listening attentively as they guided me to their orgasms.

But Wednesday nights weren't about work, they were about service. We kept our dominant/submissive agreement in a simple white three-ring binder on the desk among shot lists, porn scripts, submission forms for erotic film festivals, and paperwork waiting to be filed. The binder, labeled simply "The Handbook" in black permanent marker, was a living archive and manual of our relationship. Inside it I slipped ongoing revisions of our dominant/submissive agreement, as well as service-oriented homework assignments and research Daddy assigned me. We revised and revisited our dominant/submissive agreement every two months, setting an expiration date and a promised revisiting date for the document, then signed it.

We both were trying to learn new sets of behaviors and routines that served our relationship and our kink for service and submission. Sometimes we needed to make adjustments along the way. How long were certain rules sustainable? When I strained my IT band, causing pain and weakness in my left knee, we changed the rule "submissive will always wear heels in public when accompanying Sir" to "submissive will wear flat ballet slippers, provided by Sir, when present in public with Sir." When I wanted to cut down on my consumption of alcohol, coffee, and chocolate, I requested that it be added to our agreement that I needed to ask for and receive permission from Mr. Mogul before consuming any of the above decadent items. It was sexy for a while, and it worked. I wouldn't take a sip of wine or a bite of an energy bar that had cocoa in it, not without Daddy nodding his head to permit my indulgence. When the rule became labor intensive (with exhausting cross-country travel for shoots that required caffeine just to keep my eyes open) we adjusted. Some rules, like "submissive will ask permission from Sir before using furniture, unless refraining from using furniture will result in making someone else uncomfortable," or "submissive will serve Sir every Wednesday at 7:00 P.M.," we found easier to maintain. Nearly a year after the first edition of our agreement and my collaring, we developed a steady and adjustable routine that worked for us.

Daddy was late for our dinner on this particular evening, which was becoming more and more normal. Mr. Mogul's work often required him to stay late, Wednesday or not. I started to prepare our home for Daddy's arrival. I fetched the leather cuffs from our closet, and placed them on his chair. I crawled under the dining room table and moved my dog bed out from under it, placing the large moss-green bed, fit for a full-grown Labrador, at the foot of his chair. I scurried about, fetching clean white towels from the linen closet and placing them in the bathroom. Daddy would want a shower when he returned home. I placed my stainless steel engraved dog bowl beside the dog bed—I purchased it from the *Lillian Vernon* catalogue, and got quite a kick out of requesting the name "SLUT" to be engraved on the dish. I collected vanilla-scented lotion and placed them by the couch where I would remove Daddy's boots. There were wicker baskets full of coiled rope in both the bedroom and dining room, next to Daddy's chair, as well as large floor vases, one in each room, containing a variety of canes.

At 7:20 P.M. I hadn't yet heard from Daddy. I sunk into my latest service related assignment—becoming familiar with how to manipulate a flogger with ease. The phone rang, "Maddie, I'm so sorry I'm late. I hope you haven't been waiting long. Let me make it up to you. How does a seitan fillet at Soizic sound?"

Daddy knew the way to my heart, and I was practically starving by the time I heard his voice. "That sounds so good, Daddy. Guess what? I'm practicing my flogging."

"Watch out world, my Little Girl has got a whip! Slip on some clothes and meet me at the restaurant, okay sweetheart?" Daddy cheered into the phone, elated at making up for his tardiness at one of my favorite East Bay restaurants.

I slipped on a silk, knee-length dress Daddy bought for me in a lovely vintage robin's egg blue, without panties, and the black, flat dress shoes Daddy picked out for me. I loved being his doll, his Little Girl to dress as he wished.

Soizic was bustling with its usual late-night crowd and a loud bunch who had taken up camp in the bar area overwhelmed the space. I spotted Daddy and approached our table, discreetly standing at attention, my hands folded behind my back.

"Sir," I nodded, greeting my lover.

"Slut," he nodded greeting me back. "You may sit."

Our lives weren't always so formal. Wednesday nights were special occasions. We knew that this type of protocol wouldn't last on a day-to-day basis for the long term. There were nights when we cuddled up on the couch watching Tarantino movies and evenings we worked together in the kitchen to make Tofurkey dinner. We huddled around the dining room table to coordinate events or work on stronger infrastructure for the gallery. In our relationship as lovers and domestic partners, there was no submissive. I looked to my partner for mentorship and advice, but with mutual respect and in a space of equality. It was one of the reasons that Wednesday nights were both comforting and sexually exciting: Daddy and I tested the power dynamics in our relationship, the gender roles that prevailed in our world and society, and what people often thought of as normal, rearranging and assembling them into something that we could use. We played within a safe space we created, and in the process we tested ourselves, discovered our own psychological boundaries and touched upon some unexpected turn-ons.

19

THE PILOT DIDN'T WANT to land the plane and I couldn't blame him. Six degrees in Ohio in the winter wasn't unusual, but it chilled me to the bone. California sunshine and temperate conditions were home to me now: a moderate fifty degrees with light showers and fog that spilled in off the bay over the city like pea soup. The yearlong, moderate weather patterns in the Bay Area leave you with a feeling of consistency; you come to know the city's climate. The warmth of the Mission, the chill of Twin Peaks, and the surprisingly biting wind that comes off the ocean's waves create a sense of timelessness; the seasons seem to blend together. Six degrees was unheard of in San Francisco—at forty-eight degrees I was usually bundled up tight with a scarf and ski jacket—so James and I knew we needed to be prepared for Ohio. This would be Mr. Mogul's first trip to my hometown, his first time meeting my father and my family. We loaded up Christmas presents and armored ourselves with thick tights, sweatpants, boots, sweaters, scarves, gloves, and hats.

Packed tightly into our luggage among the warm clothes was perfume for my mother, a Velvet Underground CD for my brother, and a watch for my father. James had bought my father a nice watch with a brown leather band and large numbers big enough for my dad to see without straining his eyes. It was a gift, a token of gratitude, a firm handshake and a pat on the back. Hopefully it would help start a bond between the men in my life, my Daddies.

The roads were precarious as we made our way to the Butcher's Christmas Eve dinner. The asphalt was dangerous and iced over, not meant for cars or people. This was hot cocoa weather, stay-inside-until-it-blows-over weather. Dad had been out all day salting clients' driveways with Madison Tree Service; he often did this to keep the business solvent during the winter months, when gardens and maple trees were hibernating.

James and I pulled up to Aunt Darlene's house. The long driveway was filled with cars that had delivered more than twenty-five of my grandmother's grandchildren, along with their parents. As James parked the car and cut the engine, I took a deep breath and grabbed his hand. I looked down at the ring he had given me just that morning, a golden rope encrusted with diamonds. It may not have satiated the ache around my bare neck, but it was a beautiful symbol of our love and commitment to each other, to be worn when the collar was tucked away. He could see that I was still nervous and he grabbed a pen from his bag, hiked up my dress, and scribbled "MINE" onto my upper thigh. I smiled and kissed him deeply.

My black high heels punctured the ice and snow as we made our way up the walkway. My father's sister lived in a majestic, canary yellow house set on a large plot of land that stretched into the woods. It was a perfect playground for us as children. Built in the early 1900s, the house and the décor were traditional and worldly. The living room held an eclectic mix: a large floor vase from Asia, small sculptural pieces from South America, photography from Venezuela, and family photos.

I opened the door, "Hello?" unsure if anyone would recognize me after my four-year absence.

The house bustled with energy. Children I had yet to meet scurried about discovering all the magical, unknown places hidden in Darlene's vast home. I heard mothers call after their children, attempting to rein them in.

The large dining table was set with china and silverware. It felt familiar, yet completely foreign. It was hard to remember this life. This was Tina Butcher's life, not Madison Young's. I felt like a ghost among my family. There was a gap between them and me and it was possible that my life just wouldn't translate into their language. I took James' hand and led him into the kitchen.

"Hello, everyone."

Women filled the room, stirring the gravy and preparing the food for the buffet in serving dishes, bouncing babies to keep them from crying. Men nibbled at the food before they were supposed to. I caught my dad with his hands in the pretzel bowl and he gave me a proper greeting.

"Snaggletooth! How's my pumpkin? Give your dad a hug."

"Hey Dad, I missed you." With his arms wrapped tightly around me I was flooded with memories. Fond memories of his bear hugs and resentment toward the distance between us since my move to San Francisco. His phone calls were few and far between. His life occupied with a new family: his new wife, Lynn, only two years my senior. Lynn and her two sisters, along with her mother and father, had all moved into his new home from a small village in Cambodia. My father met their family while traveling with his best friend, Dave, and fell in love almost instantaneously. He stayed in Cambodia for two months, courting Lynn before deciding to make her his wife. It was not a traditional courtship, but very little about my father was traditional. I liked that about him. I wanted my dad to be happy, but I felt like he stopped supporting my dreams after I crossed Ohio state lines.

"This is James, Dad. He's the guy that I've been telling you about."

"You're not a vegetarian," he demanded, "are you?"

"No, sir. I enjoy a good steak."

My dad turned to me, "I like him."

"Let's go hunting next time you're in town," Dad said, then reached for the turkey and got his hand swatted away by Aunt Darlene.

"Not yet, Richard!"

"Tina, it's good to see you!" My cousin Robin came in with a smile, wiping drool from her baby's mouth as she bounced him on her hip. She was pregnant with her second child. Since I left I'd missed her wedding, the birth of her first child, and her father's funeral. A lot can happen in four years. The kitchen had been remodeled and expanded, and the spot where the kitchen table now sat was Robin's playroom when we were kids. I used to get so excited about her board games, she had every one—Candyland, Chutes and Ladders, Hungry Hungry Hippos, Monopoly, and The Game of Life. We would make slushies with her Snoopy ice machine and I would dream about what it must be like to have so many toys that you needed a separate room for them.

I sat down at the kitchen table and Robin turned to me.

"So what's going on in your life, Tina? I haven't seen you in forever."

"What's my life like? In San Francisco? I'm in love. James and I have been together for over three years now and I love him with all my heart. Um, the gallery is doing really well...We've been getting press and write-ups in some pretty big magazines...I'm doing a show with HBO, teaching workshops on art and sex, finishing my book, and Dave Navarro is hosting this show featuring the gallery and I'll be doing this aerial performance while he's there. Other than that I'm working on a few films that will be screening at film festivals in New York and Paris...I'm touring Europe this summer and reading from my book...I'm keeping busy." I rambled nervously. "Is this little Jackson?"

Robin looked at me for a minute, trying to align my schedule with hers. Her belly, swollen with another child, bulged out under her sweater.

"Wow! Those are big things. Those are California things. They aren't Ohio things."

"Yes, but love, people still fall in love here in Ohio, don't they?"

"Are you two planning on getting married?"

"I don't know."

"Do you want to have children?"

We were conveniently interrupted by my Aunt Darlene wielding a camera, "Go stand next to your dad, Tina."

It is Madison who smiled for the camera; a confident and beautiful woman standing next to the man she has looked up to since she was a child—her protector, who still smelled like rope and licorice, just a couple pounds heavier, hair thinning, glasses thicker as age had ruined his vision.

My aunts, uncles, cousins, nieces, and nephews soon gather around their food, chatting about who would be going off to college and who would be getting married, new jobs, new vacations, and the newest sales at JCPenney's. My voice got lost at this dinner table, and I eagerly filled my mouth with food to silence the awkwardness I felt.

20

THE NEXT DAY, RESTED and ready for more family time, we arrived at my mother's house for Christmas dinner. My mother unlocked and unbolted the door, already apologizing.

"Well, nothing is done...I still have to finish the cookies, the turkey still needs to go in the oven, I have no idea how to make your vegan thing and the house is a mess—a mess!"

Good to see you too, Mom.

It was always like this. My mother was always overwhelmed, stressed, and complaining. She has a lot of love to give but it's hidden under a blanket of anxiety that is contagious: the house oozes with it, constant disappointment and frantic energy. My brother was just back from rehab, suffering from depression and co-dependency, and my mother lost herself in her usual whirlwind of panic. Between the two of them they had built a cyclone of controlling, manic energy that wreaked havoc on their environment.

James whispered in my ear, "And there is no booze? I have to do this sober?"

The saving grace was my father, the voice of reason, sleepy-eyed from salting driveways all night but standing in the foyer welcoming us. My mother and father may have divorced one another years ago, but we are still a family. Their shared experiences give them a history and our holidays are always spent together. My mother may never forget my father's indiscretions but she did find it in her heart to forgive him. My father's humor is a calming compliment to my mother's fiery energy. Her anxiety comes from a well-meaning place, I know that now, fueled by the want for things to be perfect. She wants to create perfect memories, with smiling photographs and beautifully decorated Christmas trees.

James and my dad headed off to the living room, while I made my way upstairs to my old bedroom. It looked exactly the same as when I lived there. I was greeted with the same Pepto-pink walls and wallpaper, pink roses and gray ribbons. It was the first wallpaper I ever picked out and I had a comforter and sheets that matched. I closed the door and looked around. My old journals were still stuffed into my dresser drawers and the graduation cap and honors cords I earned for being at the top of my high school class still hung from my bedroom mirror. I sat on the bed, listening to it squeak, gazing out the window as snow began to fall.

That squeaking bed, like a rocking chair, used to put me to sleep. I remembered Gauge sharing the bed with me, the year I brought her home for Christmas.

We don't mind sharing a bed, Mom. We had disrobed under the covers after the door was closed and the lights were out, her soft skin rubbing up against mine, the taste of her lips sweet. My hands ached to be inside of her. We rocked slowly back and forth trying to avoid making the bed squeak, quiet as the falling snow.

My father's voice drifted into the room: "Come downstairs, *Scrooged* is going to be on in just a couple minutes."

Ok, Dad.

I snuck one last look at the world I left behind: diplomas, scrapbooks, career charts, report cards, and old loves. Photographs of a girl with braces and freckles, brassy red hair, and an awkwardness that comes from not belonging, lined the halls. I descend into the family room, where my family was huddled around the TV with Christmas dinner. We would be outcasts without our common language: television.

We sat captive to the television, reciting the familiar lines, like we had so many times before. Dad brought his voice to a high falsetto, fluttering his hands like wings and mimicking the ditzy blonde fairy on the television: "Sometimes you've got to *slap* them in the face to get their attention!"

"Ha! She's a dominatrix fairy!" My brother Reo pointed at the screen, amused by his observation. "Tina, you know about dominatrixes don't you?"

"Reo, we're not going to talk about that on Christmas!" my mother reprimanded.

"What? I didn't do anything," my brother responded, dumbfounded and defensive. "What? She's on TV talking about it. Aren't you, Sis? She knows all about dominatrixes, all that kinky shit. Dad and I saw her on what's that show called, *One Thousand Ways to Die*. Called her sexpert or somethin'."

"Richard Edwin Oliver Butcher! I will not have you ruin my Christmas. We are going to be a normal family for once and sit down together and eat our dinner and watch the goddamn movie. Is that clear?" My mom's face glowed red with anxiety and embarrassment.

"Listen to your mother, Reo."

Mr. Mogul and I stared forward, avoiding eye contact while tension thickened in the room, terrified of another eruption from my mother. James excused himself to the bathroom. I kept my hands folded in my lap, trying not to breathe or move.

21

"CHASM, WE NEED MORE ice for the bar and bring out another case of chilled champagne for our guests," Daddy's hand rested on Sarah Chasm's shoulder. She was the head house slave. She gazed upward at my Daddy and moaned as his hands traced down her naked body and struck her pink flesh with a crisp slap. She released a sharp yelp, an inappropriate reaction for a submissive who had been granted the honor of serving on The Upper Floor. I found her vulgar. Part of me pained with jealousy to see Daddy's hands on another woman, but I understood it to be part of the job, and accepted it as such. Daddy leaned in and whispered into her ear. Her mouth opened slightly and she closed her eyes. He stuffed his hand down her throat and she gagged on his digits, eyes watering. *Pathetic.* His eyes fixated on Sarah, a new toy ripe for training. He removed his hand from her mouth and slapped her slobbery face. Her eyes opened with adoration and she crossed her arms behind her back and disappeared into the hallway to carry out his orders. The camera followed James' every move.

He grabbed a black towel and walked toward Maestro, the butler of The Upper Floor, who was Daddy's right hand and had become a close friend. Mr. Mogul seemed to enjoy having a young dominant to mentor. After wiping his hands clean, he poured himself a drink, whiskey on the rocks.

"Maestro, Sir...can you make sure the slaves have properly set the dining room table for tonight's dinner?" As he brought the tumbler to his mouth, I could see his eyes pan the room full of yelping and screaming, well-lubricated guests. "And if it hasn't been taken care of to your satisfaction please make note of it and we will demonstrate an appropriate correction for the viewing pleasure of our guests." He pulled a white handkerchief from the inside of his jacket pocket, sniffled, and wiped his drippy nose. The dusty environment wreaked havoc on his allergies and the more time he spent on The Upper Floor, the worse his allergies got.

"Right away, Mr. Mogul," Maestro replied as the camera returned.

"A drink, Mr. Mogul?" Holly asked, then handed him an already refreshed tumbler full of whiskey.

We had spent Christmas day at our apartment in the Lower Haight, an apartment we acquired shortly after Mr. Mogul received a promotion at KINK. The majority of our belongings were still in boxes. With my touring schedule—directing feminist porn, on-camera porn performances, and educational speaking engagements at conferences and sex toy stores—I wasn't exactly a stay-at-home domestic submissive. I had been driving on the high of my career, neglecting to build a home for Daddy and myself. His workload had also doubled, and we were rarely around to keep house. Our kitchen lay in disuse; it was a novelty to cook at the apartment. Daddy was directing two sites: The Training of O and The Upper Floor. The Training of O was the slave training site I participated in for my own training with Daddy. The women entered with no ranking and only a desire to be trained to discover something powerful that existed within themselves. It changed many of their lives, as it changed mine. The experience created infatuations and Stockholm Syndrome responses among a handful of the women. The Training of O was an emotional journey resembling that of a makeover reality show. Mr. Mogul was the Chef Gordon Ramsey of online dominance and submission.

The second site, The Upper Floor, was the next phase—a graduation for the women. Only a select few submissives who had completed The Training of O could petition for serving on The Upper Floor. The Upper Floor was modeled after the old English Manors of the early 1900s and featured black tie events and a working staff of slaves that served as maids and butlers. Directing the site was a promotion not only for Daddy, but for anyone that he allowed into this world.

THE FIRST TIME I saw The Upper Floor was a few months earlier, at The Upper Floor Halloween party.

I was in awe. The fourth floor parlor was draped in red velvet curtains, ornate couches, and fine rugs. Rich blood-red embossed wallpaper covered the walls and a roaring fireplace heated the room. Here, every affair was an elegant affair with a mandatory black-tie dress code. San Francisco's elite celebrated here in sexy long evening gowns, tuxedos, and fine suits alongside nearly-naked bombshells in stockings, black garter belts and elegant high heels. This neo-Edwardian palace had a full bar, a humidor full of fine cigars, decanters of scotch and a grand piano in the foyer. Classical music competed with moans and yelps from participating men and women and the snap of whips and floggers.

I had just returned from tour with the Queer X Show. For two months I traveled through Europe with seven other radical feminist performance artists. We took the stage in Paris, Berlin, and Brussels, addressing sexuality and identity through raw performance art.

The gritty nightclubs and dark theatrical stages I had seen while traveling were a direct contrast to the decadence and pornification of the female body that I found at home in San Francisco. Hairy legs were replaced with smooth ones, cheap beer and burlesque costumes were replaced with expensive bottles of champagne, heels, and Wolford stockings. I left dreads, Mohawks, and tattoos on tour and arrived surrounded by platinum hair dye, Brazilian blowouts, and hair extensions.

After security guards radioed to Daddy for permission to send me up, I lugged my large suitcase up the five flights of stairs into the models' green room so I could freshen up. I powdered my face, freshened my lipstick, spritzed my body with vanilla scented perfume, and slipped into a new pair of thigh-high stockings, a garter belt, and high heels. I was jet-lagged and tired, but excited to see my Daddy. It had been months since we had last seen each other, with only patchy correspondences back and forth during my travels.

Daddy had used my time away to build a new world for KINK. Mounted cameras filmed The Upper Floor twenty-four hours a day, capturing the late-night sexual appetites of Master Peter Acworth for viewers' pleasure. Peter lived on The Upper Floor in the master's quarters. As the sun rose on the horizon, Mr. Mogul would also rise to lead the house slaves in morning workouts like lifting weights in the nude and jogging up and down the stairs while Master Peter looked on in his slippers and robe, sipping coffee, laughing, and nodding in approval.

When I entered The Upper Floor's grand parlor for the first time that Halloween night, Daddy ran to my side, grabbed me around the waist and swung me around in a circle, kissing me deeply and taking my breath away. He immediately gave me a tour, but it was a world that only they could understand completely. I was lost in his enthusiasm, delirious with jet lag, and heady with champagne.

"I can't wait to get my hands on you. Wait here, let me check in with the staff." Mr. Mogul returned with a smile on his face and a whip in his hand. He grabbed my red hair and coaxed me down to the floor, on my knees.

He pulled my coiled leather collar from his suit jacket pocket and wrapped the black leather around my neck. I closed my eyes. I felt the familiar, soft leather tighten around my neck and his hands securing the collar in place with a lock and key. I was *home*. With his index finger hooked around my collar he brought me to my feet, kissed me on the mouth and led me to a beautiful large wooden St. Andrew's Cross.

He ran his hands up my thighs, grabbed hold of my cunt and slapped it. His hands weren't nearly as rough as when we had first met, the calluses gone and his skin soft, but his fingers were still strong and knowing as they made their way slowly up the landscape of my abdomen and my ribs. His thumb and forefinger clasped around my nipples and he pulled. I smiled wickedly with appreciation as a jolt of adrenaline rushed through my body and I quickly inhaled, allowing the sensation to flow down to my cunt in a hurried rush and churn and swirl into an aching throbbing pleasure. I exhaled, releasing a slow thin stream of air through my slightly pursed lips, my eyes locked with Mr. Mogul's.

Mr. Mogul leaned in close and whispered in my ear, "I love you, Slut. I've been waiting to greet you with a nice welcome-home whipping for some time. Are you ready?"

"Yes, Sir. Thank you, Sir." I smiled, one of his hands still pulling at my pink nipple.

Mr. Mogul's whip fell repeatedly on my cunt. My vulva throbbed and ached for release. The leather implement found percussive rhythm, falling on my labia and teasing my clit. I let out a deep moan as the leather struck my inner thighs. I lifted my feet from the ground, pulling myself upward by my wrists and I felt all of the heat and energy that had been swirling about my body join forces and spasm through me in a deep tremble. Suspended, my body shook and shivered until my muscles, exhausted, went limp. Mr. Mogul's hands traced the fresh pink and red stripes that ran up and down my body. The lighter marks were already fading, but some rose to attention against his comforting and tender touch.

He released me from the cuffs and helped me to the couch. The cameraman followed and hovered over us, reminding me that I lived in a fantasy that was being filmed. The crowd parted as we walked through in a daze. A woman in a corset and her collared submissive got up from their seats to make room for us.

Sarah glared at us from across the room, her eyes stone cold and emotionless. She approached with a silver tray of champagne balanced on the palm of her hand. Mr. Mogul had first taken Sarah on as a project. She was the head submissive of The Upper Floor and worked full time for the site assisting with administration duties, post-production editing, serving, and event planning. She was like an executive assistant who also was whipped and fucked for the house and master's entertainment. Outfitted similarly to me in black stockings, heels, a lace garter belt and a house collar, she had short dyed black hair, like a twenties flapper girl. She came across as quiet and depressed, a gothic stoner. Still in her early twenties, she was discovering who she was in kink and BDSM play. Mr. Mogul found potential in her willingness to explore the outer reaches of her boundaries. She was eager to serve and learn, and she had left very little behind when she devoted herself to the castle and The Upper Floor as a full time slave. Perhaps that made her a perfect candidate for the job.

"Is there anything I can get for you, Sir?" Sarah asked, standing at attention, stoic and focused. She was so quiet I felt awkward around her. I knew over the last few months that The Upper Floor had focused Mr. Mogul's attentions on Sarah with a greater frequency than they were focused on me. I felt my hackles rise with jealousy.

"Be a good girl and fetch Madison a glass of water." Mr. Mogul issued his orders, patting his lap. I laid my head in his lap and he stroked my hair. I scowled with jealousy and unease: *I'm Daddy's good girl.*

I peered up at him, vying for his attention "Daddy...I don't trust Sarah. The way she looks at you, at us...She wants to fuck you! I know it!" I sunk my hand into his thigh, clinging onto what was mine, suddenly afraid that I could lose him.

"Maddie, do we need to do this right now?" The green-eyed monster had reared its ugly head in our relationship many times. We navigated our way in and out of an, at times sticky, open relationship based on our mutual comfort, but there was a line in the sand:

we didn't fuck our coworkers off the clock. I was highly uncomfortable with the thought of Mr. Mogul having sex with any of the models that he worked with. Those models were women that I also worked with, and I didn't want that awkwardness. James didn't want me to fuck the people that he worked with, especially his boss, Mr. Acworth, or his best friend, Maestro. Daddy also didn't want me to participate in KINK's gang-bang site, which was often made up of the many folks who worked in the KINK wood shop. It would be awkward for Mr. Mogul to have the prop maker talk about it, just as I had no desire to be in a green room hearing similar gossip from the models. Nearly everything and everyone else was up for negotiation, and negotiation was the key. When it came to Sarah, I did not want her any closer to my Daddy than was required of him, especially since he was no longer working as a sexual performer for his productions.

"You're right, she does. But I don't want to fuck her and I'm not going to," he replied. "I love you," he said, kissing me on the forehead.

"I don't know if that makes me feel any better." I muttered under my breath. I opened my eyes to see Sarah hovering over me.

"Your water, Ma'am"

THE DAY AFTER CHRISTMAS, things felt completely different. I wasn't sure how they changed, but I felt a distance stretching between Daddy and me that was getting covered up with expensive presents and dinners.

Sarah stood beside Peter and Daddy, ringing a dinner bell.

"Welcome, everyone. Happy Boxing Day and a Merry Christmas to all of our guests and our members. Our kitchen staff has prepared a beautiful dinner. We invite you all to our dining room for a delicious dinner and kinky entertainment. Cheers." Peter raised his glass and took a long drink of champagne. He wore a black tuxedo and raised his glass in celebration.

The dining table was set with fine china, and the whole KINK family of directors and illustrious models were in attendance, along with pre-selected guests from the San Francisco BDSM community. Daddy fixed me a plate of potatoes and broccoli and placed it on the floor in a corner of the dining room. A red velvet pillow lay there for me to kneel on while dining.

"Maddie, I need to go tend to the guests. I love you ,my Slut. Merry Christmas." With a smile and a light slap, he turned his attention back to the room. A devilish grin spread across my face.

"What a good slave, Puppy. I see you're eating your vegetables." Lorelei Lee approached my cushion and I swallowed my sparse dinner down with a big bubbling sip of champagne. Lorelei looked ravishing. A tight black strapless latex dress clung to her body causing her cleavage to spill out like an offering, dangerously close to my face. A modern-day pinup queen with a nervous giggle and a soothing sultry voice, I find her almost irresistible. Her fingers stroked through my hair as she asked, "How are you?"

"I'm good. Life is good. I've been traveling a bit, but it's good to be home. Mr. Mogul and I had a good Christmas. And you?"

"Things are good...exhausting. I'm back and forth between here and New York working on my MFA. I'm sorry I couldn't read at the last event at the gallery. It sounded like a great line up. My schedule's just...just, well...it's a bit much right now." I nodded, listening to her voice, while my eyes followed Daddy as he tightly cinched his ropes around Sarah. Over the months it seemed that they had become more casually acquainted with one another's dominant and submissive personalities and my anxiety was slowly growing to a boil.

Lorelei noticed my gaze. She was familiar with the complications of dating both within and outside of the adult industry and the jealousy and temptations that come as a result of our line of work. "You don't have anything to worry about, Madison. You and James are great together. He loves you, he talks about you all the time." I needed those reassuring words. She leaned in and kissed me on the crown of my head.

I nodded, "Thanks."

Sarah crawled on top of the long dining room table where dominant men and women sat with their submissive counterparts at their sides, eating Christmas dinner from dog bowls or being fed scraps from their

Master or Mistress' plate. Everyone eagerly watched as Mr. Mogul constructed a chest harness around Sarah's breasts, securing her hands behind her back and attached the harness to a connecting rope that led to an eyebolt on the ceiling above the dining table. He heaved on the rope, adding tension, and lifted Sarah into the air, making her the centerpiece for the table.

He began coiling the jute rope around her face, around her eyes and mouth, leaving her completely faceless, an anonymous bound fuck doll. He pulled a cane from the utility cabinet, a thick bamboo reed.

"Now you don't quite know what to expect, do you, Slut? I can stuff your filthy cunt with my hand or someone's cock, or I can whip your cunt or tease you with the vibrator. You're our little helpless fuck doll, just a hole." Sarah's ass swayed back and forth, itching to be touched. I heard her muffled whimpers from the coils of rope and I was aroused, jealous, and sympathetic to her vulnerability. Daddy's cane fell fast and hard on her pale, ghostly thighs and blood-curdling screams erupted as her body hung taut from the celing.

"Talk to me, Slut. Are you in pain? Do you want to go forward? Nod your head if you want more, Slave." Daddy's cane was lightly tracing up and down the landscape of her quivering body. I recognized her internal conflict: the desire for more, more sensation, so much sensation that you are carried away to somewhere far from where you are, while your psyche is rubbing against its edge. Sarah slowly, bravely nodded her head, consenting.

The cane struck again, this time on her tits, and she screamed. I saw the sensation zig-zagging through her body, and understood that she lacked the tools to process the scene she was engaging in. I had been there myself—she wanted it, but didn't know what to do with that fiery heat now licking through her body with every strike. I stood up in the corner that Daddy put me in, where my dinner was served, and walked toward Sarah, bringing my face close to hers, stroking her hair and putting my hand on her shoulder.

"You need to breathe, Sarah. Don't let the sensation control you, let it flow through you. This is nothing. It's one moment in time. What are you going to do with that moment, Sarah? Recognize it as a gift." I whispered into the mummified sphere that surrounded her head. She was still just a girl, only twenty-four, and I felt threatened by her. I felt my impending thirtieth birthday approaching like a death sentence; I tried to disregard my fears of being replaced for a younger, newer make and model.

I took a breath in and exhaled exaggeratedly as the cane again made contact with her reddening skin. "It's not pain. It's sensation, it's energy, and it exists. Let it exist."

Her sharp vocal releases transformed to deep, cathartic sobbing and I listened closely while she attempted to mimic my breathing pattern. "Okay, here comes another one. Inhale, I want you to exhale deeply on contact."

The dinner guests sat, still watching, in their seats at the table. The couples were amused and inspired by the little scene that Mr. Mogul started with Sarah. This was the intent, after all: entertainment. Onlookers touched themselves with passion or sucked their Daddys' cocks. Soon, a symphonic score of thuds and slaps, yelps, and moans filled the room, making my tiny voice even less audible.

"Inhale, and...exhale. Good, that one was much better."

I left her side.

"Too bad you can't come without penetration. Isn't that right, Slut?" Daddy taunted her and their connection made my skin crawl. *I don't want to be in the room for her orgasm.*

Sarah mumbled something unintelligible and Daddy quickly untied the ropes around her face and mouth.

"Speak clearly, Slut, when you are spoken to." His eyes locked onto Sarah's and he grabbed hold of her chest harness and pulled her in to him.

"Cock please, Sir. Please, I want your cock. Fill me with your cock."

Her words drifted into the hallway as I walked away, down the long corridor, until they were only a faint buzzing of syllables behind Beethoven's quartets.

22

I WAITED IN A long black stretch limo outside the Armory. It was clear that my hero needed to be rescued; at the very least, he needed to be rescued from work. He had been sucked into an imaginary world, fueled by energy bars, booze, and drugs. The Disneyland of KINK. Daddy went down the rabbit hole and the only way for me to be with him was to jump in myself. Wearing black lace lingerie and nude thigh highs that made my legs like silk, I slipped pedicured toes into black patent leather heels and exited the limo. I covered up with a Burberry trench coat. In my ass I had a large purple silicone butt plug. My long red hair fell in waves down my back and a diamond necklace dangled between my breasts. After collecting a very nice bottle of champagne, ripe red strawberries, and dark chocolate, I knocked on the Armory door and waited for the familiar security guard to answer the door.

"Madison Young to see you, Sir," the gentleman barked into his walkie-talkie.

"Send her up," a staticky voice answered.

I walked the eight flights of stairs, 120 in all, from the first floor entrance to Daddy's office on The Upper Floor. I knocked on the thick wooden door and turned the doorknob. Over the last five months, Daddy's office had grown from the basic desk and a white-board set-up to a full-fledged fifties bachelor studio. His room was furnished beautifully, and he brought nearly all his fetish and kink oriented books to the office. His whips and rope and canes, the implements that used to belong in our home, migrated to his castle. I didn't like what was happening, but he seemed to have a clear explanation for every move. *We don't have a laundry unit at our apartment, and I need easy access to suits and work clothes. I want all of my books close at hand for reference. Music inspires me, so I need the nice home stereo at KINK.* Always the director, Mr. Mogul hadn't only created the world of The Upper Floor; he created a cast of characters. Each of the characters, including his character as trainer, had their own narrative, and it felt as though I was losing him to his own world.

Daddy sat at his desk, staring at his computer, a nearly empty tumbler of whiskey beside him. He finished it off and exhaled deeply. When his eyes met mine they were cold and piercing. A bottle of lube sat on a vanity in the corner; beside it lay a small pile of condoms and a small hand mirror fogged with a cloud of white. *His staff of models must be using his office prior to shoots again,* I figured.

"I have a surprise for us downstairs," I said, approaching his desk, slowly unbuttoning my trench coat.

"Come on, Maddie. You know I don't like surprises." He kept his gaze on the computer screen. I saw the palm of his hand cupping the mouse and wished they were cupping my breasts.

"I'm rescuing you from this place." I slipped the coat off of my shoulders and pouted. It lay in a puddle of fabric on the floor, one less layer between Daddy and me.

"Let's get out of here," I offered, running my hands up Daddy's thick muscular thighs as I knelt down in front of him. My fingers traced the hard outline of Daddy's cock inside his perfectly tailored pants. His cock fit neatly in the palm of my hand. I gazed upward at him as he moaned. He grabbed my hair and pulled my face up the crotch of his pants, tracing my mouth up his inseam, my makeup left a smeared imprint.

I crawled my way up Daddy's body, straddling him and whispering with a devilish smile into his ear, "Daddy, there is a limo downstairs, I have a bottle of champagne, and I'm wearing a vibrating butt plug."

"And where do you propose that we go, Slut?" Daddy smiled for the first time that evening, his eyes a little softer, his hands running through my hair and fingering a dangling red lock by my ear.

I wrapped my arms around Daddy tight and nuzzled my nose into the nook where his shoulder and neck met. "Anywhere but here, Daddy."

Daddy picked my coat up off the floor and dressed me, buttoning me up, and taking my hand. As we headed down the grand Armory staircase, out the palace doors, and into the cold San Francisco night, the city and the world seemed full of fantasies not yet filled and adventures not yet had. We are gods here, heroes, and we will fuck like gods and heroes in limos with champagne; with a castle for our playground, we have nested snugly into one of the most beautiful and debauched cities in the world. Passing over the Golden Gate Bridge, being ravaged against a pillar at the Palace of Fine Arts, racing to the top of Coit Tower, our blood is warm and flowing free. For a moment, everything else drifts away and we are as young as children, full of love and free of work, titles, careers, and public personas. I am safe and home in the arms of Daddy. I am Daddy's Little Girl.

23

I SAT AT THE bar in a four-star vegan restaurant working on my second glass of red wine and toying with a small black box. It contained an antique pocket watch I bought for Daddy. It was our fifth anniversary. I watched the hands tick, indicating that Mr. Mogul was now an hour late for our dinner reservation. I turned the watch over and ran my thumb over the inscription: *Love Always Your Spaniel, Maddie.* My heart ached.

I grew accustomed to carrying a book with me to fill the minutes or hours that I found myself sitting alone at a restaurant or bar awaiting his presence. A thirty-minute delay wasn't unusual, but there had been evenings I waited for an hour, two hours, or longer for him to show up. I wanted to believe in my hero. I wanted to believe in Daddy, but it became harder and harder. I felt tears welling up in my eyes. I rummaged through my purse pushing aside lipstick, keys, and used airline tickets to find a wad of twenty-dollar bills. I left two of them for the tab, tossed the antique watch into my purse, and left the restaurant with what remained of my dignity. Taxis zoomed past on the crisp summer evening. I waved one down and slid inside. Fishing through my purse for a bottle of Ativan, I took two small pills. Along with unanswered phone calls and an absent Daddy came a rapid storm of anxiety attacks, hyperventilation, debilitating depression, and heart palpitations. My doctor prescribed me Ativan and advised that I discontinue my use of birth control pills. I swallowed the pills and attempted to steady my trembling right hand, the diamond and gold rope ring nearly slid off my bony ring finger. I lost weight and couldn't stomach much food since the onset of the anxiety attacks.

"Fourteenth and Mission, please." I cleared my throat, the Armory's address sour in my mouth. I didn't want to go there. I felt like his mother, his caretaker, like an obnoxious wife hunting down her drunkard husband at the bar. It was all too dramatic, storming the castle to win back my love. I knew I couldn't force Daddy to love me, I couldn't force him to stay, but I did believe that I could convince him that our relationship was worth working on. Daddy was lost, I could see that. This was perhaps the hardest thing for me, I was not willing to lose my Daddy again. *It's our anniversary, how can he do this?* My mind was a mess of contradictions; I wanted him to be there at the Armory so I could hold him in my arms, but I didn't want him to be at the Armory because that would mean that he had blown off our fifth anniversary.

◇◇◇

CONFUSED AND FRUSTRATED, I was in deep denial. I denied everything in our world that contrasted with the image of Daddy and me—our life together—that I had created in my mind. I didn't want to face the feelings that did not fit my romanticized notion of us, that challenged the vision of the mythically strong and able father figure I had created. I wanted, needed someone who could hold me and pet me and assure me: *It will be okay. Daddy's here now. It'll all be okay.*

Simultaneously, I wanted something to blame it on. I was desperate for something, anything, any act or issue I could pin our relationship problems on, but I couldn't see what that might be. I had discovered bags of pills and other women's panties in his pants and jacket pockets. When I confronted him about them, he launched into defensive outbursts that made him look far different from the man I thought I knew. He claimed that the prescriptions were his, that his back was in horrific pain and he had the prescriptions to cope. He said the panties were from a shoot, from work. He wanted to know why I couldn't trust him. I began to doubt my sanity: *Am I being inappropriate?* I wished that I felt like I could trust him without question, but it was becoming harder and harder for me to do so. The pills, the pot, the booze, I had convinced myself that it was recreational—for me it was, but it didn't explain the trouble he was having with holding it all together. My mind was spinning. Desperate, I repeated my mantra: everything is going to be okay. I made the decision to trust in Daddy. I needed my hero.

As the taxi pulled up to the Armory my phone buzzed inside my purse and glanced at the display, willing it to read, "Incoming Call: Daddy." Instead, it read, "Dad." *I can't speak to him right now.* I had been dodging my father's calls for the past several months, after finding out that his new wife was pregnant with a little girl. It felt like I was being replaced. I knocked on the castle door and waited for the night guard. Most of the guards knew me, since I had been in and out of the Armory nearly every day, between curating artwork for the building, performing, and visiting James, I spent a huge amount of time there. James had been working impossibly long hours, staying the night, occasionally, to pack in as much work as possible. He wanted to be ahead of the curve. Part of me thought that he just didn't feel like he had anything left at the end of the night to give to our relationship.

The guard led me to the basement, past the narrow lancet windows visible between the first and basement floor, past subterranean porn sets that portrayed a vast plethora of fantasy worlds, including an intricate padded cell with a two-way mirror for clinical observation, a meat locker equipped with meat hooks, and a neatly designed suburban apartment to cater to more traditional fantasies. Each was intended to be an impressive backdrop for different fetish fantasies. I felt like I could use a little vanilla, some suburban normality was starting to sound appetizing in this moment of chaos. My grasp of reality seemed to be getting increasingly fragile.

As I searched for Daddy, sounds of drums, bass, and guitar echoed down the castle corridors in a drunken cacophony. My heels clicked meekly down the stone hallway toward the music. When I turned the corner, my stomach churned, nauseated. Maestro was seated behind a drum set, sticks clanging on the hi-hat and snare drum. Sarah leaned against the stone wall, eyes drifting, hands tucked into a black zip-up hoodie branded with the KINK scarlet red logo. Her legs were bare and she appeared to be naked under the oversized sweatshirt. She brought a glass-blown pipe to her lips and inhaled, her purple lighter dimly illuminated the hallway with a brief flame. While she was standing there, swaying back and forth, Daddy finished off a tumbler of whiskey, his mint green guitar dangled across his chest. Beer bottles and empty glasses littered the staging area. I saw him close his eyes and pull the guitar toward him; bending down on one knee his fingers and hands strangled the neck of the guitar while he tore violently across the steel strings in an aggressive '80s metal guitar riff. Maestro looked up from his drum set with drunken, heavy red eyes and watched as I walk toward them. With tears in my eyes, I stood before him, and suddenly everything went silent, except for the muffled cries of my whimpering.

"It's our anniversary," I managed to say, red with embarrassment and completely lost. I didn't have the right words to save this evening, or our relationship, or to prevent this loss of my hero, my Daddy.

"Sorry baby, I must have lost track of the time. What time is it?" Daddy's eyes shifted away from mine as he propped his guitar on a nearby table among dildos and ropes. Sarah whispered something into Maestro's ear and took the drumsticks from his hands. They disappeared, leaving us alone in the room.

"It's nine-thirty." I looked at my watch and remembered the pulsing tick of Daddy's present in my purse.

"Woah! Really? Babe, we just started jammin' and... well, I guess we got lost in it all. It's cool. We can still grab dinner." Daddy came to me and offered a handkerchief of thin white cotton. I held my breath, afraid to exhale, afraid of what I might say, afraid of the questions I might ask and the answers I might receive.

We walked down the castle halls to a familiar set, the backdrop for my training with Daddy, and sat down on a large cement block. I glared at the floor, the same floor I crawled across on my hands and knees, the same pedestal on which I cried when his whip marred my tender flesh. It seemed like so long ago. We were no longer the same people that once occupied this room. I buried my face in his arms, crying, and tossed him his present.

At our apartment, after a hasty and hollow dinner, we fucked. It was sad and desperate sex. I was confused and alone and didn't know how to seek help for a problem that was so complicated. While I sucked his cock, his body started to feel foreign to me. Something changed. I shoved his long member down my throat, but his closed eyes made him seem far away. His mouth chewed on my nipples like bubble gum and I stuffed him into my pussy. I cried silently, wiping away tears as I bounced on his body.

Daddy threw my body away from his and pulled back my hair. I arched my back and offered my ass, and he plunged deep into my pussy, the head of his cock painfully jamming against my cervix. I inhaled and exhaled, ineffectively trying to disappear into endorphins. I wanted to let it all go, to start anew, but I didn't know where to begin.

Daddy plunged deep and moaned a low, grunting sound as he finished. I lay on the bed staring across the room at photos of us on the beach during our summer vacation in Puerto Vallarta. A beautiful charcoal drawing hangs framed on the wall. In it are two figures—me and Daddy—in the midst of a beautiful dance.

Hot come dripped onto our rich violet sheets and I looked over at him: his body limp, naked, and snoring, I wondered if I could take any more pain. I was ready for release.

Part 4

24

I T WAS THE DAY after Father's Day and a thick slab of grass-fed beef sat bleeding in the fridge. Despite being vegan for over a decade, I promised James I would prepare him a steak to celebrate. A corresponding Father's Day card sat on the bureau, unopened, untouched. The envelope read: *To Daddy, with Love. Your Little Girl, Maddie.*

Daddy and I had a tradition of celebrating our Daddy/Little Girl relationship on Father's Day, but this Father's Day my Daddy was gone.

I hadn't heard from him since our bleak anniversary. Five days without texts or calls. I heard he barricaded himself into his office, solitary in the vastness of the Armory, and that he wasn't capable of having company (at least with me).

My body was like a limp noodle, lying in a lukewarm tub of water. Reaching for my Ativan, I shook a small handful into my fist and shoved them down my throat. My head was full of white noise. I pushed my hands to the bottom of the white porcelain bathtub and stared at them.

I slid slowly under water, my long red hair swishing back and forth. Through a small window leaked a cool breeze, the smell of pot, and the sound of Radiohead from our upstairs neighbor's apartment. The front page of a weekly newspaper hung framed on the bathroom wall. The headline read "Submission Possible" in big bold lettering, a rope clad pinup girl in an aerial suspension gracing the cover. Long red curls spilled down her back and her eyes were framed in dark lashes, with a twinkling of youthful, mischievous innocence. I didn't even recognize that girl, anymore.

Do I know who I am anymore? Do I know anyone in the world that knows or cares about Tina Butcher? Is there any part of me that isn't available for public consumption? Perhaps I had made my contribution to culture and achieved what I was meant to achieve. Maybe it was time to fade away.

My phone rang, and the display read "Dad." *Not now.*

I collapsed onto the bed surrounded by an assemblage of memories: photos, objects, clothing, sex toys, cluttering the floor, spilling out of the dresser and the closet. I had texted a few close friends in a discreet attempt to seek the help I vaguely knew I needed. I needed direction and support, I couldn't make it through this situation on my own. Like good friends should in times of need, they appeared with food, compassion, and many episodes of bad television. Mev still worked as my assistant on an as-needed basis and had become a trusted friend. She sat by my side and offered a Tupperware of hot tortilla soup.

She handed me a spoon and smiled, pushing her coke-bottle glasses up the bridge of her nose. "Go on, now. You need to keep your energy up," she said, and her Texas drawl showed itself. It felt warm and comforting with the soup and the friendly company.

I swallowed each spoonful gently. It felt like the colors seeped out, like the life around me was moving in slow motion, hollow and empty. "I'm supposed to be in Chicago tomorrow, Wisconsin the next day. They're expecting Madison Young. I can't. I can't do it. I can't be her right now," I pleaded. I couldn't fathom boarding a plane, waiting in lines at the airport, and addressing a crowd of couples out on date night about how to add depth and connection to their relationship while demonstrating kinky sexual technique. I had no inspiration to share.

Maxine, Femina Potens' marketing director, and I had also grown close. She crawled to the center of the bed to hold my hand, giving me a little squeeze when I needed it to remind me I was still there.

Mev jotted down some notes. "Don't you worry about that. I'll take care of everything."

I smiled. Mev was magic, the best assistant I could hope for. She helped me with everything from video editing to red carpet costume design, from designing the gallery interior to keeping me fed. Mev is my unicorn, a one in a million girl.

I closed my eyes, trying to rest. Mev whispered a soft "Shhhhh," but all I could see was red.

"Why would he do this to me? I bought meat! A steak! It's disgusting, and just sitting in there." I sat up abruptly in the bed, fists tight around my pillow, my adrenaline pumping.

Storm, an eager volunteer at the gallery, a budding fetish model at KINK, and a new friend, leaned against the wall, texting. "He's a jerk, Madison. He doesn't deserve you. Quite frankly he's a cheat and a liar with a pretty fierce coke habit and I don't know why you haven't seen that before." I felt suddenly choked with fear. *Daddy doesn't have a problem! Is there a problem? There is a problem, isn't there?* I couldn't believe that he was an addict or an alcoholic, which seemed like something altogether different. Calling Daddy an alcoholic or addict seemed like a judgment of me, for being his partner and not recognizing it, not stopping it, not healing him. Her words were difficult to hear. It wasn't that the thought hadn't crossed my mind in the previous months, I just couldn't bring myself to listen.

"Don't say that, Storm. Are you crazy? She doesn't need to hear that right now." Maxine spoke up for the first time that afternoon with a firm voice and motherly tone.

"Well, I think she needs to know," Storm said, shooting Maxine a sharp gaze. "Anyway, I've got a client. Madison, drop James, he's bad news and he's just going to bring you down with him." Her words chilled the air even after she left the room. I feared prediction, *What if she's right?* The room went quiet as I stared blankly at the doorway Storm had vacated.

"He's got allergies. He's allergic to dust, that's why he's always sniffling. He didn't fuck anyone. He would have told me. He would have told me, right, Maxine?" I nervously ripped apart my cuticles, spitting them out onto the dingy, stained white comforter.

Maxine looked up at me with a reassuring response, but in her eyes I saw a glimpse of doubt, "Of course he would have, Madison. He loves you." Her words were kind, but I found it hard to believe her.

"Forget about him, just for this moment, and let's do something for you," Mev softly pleaded.

From her canvas bag she revealed a velvet maroon sack full of tarot cards. Shuffling through the deck of cards, she handed them to me.

"Shuffle them and then pick a card and turn it over. What do you love, Madison?" Mev asked. I held the cards to my chest and closed my eyes, wishing for an answer.

"Work. I love what I do for work but I just can't..." I shuffled the cards back and forth in my hands, opening my eyes.

"No. Something that isn't work." Mev interjected and I turned over my chosen card. The Sun card. My mind drifted off to my father. During warm, humid Cincinnati summers I used to dig my fingers deep in steamy mulch to spread the moist bark chips across our flowerbeds, covering the top soil and improving the fertility of the earth. My dad dug holes deep in the ground to plant saplings and flowering bushes. We seemed to be surrounded by life during those summers.

The life of simplicity, inhaling the smells and sounds of nature, was one of the feelings that had first aroused my interest in the fibrous organic rope I now cinch tightly around my body

"A garden," I shared, and with a small, hopeful smile I turned the card around to show Mev.

"There you go! A garden. Now don't tweet about it, don't Facebook about it, don't blog about it. Plant a garden, Tina, and let it just be for you."

WITH THE SUN PEEKING out beneath the San Francisco fog, I knelt in reverence on my bare knees on the stone patio that made up our Lower Haight backyard. To my right was a large pile of top soil—rich, dark, moist earth—and to my left, trays upon trays of flowers, herbs and vegetables waiting to be planted in their respective homes among my raised flower boxes. I took Mev's suggestion and decided to plant something that was mine. I needed to be surrounded by growth and life. I needed to tend to something that wasn't for public consumption, something separate from my Madison Young identity.

I drove my hands into the soil and felt the cool earth sift through my fingers. A peek at my fingers revealed chipped red fingernail polish and cuticles that need tending, signs of my personal neglect. I felt soft and vulnerable, like a crustacean without its shell. There had been no word from James for nearly two weeks, and I didn't know if there ever would be, again. Slowly burrowing small holes, I placed sage, basil, mint, and thyme in the flowerbed, filling in the indentations and covering the roots with fresh new soil. With each plant I said a small prayer, a mantra, an affirmation, a wish. To me, this wasn't just a garden, it was a hope chest for the future.

"Thank you, basil. I have hope and faith in you. I know you will thrive; that you will grow; that you have life. I will nurture that life and care for you. I will mother you. Your life is worth nurturing. Sink your roots and breathe deeply. This is your home." I placed my hands around the earth that surrounded the basil and closed my eyes, inhaling deeply and exhaling the grief and toxic pain that had been filling my body. I held my hands to the earth, feeling the pulse of the plants, tears falling into the soil.

I plucked the tomato plants from their trays and sunk them into the holes I had dug for them. While covering their small, stringy roots with nutrient rich earth, my mind wandered to my father. I hadn't spoken with him in months. On weekends, as a teenager, I often found myself in the same position, kneeling and bowing to gardens full of rich earthy soil, while I assisted my dad with landscaping jobs. During this activity, I found myself at absolute peace, with earth beneath my fingernails and the warm scent of moist mulch in my nose.

Small strawberry plants stood short and sturdy, one after another, as I scooped soil and patted the earth around them slowly and intentionally. Only three weeks before, Daddy and I had eaten the sweet red fruits from one another's hands while we tasted the sweetness of each other's bodies. We devoured one another with lust and appetite. I found a glimmer of hope thinking of Daddy in that moment and wishing—no, trusting—that we would both survive this dark period of our lives.

25

"HELLO EVERYONE, MY NAME is Madison Young and I am a Sex Positive Tasmanian Devil. I travel all around the world advocating for healthy sexual relationships through workshops, by documenting authentic sexual pleasure on film, and through fierce feminist performance art. Tonight, I'm here to discuss with you the topics of deep throating and oral sex."

About seventy people crowded into the small basement of an adult store in Denver. It was hot and stuffy, home of the store's administrative offices with plenty of boxes of inventory.

I felt lost in the sea of audience members who had gathered in the basement. They filled the folding chairs and the aisles, and some camped out on the steps of the stairwell to catch a glimpse. I could recite this presentation in my sleep. I was on autopilot, slightly less focused than usual, my mental and emotional capabilities handicapped by the new information I had received only twenty hours ago. I was pregnant.

◇◇◇

IT WAS QUIET AND still in my San Francisco apartment. Mr. Mogul was gone. He hadn't answered his phone in a week. Calls went unanswered, voice messages stayed unheard. My garden was taking root in its new bed of soil but I felt utterly misplaced in our bed with his body so far from mine.

I went to the bathroom to pack my toiletries when I glanced over at my tampons and menstrual cup and realized, I couldn't remember my last period. When was my last period? I pulled out my phone and checked my period tracker app. I was seven days late. It may have felt like an eternity since we'd been together, but we had fucked several times that month.

In a panic, I slipped on ballet slippers and headed to the corner store for a pregnancy test. It was cold and there was a light rain. I pulled the hood of my green sweatshirt over my head and hurried.

When I arrived, I roamed around throwing assorted goods in the red grocery basket—vegan chocolate chip cookies, sparkling lemonade, a douche, vaginal wipes, enemas, another tube of red lipstick, a box of chai, and two pregnancy tests.

The store owner, Fahah, was a Syrian man in his mid-forties with an enchanting accent, warm smile, and round, loving face. Pictures of his wife and children were taped to the register and a small gray kitten lived in the store, wandering the aisles while customers filled their grocery baskets. It was about 10:00 P.M., but Fahah was still hard at work, stocking soy milk and beer for the flow of customers that poured through his market.

I held my basket close to my hips, hoping to make my transaction quick and discreet. A couple, man and woman, stood in front of me in line. Her dark brown hair was wet and kept falling in her eyes, causing her mascara to drip. The boy, tall and lanky, with an awkward mustache above his upper lip that seemed unfit for his youthful appearance, wore his chestnut colored hair swept to the side, and wrapped his arms around his giggling girlfriend.

I dropped my basket on the counter, and Fahah smiles at me, "Young love, eh?".

"Huh? Oh...yeah. Young love." Avoiding eye contact, I fidgeted with the display of herbal supplements at the checkout counter. Fahah sensed my nervousness, and kindly put my items in a plastic bag. "Good luck, Maddie." He said, with a warm smile.

After a few minutes I was standing in disbelief in my small, white tiled bathroom, pink satin panties at my ankles, jeans and ruby slippers discarded in the long hallway. One pregnancy test between my thumb and forefinger screamed at me: "PREGNANT." Another sitting on the bathroom sink read the same: "PREGNANT."

I can't be pregnant! I needed to pack for my trip. It was near midnight and I was going to be picked up at 4:00 A.M. to be shuttled to SFO.

NOW IN DENVER, STANDING before the large crowd on top of a chair, I proclaimed: "Wow! What a pleasure it is to be here in Denver! Now, the first thing that I'd like us all to do is get into our body. We need to warm up our muscles and relax the muscles that we are going to be using for our oral sex techniques."

I picked up a realistic anatomical dildo that sat on the propped table and glanced down at my phone. Daddy still hadn't returned my voicemails or text messages.

"This is a cock. In order to pleasure the cock to the best of our abilities, we need to first learn the anatomy of the cock. Specifically, I will be pointing out to you the areas of the cock which are the most sensitive and pleasurable for stimulation." I projected my voice over the crowd, holding up the silicone object. Ivy, my assistant for the evening, strapped on the dildo and I paraded her up and down the crowded aisle, pointing out the anatomy of the cock. We'd only met that day, but she seemed giddy with the prospect of being paraded around by Madison Young.

My voice was enthusiastic, sultry, and humorous, but my mind was in the midst of a breakdown. *Can I do this? Can I be a mother? Do I want to be a mother?*

I relaxed my throat muscles, submerging the cock in my throat while making a mental list of my heroes and noting which of them were parents.

"Now, this technique is called the lollipop." I wrapped my lips around the head of the cock, then made a popping noise when I removed it from my mouth.

Going through my list of my heroes, I pondered. Annie Sprinkle: she didn't have children. Emma

Goldman: she never had children either. Carol Queen: childless. *Is it possible to be immersed in sexual culture or be a radical activist and also be a mother?* I drew a blank.

"Now, if you notice here, on the underside of the cock toward the head, there is a little sensitive bit called the frenulum. Get to know it. Get to love it. It's similar to a woman's clitoris. This is where the tongue circles you were practicing earlier come in handy."

Daddy didn't want to be a father. I knew that. He had expressed his disinterest in marriage and children in the past, but as for me, I was not so sure. If I was going to become a parent, I would have to be completely okay with knowing I would most likely be doing it on my own. I came from a long line of single mothers, four generations in fact. Four generations of strong-willed, independent women. *I can do this on my own. But do I want to?* I thought about the way I felt when I nurtured the plants in my garden, or when I mentored a young queer artist just starting out on their own path. Perhaps now was the perfect time to nurture something inside me, something greater than me. This child would be a change, that was for certain. And change was something that I needed, more than ever. I was growing a personal revolution in my uterus, in my body.

"Enthusiasm, my friends. Don't forget enthusiasm, communication, and eye contact. You want to be enthusiastically connected with your partner. You want to devour their cock like it's cotton candy and diamonds."

I kept going with the list: Susie Bright...Yoko Ono...Shar Rednour...Thea Hillman...Catherine Opie. All mothers. *I can do this.* I had recently completed a documentary-porn on pregnancy and sexuality. The mothers I met were some of the strongest and most amazing people I had met in my career.

Yes. Yes, I wanted to be a mother. I wanted to be a mother to this child. I could do it. I would do this!

I watched as the audience awkwardly slid their mouths around the bananas that Ivy passed out to them. I was nauseated, but unsure if it was the morning sickness or anxiety. This wasn't going to be easy.

"Great job, class. I will be around the store for about an hour so feel free to come up to me afterward and ask questions or have a DVD signed."

A young woman and her partner walked up to me and handed me a cupcake with pink frosting. "Thank you! That was a great class and we are just awestruck. You have been such an inspiration to us. Especially your work on *The Training of O.* We've never seen porn that was also a love story before. We would love to take you out tomorrow if you have time to chat?"

I graciously accepted, I needed a little kindness right now. I needed to believe that I could be my own hero, that I could be my child's hero. I needed to have someone take me out for ice cream and fill me with affirmations and tell me that my journey had made an imprint in the world. I wanted to believe that my journey was only just beginning.

26

I SAT IN FRONT of my laptop in a dimly lit café in Melbourne, Australia. Tomorrow, I would be giving the keynote speech at the Femme Conference and I was struggling to find my words. I ran as far away from the comfort of San Francisco and the arms of Daddy as I possibly could. Out of my depth, I ran from the familiar things and people and places that reminded me of him. While preparing to head to Australia, I naïvely imagined a wild landscape of koala bears and kangaroos, duck-billed platypi, and an open wilderness in which I could walk about and embark on a journey of enlightenment.

Colorful graffiti and murals filled city streets lined with pretentious cafés and overpriced clothing boutiques. Streetcars transporting locals and tourists from one stop to another reminded me of the city I had just left. Mev was going to meet up with me here. She had a lover in Melbourne and would take the same journey to Australia to follow her heart and her lover. I was grateful for her familiar face and warmth. I would feel less alone with Mev by my side. She had become one of the only people in my life that I truly trusted, and it felt like she had always been there.

Holding a yellow ceramic mug of soy mocha in both hands I glared at the half-written speech. *Try to stay busy, stay focused.* It was those moments of silence and stillness that were the hardest. I couldn't let myself think much about where I'd just been or where I was going next; for the sake of my daughter and me, it was crucial to be in the moment. I tried to fill my days teaching classes on sexuality, speaking at conferences, giving interviews, Internet conferencing and grant committee meetings for the art gallery, and performing. The wardrobe I packed for my nearly two months out of the country no longer fit my growing abdomen, so I was repeating the same three outfits. I had to get a bit creative with my performance outfits, mixing and matching colors and skirts in a patchwork of funky, artsy style that matched my awkward, shifting body.

A waitress approached the table and delivered a big stack of pancakes smothered in maple syrup.

"Thank you," I smiled up at her, a young girl likely no more than twenty-two. I closed my laptop and moved the pancakes closer. With a bite of warm, doughy sweetness in my mouth I closed my eyes, smiling at the thought of my future daughter laughing with chipmunk cheeks full of pancake.

I opened my journal, inspired, and found her image staring back at me, her recent sonogram. I ran my finger across the black and white photograph, picturing a healthy baby girl growing in my uterus, then moved my hand over my belly to feel the fluttering of my daughter, a faint but rapid beating. My eyes swelled with tears as I recalled the doctor hovering over my body and sharing the sex of my child to be.

◇◇◇

IT WAS MY THIRTIETH birthday. I felt old and alone when I lay back in the stirrups and chair in a small examination room at San Francisco's Kaiser Permanente, my mother by my side, holding my hand. She traveled to San Francisco from her home in Ohio to be there with me. She missed me and was worried about me, and knew that James was rarely around. Even though she didn't always agree with my way of life or decisions, she loved me deeply, and always called a minimum of three times a week. As mothers always do, she seemed to intuitively know when something was wrong, even from 2,500 miles away.

The doctor left the room to print out the sonogram photographs and my mom squeezed my hand, her eyes full of liquid.

"I love you, Tina. You're going to be a good mother. You know that?" My mother's hands were soft, her skin having lost most of its elasticity, freckles spotted her ivory flesh. Short, thin nails painted pale pink hid callused fingertips. My fingers trembled, enveloped in her hands, frightened by the impending possibility of failure.

I tried to smile and nod at my mother's assuring words, uncertain what exactly it meant to be a good mother.

"You know, my thirtieth was a hard one, too. That was the year your father left. I was heartbroken, but I knew I had to keep pushing through, to keep on going, for you kids. There was a guy I was dating, Terry. I don't know if you remember him?" My mother awkwardly cleared her throat and folded her hands in her lap. For a moment, she stared at her hands as if the memories of my father were stored there, like her hands could tell the story on their own. With her thumb she traced the ring that I gave her. It's set with my and my brother's birthstones, as well as a diamond from her engagement ring.

"Yeah, I remember Terry. He was a real jerk." I felt a chill run up my arms and down my legs at the memory of my mother's one-time boyfriend.

"Yeah, he was a jerk. But I needed someone, Tina, and sometimes a jerk is all you got. Anyway, for my thirtieth birthday Terry was supposed to take me out to dinner. Somewhere real nice, like Montgomery Inn, where they have those delicious ribs, you know the ones that were endorsed by Bob Hope?" My mother's hands remained in constant motion. As she was talking, she nervously bit at her cuticles, mumbling her speech.

"Well, I put on my fuchsia suede dress and curled my hair, sprayed all up with AquaNet, and you watched me in the bathroom as I put on my eye makeup. You said, 'Mama you look so pretty, like Barbie, I want to be pretty like that one day, too.' You always knew how to get my waterworks going, Tina. I had to dry my eyes and fix my makeup. Your sitter showed up and I slipped on my black suede pumps and put on a movie for you kids and waited and waited. Terry never showed up. I sent the sitter home and put you and your brother to bed and spent the evening crying and cursing in the bathroom. I swore after that I'd never spend a birthday with another man. I'd go out with my girlfriends on my birthday, I could count on them." She returned her hands to her lap, her thumb grazing the ring that was once a symbol of my father's commitment and love for her.

"I just keep thinking about that, Tina, and for the life of me I just couldn't stand by and allow that to happen to you, I didn't want that to be you, my little girl and your little girl." She looked at me with a piercing gaze. I'd never heard this story before, and I thought I knew every story my mother had to tell. My journey toward motherhood was already bringing me closer to this woman in unexpected ways.

"I'm not alone, Mom. I love you. I'm so happy you're here for this."

I EXHALED DEEPLY AND took a big bite of my Australian pancake, closing my eyes. I allowed the tears to run down my engorged breasts and changing body, the same breasts that Daddy once held tight in his ropes, circled in his arms, cupped with his hands. I pulled big black sunglasses from my purse to shield my blurry eyes from the gaze of other customers. The large, dark lenses had come in handy over the past year to hide my red sad eyes, dripping mascara, and sleepless nights.

While rummaging through my bottomless purse I found one of Daddy's handkerchiefs. The same handkerchiefs that used to gather like leaves in my purses, bags, and coat pockets, usually stained and occasionally crusted with dried mucous from my blubbery meltdowns. They were like love notes that had been left for me everywhere, except they were soaked with past sorrows and tears.

The tears that were running down my face at this moment sprung from hope, the aching, sore instincts of survival. I stared down at my baby's image: the little alien-like body curled up like a kernel of light in a dark abyss. With a deep breath in, I allowed the palm of one hand to rest on top of my belly. Her faint movements blew me a kiss from inside my uterus.

I scribbled a list of names into my journal.

Potential Names for Baby:

Rilke Anne

Caitlin Rainer

Rilke Virginia

Virginia Rilke

Emma Louise

I had been combining the first and last names of my literary and political heroes. I kept gravitating to Emma. Emma Goldman had been one of my feminist heroines since my early college days. Her spirit of fight and fearlessness in the face of social change inspired me in all of my endeavors. She was so precious to me that I adapted her famous quote, "If I can't dance, it's not my revolution," into my own, more sexually explicit declaration, "If I can't fuck, it's not my revolution." In black Sharpie I signed my slogan on DVD covers and the walls of bathroom stalls. Louis has extra resonance, it's both my dad's middle name and the surname of the only family James ever talked about with love and adoration, his leather Daddy, Drake Lewis.

I plucked a small stack of postcards from my journal.

Dear Dad,

I miss you and love you. I made it to Australia and have been incredibly busy with work. I'm speaking at a conference tomorrow, giving the keynote speech. I'm finally starting to look pregnant and I'm feeling a little fluttering.

Your little red-headed angel,
Tina

Dear Mom,

I made it to Australia. It's raining but the people here are wonderful. Work is keeping me busy. I was just thinking about your visit. I'm so grateful to have you in my life.

With love,
Tina

Finally, I prepared James' postcard.

Dear Mr. Mogul,

My heart aches for you, my love. I'm starting to feel our little girl kick. It's raining here. I miss you so much. I love you and I yearn to be curled up at your feet, on the floor, in my place.

Your devoted Spaniel,
Maddie

I stuck them back in my journal for safekeeping until I could locate a post office. With care, I put my journal back in my purse and pulled my laptop back. I opened my email, holding my breath as I wished for a word, a bit of hope or encouragement, from Daddy.

My inbox overflowed with correspondence. My cell phone bill was due, grant application deadlines approached, editors were asking for submissions to their anthologies, organizations and conferences were inquiring about teaching classes, artists were asking about upcoming exhibitions, volunteers and interns were seeking direction while they pulled together to run the gallery during my absence. I scanned through the emails for the only one that really mattered to me in that moment, the one from Daddy.

> Hi Maddie,
>
> I miss you so much baby. I hope you get this note well. I miss you terribly! It's been a really hard week here with lots of draining shoots. When I feel I can't keep up I just think of you and our little girl and it drives me to do the best I can.
>
> Do you have a flight number or the airport that the flight departs from so that I can track it and confirm arrival online?
>
> Do you have money? Are you well?
>
> Miss you, love you, and I will see you soon.
>
> J

I had left the country in a flurry, an attempt to escape constantly thinking of him, to make the aching go away. It didn't work, he was still constantly in my thoughts. A child created by us was growing inside of me everyday. I didn't know if we would be together when I got back, but it had become incredibly clear that I couldn't care for him or fix his problems. The only thing I could do was care for the child growing inside of me and let him know that I still loved him, and that if he needed me, I would be there to support him.

Hello Mr. Mogul,

    Wanted to let you know that the pregnant lady made it to the other side of the world in one piece. The hotel that the convention is set up in (and that I'm staying at) is amazing. They are totally treating me like a princess. There was a mix-up with the organizer on what time I was arriving so they forgot to pick me up but luckily Mev landed about an hour after me and found me randomly in the airport and her friends gave me a ride to the hotel.

    The hotel is downtown with a great view, and they are very accommodating of my diet, and the convention is covering all food costs for the weekend. I bought a swimsuit and I'm going to utilize the pool. I hear swimming is good for me and the little one. Between my baggage fee and having to buy a travel visa in order to get in the country it took a chunk out of my account.

Do you know if any of my checks arrived at the house yet? Also if you could, let me know which day this week you can drop off the artwork so I can arrange for my volunteers to install it. Thank you so much.

I have to do Internet from a public area during the convention so it might be best to wait until Monday evening to do a video chat. Does Monday work for you? If so let's make a date around 10:00 P.M. your time on Monday.

I love you.
Your Maddie

I checked my watch, 3:00 P.M. It was nearing my call time for a shoot I scheduled with a local sex-positive porn company. Speechwriting would have to wait. One local in particular was exciting to me: Gala Vanting. Gala was a twenty-three year old queer feminist pornographer in the making. I gathered my belongings and shoved everything into my purse and bulky backpack alongside dildos, vibrators, makeup, lube, and what lingerie my body could still squeeze into, and left the café.

27

My heels clicked along the wet sidewalk, rain pouring down on me. My chocolate colored dress with petal-pink polka dots, soaking wet, hung heavily on my curves. My makeup was running down my face, streaks of mascara and blush bleeding on my pink cheeks, and the wind plastered my hair to my head in cold, wet clumps. My bags were soaked. The cold, Australian rain fell with fury in a rapid, spinning succession, like the sky had opened up and was having one big childish temper tantrum, especially for this trip. I took a shortcut through a children's playground to get to the streetcar and encountered a large, pond-sized puddle in my way. I stopped at the puddle and dropped my bags on the muddy, grassy earth. Looking upward to the clouds, huge drops of rain beat down and stung my face, I smiled and screamed up into the sky.

"AHHHHHHHHHHH I'm ready! I can do this. You think this is a challenge? Do you know who I am? I'm Madison Young! I'm a super hero. I'm this little girl's mother. I am capable of greatness. I can do this!"

I tore off my heels and tossed them in my bag and dropped my purse and backpack, now not just soaked in rain but also doused in splotches of dark earth. Mother Nature was attempting to baptize me and I had been putting up a fight. I looked at the large puddle, sixteen inches deep and at least ten feet in diameter. *Can I go around? Yes. Will I? No.* I sunk my toes into the muddy green blades of grass and recalled my first baptism, an eight-year-old girl wearing a pink ruffled Lycra swimsuit, standing among a congregation of farmers and factory workers, schoolteachers and grocery clerks. Our pastor called me forward and my mother gave me a little push in the direction of the chlorine-soaked backyard swimming pool.

I knew that this muddy puddle was my pool, the pool into which I needed to descend, and I jumped. My bare feet landed full-force in the water, causing a wave of reactions, and I jumped again and again laughing, crying, laughing hard and loud, and crying with laughter. I danced through the puddle, nymph-like and fearless. My body shivered and trembled as I spun in circles, water running from my head to my feet, purifying me. I felt one with the throbbing, pulsing, wild passions of the earth. I knew there was nothing clean about life, but there was joy and fear and pleasure in life and I was in the cyclone of it all. I felt ready, cleansed and prepared for everything that might come my way. I found my breath. I felt ready to let go of all the sadness that had accumulated in my body, ready to cast off this shell.

A few minutes later I stepped into the production studio. The waiting room was serene and powerful. "You must be Madison. Oh dear, it looks like you really got soaked out there. Why don't I show you where our bathroom is in the guest quarters and you can take yourself a nice hot shower. I'll have a hot cup of tea waiting for you when you get out. How does that sound?" The welcome in the receptionist's voice warmed me immediately.

After freshening up, I pulled a lavender polka dot slip over my head, careful not to smudge any of my freshly applied makeup. My breasts were sensitive to the touch, full and sensuous. I was in the throes of a second puberty and became amused and distracted by my transforming body. I always loved my small A-cup breasts, breasts that didn't require a bra for support to stand up like perky pyramids with pink, gumdrop tops. Now, I had a new toy, a new body to admire and to love. My breasts were spilling out of my satin rose-colored bra and for the first time in my life, I had cleavage.

The bathroom mirror was still steamy and the air warm from the hot shower. I inhaled the humid bathroom air and spritzed sweet, citrusy perfume on my pulse points. My ruby-colored lipstick felt out of place with the soft, lace detailing of the thrift shop slip. My long red hair had started to grow thick, and I felt like a curvy goddess with a new body that overflowed with life. I opened the bathroom door and stepped into the production studio where Gala sat on the bed in a similar satin slip.

I felt comfortable with Gala. She was an intelligent young woman, trying to make way for a woman's voice in the world of pornography. She represented the next generation. I saw her push her glasses up the bridge of her nose and tuck her shaggy brown locks of hair behind her ears, her unshaven legs tucked up toward her chest.

"So, I think Richard will be back in fifteen minutes or so...he had to take a phone call down in the office. But I thought maybe we could talk a bit about the scene," she said, carefully picking up a hot cream-colored teacup from beside the bed.

"Yes, I'd like that. Do you want to start?" I smiled, impressed by her proactive nature for negotiation. An electric kettle began to whistle from a table in the corner of the studio and I followed its sound to prepare my own cup of tea. My bones were still chilled from the cold, rainy morning and impromptu puddle-jumping.

"Sure. Well, I brought a few toys. I saw your stash on the table...it looks like we both brought Magic Wands. I love vibrators and hands. I'm a big fan of hands. And I ejaculate. I know you really like kink and I thought maybe we could incorporate some kink into the shoot. What do you think?" I nodded, slowly sipping my tea. Gala pulled out pretty pink vibrators and sparkling pearlescent dildos from a canvas tote that read, "Well Behaved Women Rarely Make History."

"Cool. That sounds great. Well, I love hands, too. Did you bring gloves?"

"Totally. I brought some black nitrile gloves and a lube that I really like, it's organic." Gala's eyes lit up as we continued our conversation. I could tell that, like me, she was not someone who just enjoyed pleasure and sex, but was a sexual enthusiast.

"Perfect. What about condoms for toys, or should we just use our own toys?"

"I did bring some condoms if you would like to share but I'm pretty comfortable just using my own toys...or just hands. Hands are my preference."

"I'm comfortable without dental dams since we are both tested. Did you see my test downstairs?" Gala asked while methodically organizing her dildos and vibrators into a straight line on a clean towel beside the bed. We were just two girls sitting on the bed talking about sex. I was excited to be touched again, by hands other than my own.

A few moments later, Richard returned and adjusted the lights. "Did you two have a chance to talk?"

"Yes, thank you, Richard." Gala smiled and adjusted her bra strap, which had fallen from her delicate shoulders.

"Is there anything specific I should keep in mind?" I asked. It was my first time working with him.

"If you can try not to face that corner, we don't have a lot of light in that direction. But other than that, just take your time and be yourselves. I'm going to turn on the cameras and then I'll go downstairs to give you two your privacy. I'll come back up in forty minutes. Sound good?" I nodded my head and placed my hand on Gala's bare thigh.

Richard's smile was warm and comforting. He was the antithesis of a typical pornographer, polite and political while at the same time a businessman. He didn't feel like an artist or a capitalist money-driven pornographer, his was a personality that was hard to pin down. He had built a strong, confident, successful business, and employed a team of ten twenty- to thirty-five-year-old confident, intelligent women, all of whom wanted to make a difference in the international conversation about sexuality. Their network of sites was tasteful and filled with beauty: faces of mostly unknown women and men who courageously stepped in front of the camera to document honest moments in their sex lives. It was a wonderful message amid a culture that lacks the language to talk about desire in a healthy, non-shaming manner, and Richard wanted to help change that. I was excited to be part of his endeavor.

My body tingled as Gala removed my slip. I was in my fifth month of pregnancy and my rotund abdomen was taking shape. I took several pillows and used them to prop myself up, Gala watching with a girlish grin. Reclining onto the pillows, I slowly spread my thighs. I reached for the massage oil and drizzled it onto my breasts. My eyes closed and I exhaled as I cupped my tender breasts in my hands, massaging the warm oil onto them. I purred, getting lost in the moment, the sensitive, supple flesh rippling under my curious fingers.

I opened my eyes to find Gala's patient, eager, attentive eyes transfixed on my body, enjoying the show. I called her forth with come hither fingers and a ravenous voice that reverberated from deep within. "Come here, I want you close to me."

Her hands cautiously touched my thighs and I nodded, smiling, "Yes, please." She smiled back, her eyes connecting with mine, reading my body language.

After the young woman pleasured me, I rolled over on my side, exhausted, flushed with endorphins and feeling blissful and at peace with the world. Gala's naked body was coupled with mine. Her arms were wrapped around me, holding me close, and I felt safe in this woman's arms even though we'd only just met. I took her hand from my shoulder and kissed her palm. Every touch was full of intention, warmth, and kindness. I felt like she needed affirmation and love as much as I did. I rolled over and pinned Gala on her back. I was a cat with a delicious bird in my yard and I intended to swat her around before I devoured her in a petite mort.

With a smile I looked at her, really looked at her. I looked into her eyes, green and full of life; she had excitement and a future sure of success; bright and inspired, I couldn't wait to see what she would accomplish.

"Yes, please," she said quietly, pleading. I was enraptured by her simple, raw, unaltered beauty. I slapped her lightly and gauged how she processed the new sensation. She moaned and her eyes danced with adrenaline. I laughed and slapped her harder. I squirted some lube onto my hand and slid my hand inside her, drizzling more lubrication onto her cunt, which quickly blossomed and engulfed my fingers. Gala moaned as I massaged her vulva, periodically dipping into her cunt. She reached for her Magic Wand and used the vibrator on her clitoris. With my gloved fingers I curved around her engorged g-spot and explored her with a handful of techniques, gauging her response, moving with confidence. Gala grasped onto the sheets and tears streamed down her face as my hands moved, stimulating her and pumping in and out of her cunt. Her small mouth opened and a scream escaped as hot glandular fluid flooded onto my hands and thighs. It continued to fountain from her, spraying my face, my breasts, and dripping down my baby bump. I lay down next to her drenched, shaking body. It was the second time that day that I had been baptized. Covered in sweat and sex, I brought her lips to mine, kissing her and stroking her hair. I felt the fluttering of a new generation of women just emerging, and the light movements of my daughter in my uterus.

28

SITTING AT A SMALL kitchen table, scribbling notes in my journal, I looked out the window onto the wet cobblestone streets of Amsterdam. Women and men on bicycles pedaled past the narrow three-story apartment. Autumn leaves were falling from the trees that lined the canal, creating pillows of muted warm golden hues and earthy oranges that drifted past the small boats that filled the canal with visitors.

I'd arrived at Jennifer's apartment three days earlier. The flight from Australia was long, over twenty hours spent on multiple planes with a long layover in Malaysia. I had suffered nosebleeds from the altitude, the dry recycled airplane air, and the increased blood supply circulating through my pregnant body. Still, I made it to Amsterdam and found my way to Jennifer's cozy apartment safely. A single room provided a space for family, dining, and a kitchen; a nursery and bedroom occupied the upstairs.

Jennifer was a new mother and erotic filmmaker living in Amsterdam with her husband, Jeffrey, who worked for an advertising agency, and their six-month-old daughter Madelief. Originally from the Bay Area, she made annual visits back to visit family and connect with other feminist pornographers. Jennifer is short in stature with a radiant smile, warm eyes, and chestnut tinted locks in a pixie cut. I met Jennifer while she was pregnant and in San Francisco working on a documentary on feminism and submission; she asked to interview me for the film. I instantly adored the independent and sharp-witted artist. She's a politically fierce feminist with the brains to back up her politics.

> Needs for tonight:
> *Grape juice*
> *Grape flavored bubble gum*
> *Enema bottles*
> *Lube*
> *Grapes*

I was jotting down a shopping list for the evening's performance in my journal. I would be leaving in the next hour for the all-day private event, in which I was presenting a performance in collaboration with Annie and Beth's purple wedding. Annie and Beth were marrying the moon this time, in association with the purple chakra. They were being married in Los Angeles at Highways Theater and although I wouldn't be there in person I agreed to do a performance in Amsterdam in conjunction with the wedding.

Jennifer came carefully down the stairs, Madelief held close to her chest. She exhaled in a calming shhhh sound, which seemed as much for the baby's benefit as to calm her own nerves. A sleepy grin shaped her mouth and grew into a yawn as she stared down at Madelief. She looked tired.

I shut my laptop, fascinated by the small child, who had abandoned her rattle and raised her body up into a downward dog-type of yogic position, which seemed impressive for an infant not even six months in age. *Is it impressive? Is it typical?* I wasn't really sure, I hadn't gotten that far in my reading. I was still struggling with my changing, pregnant body and the looming, mind-blowing concept that I would be pushing a seven to eight pound person out through my vagina. I had to take each moment as it arrived.

I smiled and sat down on the floor beside Madelief. I was taken by her complete wonder at everything. Her eyes were wide and dancing while she giggled and rolled. Her young life was small and safe and filled with the wonder of discovery and of testing her limits. I closed my eyes and held my hand to my belly. *I'm growing one of those.* I would be bringing something beautiful and simple into this chaotic and complicated world, and I knew I would give her all of my love.

"You can touch her. It's okay. She's not going to bite." Jennifer laughed as she curled up onto the couch.

"Do you want to hold her?"

"I'm afraid I might break her. I've never really held a baby before." *How exactly is it that you hold a baby?*

Isn't there something about their head or their neck? Parts of their bodies are still forming. I was terrified.

"You're not going to break her," Jennifer assured me and plucked Madelief up from the ground to place her in my arms. She was warm pressed against my chest. She examined my face with her tiny hands and grabbed my long hair. I laughed and at the same time felt a bit panicky. Madelief's face scrunched up like she was about to sneeze, but instead white fluid projected from her mouth onto my sweatshirt.

"Oh, wasn't expecting that," I said. "I guess that's something I'll have to get used to." I held the baby away from my body and an amused Jennifer returned her to her crib. She wiped the spit-up from the corner of Madelief's mouth and handed me a soft, pink tissue. I wiped the mess up and tossed the soiled sweatshirt aside. I rummaged around for something to wear for the evening's event; it should've been purple to fit in with the theme.

"Do you need something to wear for tonight?" Jennifer asked. It seemed like every day my limited wardrobe became even more limited as pants became tighter and dresses became obscene on my ever-expanding body.

Jennifer handed me a deep purple, empire waist dress, "I was going to get rid of this, but if you fit it, you should wear it tonight. It's one of my maternity dresses. I wore it to a wedding I went to when I was pregnant."

I loved it. I loved the dress and the memory we would share with it. It felt loving and nurturing to have support from someone who had been in the aching throes of pregnancy not so long ago. By chance I had fallen into the warm home of an erotic filmmaker who was balancing both a family and a sexual life.

I shed my tights and dress. My skin was stretched tight around my protruding abdomen. I was round, bottom, belly, and breasts. Jennifer unzipped the purple dress and I stepped into the loose flowing fabric, it felt light and delicate on my skin. I felt confident in my expanding body, like a new goddess was forming, imperfections and all. I knew that not everyone in the adult industry would share this same acceptance of change and flaws, but none of that seemed to matter.

"You know, I still feel pretty clueless about being a mom, too." Jennifer gave me a reassuring smile and zipped up the dress, resting her hand on my shoulder. "Biology has a funny way of kicking in and teaching you a thing or two. We are meant to survive." I smiled and nodded, less than certain about what my own journey to motherhood might look like.

29

"YOU CAN'T TAKE LIQUIDS on the plane, Miss."
The airport security agent pulled a thermos filled with frozen breast milk out of my carry-on. My pornography DVDs and compartments full of assorted dental dams and condoms went untouched and unnoticed, but traveling with a thermos full of Jennifer's frozen breast milk raised red flags. I was on my way to the Berlin Porn Film Festival where seven films that I had either directed or starred in were screening. This year there would be a special honor. I was one of two filmmakers "in focus" and was giving a special presentation on my body of work as well as screening a small selection of my favorite scenes from films that I directed over the years. Jennifer asked if I could bring more of her frozen milk from the apartment to her and Madelief, who were already in Berlin.

"It's not a liquid. It's a solid. It's frozen breast milk." I looked at the TSA agent, indignant and frustrated. I've never done well with authority figures; I don't trust them. My story has never been one where officers were fighting for justice. I've come to know officers in a different role. In my circles, officers are not there to build community or provide safe harbor for creativity. They're there to police it.

"I'll need to consult with my manager about this." The stocky, broad-shouldered man towered above me in his white uniform and cap as he radioed his manager.

I looked down at my watch, the silver bangle a gift from Daddy. Only thirty-five minutes until my flight was going to depart from Amsterdam to Berlin. I didn't have time. He moved my thermos and backpack onto another table away from the conveyer belt where passengers were quickly gathering their scanned belongings and scurrying off to their respective gates of departure. I felt helpless, like a threatened child, still reliving the pain of hard-to-swallow memories.

I WAS FOUR YEARS old, sitting on a long wooden pew in the courtroom, holding onto my Grandma Virginia's cold, bony hand while officers of the law decided whether or not my Dad was allowed to see me. The bones in my grandmother's right hand had become sculptural, protruding and angular, the results of a time when my mother's birth father, Bill, tried to sever my Grandmother's hand from her body with a butcher knife in a drunken rage. My mother, then only five years old, buried her head under her pillow in hysterics. The police never came, but Bill left the apartment never to return. My Grandmother's neighbor drove her to the hospital where doctors tried to mend her mangled hand. After months of rehabilitation she still needed to learn to write with her left hand. I loved my Grandmother and I loved her strength; I clung on to her misshapen right hand and watched as my father was ushered into the courtroom by police officers to a chair beside the judge's stand. My mother was seated beside her lawyer as the custody proceedings continued. I remember the uniformed officer's cold, dark stare instilling fear in me while my father's visitation rights were decided by a system I was powerlessly subjected to.

"TRY TO CALM DOWN, miss, and we will get you on your plane. Can you show me your passport, please?" I scowled and handed the officer my passport.

"So what seems to be the problem here?" The officer's manager asked as he approached. My heart was already racing, adrenaline pumping furiously through my veins, blood rushing to my head. My mouth was parched from the long wait and mounting anxiety about missing my flight.

I was beginning to draw attention from the eyes of other passengers, which made me feel trapped and vulnerable. The two officers towered over me, "I'm trying to get on my flight to Berlin. I'm presenting a film there tomorrow and I'm bringing this frozen breast milk to my friend for her child. She's at the same festival and she forgot the breast milk at her house."

The officer thumbed through my passport and investigated the frozen breast milk, banging the frozen packets against the table, "So where is the baby?"

"With her mother in Berlin! She needs this breast milk for her baby, that's why I'm bringing the milk! Oh my God, this is ridiculous."

"Wait here." The officer replied and walked away, leaving me to wait for a decision. *I know their minds are made up. I'm not getting on that plane.* The only question that remained was how, exactly, was I going to get out of this situation.

"Yeah, Ma'am, we are going to need to take the milk. We can't allow you through with that. It's a liquid. We will give you your passport once you calm down." The manager placed his hands on my shoulders, leaning down close to my face softly whispering. "You should really try a breath mint. Your breath stinks."

I closed my eyes and cringed in embarrassment. The on-lookers peered from the security line, but no one dared interfere. I filled with rage as I looked at the blank stares on the faces of these smug white men. I became intimately familiar with power exchange as Daddy and I delved deep into the world of dominance and submission, but our power exchange came from a place of love and trust, and was met with mutual consent. A uniform and a shiny badge seem like nothing more than an outward declaration of unearned power and exemplified ego. There was no consent.

30

A T A TABLE IN the food court, peeling rubbery cheese off of a slice of vegetarian pizza, I booked myself a train ticket and emailed the director of the film festival. I wouldn't be arriving until the following afternoon, but I would have Jennifer's breast milk in hand. I was beyond exasperated by what just happened, and vividly recalled my last confrontation with the police, at a recent performance art piece staged by a queer Japanese-American artist at a bustling exhibition at my gallery.

THE GALLERY WAS FULL of people dressed to the nines in latex and corsets, admiring photography by legendary photographer and fetishist, Fakir Musafar. Fakir had been at the cutting edge of body modification, corsetry, scarification, and ritualistic hook suspensions fifty years ago when the world was even less kind to those existing outside normativity. He was a brave pioneer, a sexual outlaw, and now this seventy-year-old vivacious sprite of a man was exhibiting legendary art works on the walls of Femina Potens. Onlookers laughed and smiled, drinking champagne and watching impromptu rope bondage and performance art. I was naked, pink rope marks still imprinted around my thighs, wrists, and wrapped around my torso. I was monitoring the audience, the volunteers, and the elegant performance that Midori produced with the collaborative efforts of her rope bottom, Nikki Nefarious. I was watching, mesmerized, as the two danced with the rope in a lovely intimate tango, when the San Francisco Police Department barged abruptly into the midst of their dance, dressed head to toe in riot gear, and dragged audience members kicking and screaming from our safe haven into the street. I was paralyzed with fear, naked and shaking, in a state of complete vulnerability. While I tried to gather my thoughts and dress my naked body, Amnesty International pamphlets were tossed into the air and Midori disrupted the panicked audience with these important words, "This was a reminder my friends. Consensual kink is a privilege not to be taken for granted, but a lifestyle to cherish and protect."

I FINALLY MADE IT to the Berlin Porn Film Festival and I had to pee. I squirmed back and forth on a metal folding chair behind a long wooden table. Row upon row of red velvet theater seats in a large screening room were filled with people. A microphone sat before me in the off position, awaiting my commentary on the scene that was playing in the movie theater.

My frequency of urination increased drastically in a matter of only a few weeks, but at this point there was no way out. The audience was immersed in a scene between Daddy and me in *The Curse of Macbeth*, a kinky post-apocalyptic re-envisioning of Shakespeare's classic tragedy. I would be answering questions from the audience after the screening.

Sadie, my fellow Queer X Tour alumna and performance art compatriot, was sitting in the dark theater in the front row, smiling. Sadie recently moved to Berlin after the Queer X Tour and it was comforting to see her familiar face.

As a theater major in college, I felt personal gratification for fulfilling the sought-after role of the power-hungry Lady Macbeth. The image of my seductress self projected onto the huge theater screen felt distant and removed from the world I now lived in. The reel felt like a collection of remote images of my previous life. Lady Macbeth embodied sin and indulgence, but I didn't need to play the role of leading lady anymore. I felt content in building my own world, a little less glamorous than post-apocalyptic Shakespearean porn, but much more intimate and personal.

As the character played by James stumbled to his tragic death on the large screen, I was boxed in behind the table with no escape. It seemed ironic and darkly humorous. It felt like part of Daddy had died and I had to wonder if I was just torturing myself, trying to resuscitate a body that had been left behind; I would find out soon enough. In a few days I'd be home again, and I hoped I would find a spark of life in Daddy's eyes again. Right now, I needed to get out.

I looked around me to see if there was anything that I might pee into. *A cup? A popcorn box?* The water bottles that were left at the table for filmmakers and panelists have too narrow of an opening. I looked behind me at the glowing red exit sign. *Can I make it out the door without anyone noticing? I have to try.* I snuck out the theater's emergency exit and into the alley, slipping off one high heel to prop open the emergency door.

I hiked up my dress to around my belly and removed my black and white polka-dotted panties. Propping one foot up on a pile of dismantled cardboard boxes and plastic milk crates, I exhaled in relief as my pee sprayed forth onto the cement alley wall blemished with spray-painted tags. As I watched the golden shower run down the wall, I felt powerful. I was no dainty porn princess anymore, nor was I a fragile, pregnant housewife in need of coddling. I owned my pregnancy, my body, and I would learn how to parent in my own way. I hoped that vision would include James. I was familiar with the ache of growing up with a distant father and I didn't want to pass that pain on to my daughter.

I could hear my Lady Macbeth's moans spilling, muffled into the alley through the crack in the door. I knew the scene by heart, and it was almost over. I pulled up my panties, slipped on my shoe and slipped back into the cold metal folding chair. I gazed out at the dimly lit audience whose mouths hang open as, onscreen, I screamed out in orgasm.

31

WATCHING THE LUGGAGE CAROUSEL going round and round from my seat on the musty, carpeted airport floor and surrounded by a protective wall of my luggage I texted Daddy, "Are you coming?" It had been an hour since my plane landed in San Francisco, and nearly two months since I had been home. There was no sign of him.

Daddy promised to be there, but these days I tried not to invest too much into his words. I was treading forward with caution. I watched as a young man in his twenties with dark curls and black Buddy Holly eyeglasses shuffled back and forth awkwardly near the carousel, likely awaiting the arrival of his lover, with a bouquet of cheap red roses. I glanced down at my phone again and hung my head. I didn't know where to go. I was waiting for Daddy. *Will he ever come?* It had been months since I'd seen his face but his sporadic emails and texts expressed his love for me and had given me hope. I looked down at my belly, six months pregnant; the feel of thumping fists and feet in my uterus reminded me that another life was taking shape. I closed my eyes and held my hand to my belly, awaiting her response.

"Hi, Maddie." The sound of his voice was so textured with emotion and turmoil that I couldn't open my eyes. *I'm not sure if he's really there, but I don't want this to be a dream.*

"Daddy?" I asked, smiling.

"Yes, Maddie. Daddy's here." He rested his hand on my shoulder and in that moment I felt her kick.

"Daddy, she's kicking." His familiar callused hand gently landed on my belly, my fingers threaded between his. I opened my eyes, my hand in his, and looked up at him.

I WATCHED AS A young woman on a bicycle dismounted in front of our building from my seat in the window. I speared another piece of pineapple and look over at Daddy to see if he would answer the ringing doorbell. He was engrossed by the glowing screen of his laptop, watching a black and white World War II documentary.

I crushed chunks of fruit between my teeth in an attempt to hydrate my constantly thirsty, ever growing, pregnant body. Depositing the fruit on the hope chest, I grabbed two twenties from an envelope in the top desk drawer and slipped on my pregnancy shoes, Mary Jane style reinforced heels made with a charcoal gray tweed fabric. Slowly, carefully, I descended the staircase to meet the delivery girl who brushed her dark, choppy bangs out of her eyes and handed me a large brown paper bag.

I returned with the bag full of food from my favorite taquería in the Haight. I lay the food out on the table like a buffet. Chips, guacamole, a vegetarian burrito with avocado and mango salsa, lemonade with three cubes of ice, and a side of pitted olives marinated in spicy chilies.

I gained forty pounds in seven months and was stretching all of my sweater dresses and empire waist gowns to accommodate. The doctors assured me I was healthy and that my baby was healthy, but it looked like I might be expecting a larger than average baby. Nothing about me or James has ever been average, so why would I expect that our child would be any different?

Even seven months pregnant I was making trips down to Los Angeles to perform in pornographic magazine shoots and lesbian erotic films. At my last porn shoot, I studied my naked body in the bathroom mirror, watching as my shape shifted, my little girl poking through with an elbow, a punch, or a kick. My hips were thick and wide, my thighs and ass full. I closed my eyes and touched my body, repeating a little mantra: "You are beautiful. You are radiant. You are full of life. You are just as you should be," before stepping onto set with a nineteen year old who still wore a size zero and weighed in at under a hundred pounds. It took courage for me to reveal my body next to hers, to feel as if I had something to offer.

As I made my way into the beginning of the third trimester of my pregnancy, I found that my cravings became more intense. I needed sour, sweet, spicy, and creamy, my needs and desires shifting by the moment. In one minute Chilean vegan hot dogs topped with tomatoes, creamy sliced avocado, and vegannaise were all that I wanted, the next moment I found them revolting. One minute I craved Daddy's mouth on my tits and his hands at my cunt and the next I couldn't forgive him and his face nauseated me. There was only one constant: pancakes. I *always* wanted pancakes.

I sat down on the couch and draped a pink crocheted baby blanket over my legs. I carried this blanket with me my entire life. I can recall my mother tucking me in at night under it, I used to recite my prayers and wish on the bright stars that I could see from my bedroom window for my dad to come back home. Even when my mind wandered over his absence and my heart ached, under that cover I felt safe and secure. It was an object that held memories of my life before he left, when our family was complete. I looked forward to passing the blanket down to my daughter in only a few months.

The thirty-two inch flat screen television offered a welcome distraction to the tension that filled the apartment. The apartment had gone quiet in Daddy's absence and the absurd reality shows that littered the television networks offered a reprieve. It was the first television that I had owned in the nine years that I lived in San Francisco.

I bit into the thick burrito causing a small avalanche of beans and salsa. Anything that landed below my belly no longer existed. I could barely see my feet when standing up. I was watching a movie in which a young couple, a boy and a girl around eighteen, were laughing together and running down a wet and rainy street. He scooped her up in his arms and twirled her around in circles, pulling her close, looking into her eyes, and kissing her passionately. I scooped another chunk of guacamole and glanced over at Daddy.

The boy and the girl in the movie were being kept apart by their families, one coming from nothing and the other from wealth. A riff on *Romeo and Juliet*. I never tire of stories about star-crossed lovers. James' documentary exploded from his computer speakers, gunfire beginning an audible battle against the sobbing and emotional urgency emanating from the television.

"Ahhh! James can you turn that down?" I shouted, pelting a spicy olive at his hooded head. He stood up from the desk and threw me a piercing look with cold, sharp eyes, then retreated to the bathroom with his laptop.

James and I were in our own war, our own face-off. I was waiting for his return, not quite knowing what to expect. As I watched him storm down the hallway and slam the bathroom door without a word, I just wanted acknowledgment. I missed being loved, being held, I missed Daddy, *my* Daddy. I stood up and tiptoed over to his desk, where I rummaged through his drawers, hoping for a clue. I opened a familiar envelope that read "To Mr. Mogul, From your devoted little girl." Unfolding the letter that seemed like it was written so long ago, I realized I composed it when I was three months pregnant. At the time, I hadn't heard from him in ten days and I was worried. I wrote the letter and shoved it under his locked office door at the Armory. In the vastness of a castle, my letter seemed as useless as a message in a bottle. "I love you Daddy and I believe in you. I will always believe in you. You are my family and family doesn't disappear when things get rough. I'm here for you. Yours always, your devoted Little Girl—Maddie."

Until now, I hadn't even been sure that he ever got the letter, or that it meant anything to him. I allowed my fingers to linger over the words, smiling at the thought that, perhaps, this letter gave him hope, and returned it to its place.

I heard James steps coming down the hall, his feet squeaky on the wooden floor. He watched me watching the movie from the doorway for a moment before entering with a pint of vegan ice cream and a spoon.

The protagonist in the story grabbed the woman in his arms, "Look around, Allie. I built this house for you, for us!"

James interrupted the movie, standing next to me. "Is that what I need to do? Build us a house? Would that make it all better?"

I've fantasized about James building a house that we could live in together many times. He worked in construction before he began to do porn and sometimes I touched myself while visualizing him out in the hot Virginia sun hammering nails and hanging drywall. It was part of the plan: work at KINK long enough to have money in the bank to buy houses, remodel them, and flip them for a profit. But the economy had only continued to plummet, slowly unraveling our plans for leaving KINK.

"It wouldn't be so bad to have a house for our family. I guess that would be a start."

"I have our whole lives to make this up to you, Maddie. But I need you to give me a chance." I felt suddenly breathless. *It isn't easy to trust again.* Daddy had been gone for so long, and in his place was a ghost of the man I once knew. I was not quite sure how to make our way back to the love we first knew. Seattle mornings filled with rope and bodies and bottomless cups of hot cocoa seemed so far away. I wasn't sure what our future held, but I hoped that we could find our way back to *us*.

"This is your chance, Daddy. This is our chance." I looked up at Mr. Mogul, speaking softly, my eyes drippy with tears. We had both been swept away by our careers, by the expectations of others. The pressure had ripped us apart, and we needed to find our breathing room together, to find where we could exist together.

"I'm sorry, Maddie. Ice cream?" Daddy earnestly extended the pint of chocolate brownie soy ice cream.

I nodded in agreement, gently wiping tears from my red-rimmed eyes, and reached for the cold carton.

"Is there room for me on that couch? Can I watch the rest of the movie with you?" Daddy sat down next to me, holding my hand, and the touch of his fingers threaded through mine brought back feelings from our first date.

"You'll hate it, Daddy. It's a romance." I looked up at his face and, for a moment, I thought I recognized him.

He brought my hand to his lips and kissed my quivering fingers, "I don't mind."

Maybe Daddy had finally come home.

32

I WOKE UP IN our bed in a sweaty panic, feeling out of place, alone, and wondering where I was. My body was naked and smooth. I closed my eyes and allowed my hands to run down my growing breasts and belly. I smiled, remembering the night before. I could smell pancakes, and I peeked out from beyond the covers to see his black boots. He knelt down, looked me in the eye and stroked my hair with tenderness and compassion; I was desperate for his touch even though, at times, it still felt hollow and forced. It broke my heart, but I could think only of my daughter and myself.

When Mr. Mogul spoke to me his voice was quiet, but it felt like a chorus of hope. "Maddie, I can't do it any more. I can't work at that place. I can't be there and be a father. What do you think? I need your support if I decide to do this." It felt like he had opened his eyes and chosen life; like he might be ready to raise a family with me. I smiled and nodded, sitting up in the bed, and pulling him close to me.

"Alright, I need to go in and get my stuff but I'll be back." He leaned in and kissed me on the mouth as my eyes watered up and I was filled with hope. I exhaled deeply when Daddy headed down the stairs of our apartment, descending into the Mission to enter those heavy castle doors that once lead the way to what seemed a palace but became our prison, for the last time.

I TOOK A LONG bath, lathering my body in delicious lotions and spritzing vanilla and grapefruit perfumes onto my wrists. I rubbed jojoba oil onto my round belly and taut skin. I slipped into a long peach-colored empire waist evening gown that my mother wore when she was twenty years old, in 1974. I applied fresh makeup, lining my eyes, and opening my mouth to fill in my plump lips with rich, deep red lipstick. I smiled in the mirror, looking at my face, now thick with pregnancy, my vibrant red hair falling in waves down my back. I stared into the mirror reciting the difficult speech that I had to give with a smile, "Welcome, and thank you for coming to Femina Potens' award-winning literary series, Sizzle! Tonight we will be indulging in two of my favorite topics: cupcakes and Kink, yum. And we have a star-studded lineup this evening that includes the brilliant Laura Antoniou, Lorelei Lee, and Tina Horn. I will also be reading from my upcoming memoir." I know how to warm up a room, I can excite an audience with a dash of humor and a whole lot of energy and cleavage, but these next words wouldn't come with such ease. My stomach ached and I questioned whether this was growing pains from making a mature and responsible decision, or if I was giving up without enough of a fight. " As you may have..." I lowered my eyes in shame and cleared my throat. I needed to do this with dignity and leave the audience with hope. "As you may have heard, tonight will be our last event at this location. Although goodbyes are never easy, I know this is only a transition as Femina Potens moves onto something even more brilliant. Please know that the power and strength in our community is not limited to a single home, we are ever changing, ever evolving, and we wouldn't exist if it wasn't for all of you, our dedicated volunteers, our incredibly talented artists, and you, our community, our support. This dialogue will continue. So grab a cupcake, sit on down and let's get kinky." Tears streamed down my face. I wanted to believe the words as I spoke them out loud. I wanted to believe that our organization wasn't dependent on my anal scenes and porn career alone. *So much is changing so quickly.* The rent had gone up again on the gallery and the number of porn scenes I could perform at seven months pregnant was limited. It was becoming increasingly clear that if James wasn't working at KINK and I was not performing on a consistent basis we could no longer support the hefty rent and expenses of a storefront gallery in the Castro. It was time to say goodbye.

I stood outside of the gallery on that familiar corner of Sanchez and Market, a weathered gay pride rainbow flag waved majestically in the cold San Francisco wind. Men with fresh buzz cuts and well groomed beards sporting leather jackets and dark denim blue jeans walked out of the neighboring barber shop, Male Image, a cornerstone in the old-guard gay male culture in San Francisco. The gallery lights were shining brightly, illuminating the buzz of activity visible from the large storefront windows. Several volunteers set up folding chairs in rows, while another adjusted the microphone height and plugged in a small guitar amp. Pink vegan cupcakes with icing pictures of handcuffs sat out on thin silver-coated platters from the dollar store. Maxine was sitting at the door with a cash box and a flier for that night's event. A red carpet had been duct-taped to the sidewalk to lead guests into the warm, glowing beacon.

"It's the one place in the city where truly anything can happen. That kind of potential is crucial for the San Francisco art community," one woman on a recent grant-funding panel had said of the organization. It was true. Anything could happen in the safety of those walls, and it did. Now, I was ready to build new walls and tear down old ones. I had a new family to protect, Daddy needed me now, and so did my baby to be.

33

ON MARCH 2ND AT about 4:30 A.M., a blood-tinged, snot-like mucous plug dropped from the hole of my cervix into the toilet. My focus shifted. For two weeks I'd been having pre-labor contractions and frantically attempting to finish all of the dangling projects and meet impending deadlines before the real labor began. From this moment on, any essays, deadlines, or press inquiries would be swept aside; I would focus on guiding my daughter into this world one contraction at a time, one breath at time, one painful stretch of the cervix at a time.

My uterus started to tremble, undulating waves of sensation and pressure spread throughout my organ that was now the size of a watermelon. My daughter's head pressed hard and heavy against my cervix. We were both fighting to make our way into a new world.

I watched the green digital LED clock on the kitchen stove as I sat cross-legged on the linoleum floor. Every five minutes a contraction hit my body. I eagerly awaited each new contraction; I would let Daddy keep sleeping for now. As the sun came up I watched him snore in the family room on the mattress on the floor; his long, lanky body rising and falling under our deep violet satin sheets. I smiled as I listened to the nasal, wispy exhale seep from his gaping mouth. It gave him a charming bit of humanity.

I sent a simple text: "Labor has started. I lost my mucous plug. I think this it," to our doula, Dani, as well as to Annie, Beth, and my mom. My mom would tell my dad.

I could feel my insides pushing their way to the outside: fetus, placenta, and all my love and fear tied up in blood vessels and nerve endings that would soon be exposed. *I wonder, am I ready to let it all go? Am I ready to be torn wide open?* I was not sure if I was willing to release all that fear and trauma yet, I had been holding onto a lot emotionally. All of the words left unsaid between James and me that once stuck in my throat had grown over the past year, burrowing deep into the bowels of my body.

Daddy woke up as one of the contractions subsided and I closed my eyes as he gently and tentatively touched my shoulder. I wanted to vomit up our recent past, but when I looked at him I had hope. I knew that if I kept space for him to return to, he would come back. It was my turn to take care of Daddy, and right now that meant waiting while Daddy found himself and knew himself, not just as my hero but as a man with flaws and scars and stories and histories that shaped him into a person I still loved.

Daddy was from the Emerald City of Seattle—the man behind the curtain, with a larger-than-life image. He was my hero when I needed one, when the questions seemed too hard to answer. The reality is that we all have heroic moments. Sometimes, we have to be our own heroes and sometimes our heroes need our help. They are, after all, human, too.

THE SUN WAS JUST peeking up over the horizon and I was approaching twenty-seven hours of labor. It had been a long day and night of waddling up and down the squeaky wooden floorboards in the hallway. When a contraction started I leaned up against the white walls of our apartment, pressing my face against the cool plaster and stared into the eyes of a painting that hung on our wall. The square stretch of canvas portrayed a girl with waves of red fiery hair, scarlet lips opened in a pouty display of pleasure, rope cinched tightly around her breasts. It was the girl I once was. I inhaled that image and exhaled something different, the swollen, throbbing discomfort of change.

I was seated on the mattress, and Daddy settled behind me. His body enveloped mine, his lips on my neck, his arms cradled around my hard round belly, as we breathed together through each contraction. I sobbed as I felt the past melting away, the intimacy and closeness I hadn't felt in so very long felt as though it was returning. Daddy seemed intertwined with my pain,

I could breathe through it with him there whispering in my ear, "Breathe...breathe...you can do it, Maddie. You can do anything." I believed him.

When the sun came up for the second time during my labor, I was ready to go to the hospital. Daddy called to let them know we were on our way. James grabbed our hospital bag equipped with all of the necessities: toiletries, clothes, my waterproof vibrator, clothes and blankets for the baby, snacks, and water bottles. *We're ready.*

He held my hand as I carefully made my way down our apartment staircase. The next time I entered through this door, we would be a trio. I looked up at James with this realization and smiled.

Dani was downstairs waiting for us. She smiled and looked up and at James and me. Her hands were wrapped around a gold, glittery thermos of coffee with a drawing of a pin-up model reading a book. Above the figure read in bold typed font: "BRAINIACS ARE SEXY." It was a drizzly morning and she was bundled warmly in dark denim jeans, a white long-sleeve thermal shirt, and a green puffy vest. She leaned in to me, kissed me on the cheek, and looked me in the eyes.

"How are you feeling?" she asked, placing a hand on my shoulder as the cab pulled up to the apartment.

"I'm ready to have this baby, Dani." James opened the taxi door and we both awkwardly maneuvered our bodies into the back seat while Dani settled in front with the driver.

When we arrived, James and Dani led me down the long, sterile hallway of the maternity ward. The walls were a sunny yellow decorated with beautiful black and white framed portraits of small, wrinkly babies with squinty little eyes. I held Daddy's hand tight as I watched a woman being wheeled out of a birthing room wearing a baby blue hospital gown, their newborn baby followed in a small clear plastic basinet. The baby was tiny and swaddled tightly in a blanket, its violet face scrunched up and screaming. The mother looked exhausted, red and sweaty, her hair in tangles, her expression resting somewhere in between a look of severe pain and a weak smile of bliss.

Her husband, standing next to them, was smiling ear to ear. He must have seen the look of pure fear on my face as I walked past; he laughed, taunting, "I'd turn back if I were you."

I exhaled and nodded, forcing a smile. Grasping now both Dani's hand and Daddy's, Dani looked at me with a sweet smile. "Maddie, just remember there are plenty of people out there without much brains that do an awful lot of talking. Especially men." I looked up at her and laughed, a welcome respite.

In the birthing room, Daddy helped me slip on my hospital gown while Dani unpacked our hospital bag. Out came photographs, angels, oils, flowers, vibrator, and birthing plan. A young doctor walked in. She was beautiful, with a short bob of blonde hair and pools of blue eyes. I carefully pulled my way up onto the stirrups and table and spread my legs. I was in labor but my cervix was only dilated three centimeters; at ten centimeters we pushed. We had a while to go.

I WANTED TO BE immersed in warmth, in water. My muscles ached and my joints creaked, so, delirious with exhaustion, I lowered myself slowly into the bathtub in the hospital's birthing suite.

Annie and Beth arrived from Santa Cruz, and eased their way into the room.

"Knock, knock. How is our beautiful mama?" Annie knelt down beside the tub of water.

"I'm so happy you're here, Annie. I love you both so much." I took Annie's hand as a contraction came and we breathed together.

"I brought something for you." Annie said. "It's a scented oil. This one is lavender. Would you like me to place a little of it on your heart chakra?"

"I'd love that, Annie. Thank you." She dabbed the lavender oils on my chakras and pulse points and I felt calmness and comfort set in. My heart was at ease in her presence.

Beth guarded the door, keeping staff and doctors from invading the intimate space we were creating for this birth. James set the mood, dimming the lights, setting the water to the perfect temperature and arming me with the waterproof vibrator. I touched the vibrator to my clitoris and practiced a deep exhale. Daddy, Beth, and Annie all joined in. Annie and Beth vocalized oms and chants while they shook the ritual percussive instruments they brought along for this special moment.

Daddy's always good at details, it's a talent of his. He knelt by the tub and combed his fingers through my hair, tenderly tracing my face with his hands. The doctors knocked on the door and Beth looked to me for the go ahead to let them in. She was my courageous lioness and I felt safe under her guard. As my labor continued hour after exhausting hour, we all feared the doctors would start to push for a caesarean. Beth knew I wanted a vaginal birth. I wanted to be present and connected for every long and exhaustive moment of the birth and labor.

The blonde doctor poked her head inside our small retreat and was embarrassed by the vibrator. She had seen the battery-powered device lying on the table in the birthing room a few hours earlier and jokingly asked if I was planning on singing some karaoke during the labor.

It was time for another examination. I toweled off, slipped on my gown, and headed back to the stirrups and table.

"This might be a little awkward," the doctor commented while inserting her gloved, lubed hand. This was the least awkward part of my laboring experience. She removed her hand and shakes her head, "Hmm, well that's not good..." then jotted something down in my file.

"What?" I started to panic, assuming something must be wrong with the labor.

"Well...your cervix is swelling. You have been laboring so long and so intensely that you're now down to only two centimeters of dilation in your cervix, due to the swelling." I wondered what this meant for the baby and me. Daddy held my hand and Annie, Beth, and Dani all huddled close to my shaking body. I started to cry. I was now forty hours into labor, I had been traveling down this yellow brick road for nearly two days; the door was closing in my face and I felt helpless and defeated. There was no turning around, I needed to be the one to release this child. I wanted to bring hope and life into our world through my own breath, through my own power. As the doctors started to swarm like flying monkeys I cried, nodded and accepted an epidural.

Annie dabbed a little lavender oil on my pillow, kissing my tear-streaked cheek.

I WOKE WITH DADDY by my side. He pulled a red Popsicle from a plastic bag, "I have a little something for you." The strawberry popsicle melted in my mouth, sweet frozen perfection in my foggy state of consciousness. "She's awake, Doctor."

I had only been asleep for an hour and a half, but it was the first hour of sleep I'd had in two days. I woke up feeling reenergized and reinvigorated, with a renewed sense of accomplishment. The doctor examined me once more and smiled, "We're ready to push. Are you ready for this?" *I don't know that I'll ever fully be ready for this moment, but this is my chance.* My moment for transformation, the beginning of my journey back home began. I looked up at the room full of people who loved me and believed in me.

"You can do this, Maddie." Daddy said, holding my right hand, while Dani coached me through. My breathing and pushing and contractions approached one after the other. Annie chanted and Beth shared courageous, encouraging affirmations.

"Go for it, Maddie. You can do it. I know you have this in you." Daddy said. His eyes had changed, they twinkled with life, and I felt so much closer to him. He stepped out from behind his curtain with a new bravery that I hadn't seen before. His eyes teared up as his lips met mine. He pushed my tangles of hair aside and whispered, "You are my hero, Maddie. You are my hero. You can do this, baby. I believe in you."

Emma's head began to crown and I pushed with love and courage and fight. The doctors scurried about and caught her, then cut the umbilical cord. Daddy, remembering that I wanted her placed on my breast immediately after the birth, ripped my hospital gown open and revealed my swollen milky breasts and still swollen belly. Emma latched her mouth around my breast and suckled. I looked up at Daddy and cried, "I did it, Papa. I did it."

Daddy smiled with love and vulnerability that was new for him. He was a father, I was a mother, and our world was changing. We created something so much greater than ourselves to serve and care for.

"Can I hold her?" James asked, gazing down at our small, reddish-purple child, her head already covered with dark black hair and a streak of blonde running down the middle.

Part 5

34

I PLANTED MY HANDS firmly on the cool, gray cement of the shaded patio floor. My legs stood tall, rooting me deeply into the earth below. My spine sloped from my hips to the crown of my head in downward dog. I gazed over at my toddling child mimicking my yoga position.

"Very good, Em. That is downward dog." Her long, snowy blonde hair fell down over her blue eyes. Her cloth diaper bulged around her butt and poked its way out around her tan, chubby thighs.

"Dog," she repeated, then stuck her tongue out and panted like a puppy. She maintained her yoga position until I moved into cobra. My belly touched the floor, my palms firm against the ground. As I arched my back I felt a strong bolt of radiant energy release from the crown of my head, pulling me upward toward the intense light of the sun.

I looked forward and focused my eyes on Daddy working in the garden. He was a tall tree of life among a landscape of dry lifeless desert in Southern California's Inland Empire. It had been five months since we unpacked our complex San Francisco lives and moved into the large ranch-style suburban home in San Bernardino County. Here, our neighbors were retired police officers, United States generals, people who nailed crosses to their front doors and stuck Romney for President stickers to the bumper of their oversized pickup trucks. Much of our belongings remained hidden away in boxes and crates in storage. Without Daddy's position at KINK and my active touring schedule of workshops and filmmaking, our finances had run dry.

When we realized we couldn't afford to stay in San Francisco, James picked up the phone and made an uncomfortable phone call to his older brother, Ed. They hadn't spoken in ten years. Ed was a service man, a high-ranking lieutenant in the military. As a child, Ed was James' hero—he had left their home in Massachusetts when he was eighteen, and James was only eight. Ed went out to see the world, serve his country, and escape their dysfunctional family and their alcoholic father.

Much of my adult life had revolved around a ten-block radius of our San Francisco apartment. It was a huge loss, and we were propelling into a frightening unknown. James and I were changing in every way possible. My belly was tiger-striped with stretch marks and I cut off all of my long red hair into a pixie cut since it had started falling out, a phenomenon known as post-partum shedding. My round, awkward body still clung onto twenty pounds of post-partum weight. When we left San Francisco, I felt like I was leaving behind a part of my identity; who was I if I didn't reside within its queer, tattooed bosom?

Ed opened his home to us and graciously extended himself in every possible way. I tried to swallow my ego and accept the challenges we were handed. This could be a gift, a chance for James to reconnect with family and find a reprieve from the everyday triggers that reminded him of his recent unhappiness and posed a threat to his sobriety.

Now, James was turning the soil in Ed's yard, seeding new plants in one of the raised beds, watering baskets of flowers and pruning overgrown basil and oregano. James wanted to grow a garden, to grow something for us. He wanted to cook and to nourish us. He saw the garden as something he could build and grow and then hand over to his brother when we were ready to leave. It was his tacit thank you.

I smiled and exhaled when he glanced back at me. Emma was squatting close to the floor. She studied my face and my smile, then reached out with her paint-covered hands to touch my cheeks, petting them gently: "Gentle Mama."

Abandoning yoga, Em's fingers pulled at her fair locks with great tension. Her hands fell with volition to her painted thighs, smacking her plump flesh with frustration at her sleepy body. I pulled her body to mine and whispered softly into her ear, "Shhhhh. Em, gentle. Be gentle with yourself. Be gentle with yourself and with those around you, my sweetheart."

SHORTLY AFTER EMMA'S BIRTH, my father came to visit us in San Francisco for the first time in the ten years I'd been living there. With the birth of his granddaughter, there were no more excuses. We were strolling slowly along the bay while James was busy securing a table at a seafood restaurant. I was holding Emma close to my body, as she was enveloped in a black fleece sling.

My dad stopped walking and looked out at the sea lions. It was windy and cold by the bay.

"Do you come say hello to the sea lions very often?" He plucked a handkerchief from his pocket and loudly blew his nose.

"No, Dad. This is pretty much for tourists." There was an awkward pause. Between the waves crashing and the crowded Fisherman's Wharf tourists, sound filled the air with a marriage of voices and white noise, but from the only voice I really cared to hear at that moment, there was silence.

"Why didn't you ever come to see me, Dad? Why did you wait until now? My life is a mess right now. I wanted to make you proud of me."

"I am proud of you. I'm proud of that little girl. I haven't always been proud of myself. I know I haven't always been the ideal father. But I love you. And of course I'm proud of you. How couldn't I be proud of you? You followed your dreams. Now, those might not be the same as my dreams, but you followed them, and

I love you for that. Hell, I love your brother and that boy can't even find a dream! You're family, you're my daughter and you'll always be my daughter, even when your life is a mess. I want to know that you're okay."

"I'm okay, Dad. Life is just a little scary right now."

"Yeah. Life will do that, Tina. And it just gets scarier when you've got kids because then you start being scared for them."

"You should move out to San Francisco, Dad." I smiled, laughing at the thought of my father trying to fit into this environment.

"Nah! If I lived in San Francisco where would I vacation? When you live in a place like Cincinnati you have a reason to want to leave and visit other places that are more exciting. Come on, let's get you and that little muskrat inside. I'll buy my little girl a Shirley Temple. You still like those?"

"Sure, Dad." And we stood, looking out at the ocean together, watching the sea lions on the rocks as they barked and pointed their noses into the air.

EMMA SOUNDLY SLEEPING, I tiptoed out of the nursery and made my way into the master bedroom, which served as both an office and a pocket of space for wakeful nights of sleep. I sat down in my office chair in front of the computer. My heavy antique desk was one of several items of furniture James had hauled into the moving truck to bring along to the desert. It was cluttered with papers and DVDs of pornographic footage waiting to be edited. Model releases, grant applications, artist submissions, and outlines for workshops lay in heaps on top of parenting books. The wall above the desk was pinned with collages and photographs, inspiration boards, and shelves full of feminist porn awards.

On the desk there was a photo of Daddy and me leaning against a tree in a beautiful amber field in Marin County. Next to the photo was a valentine he gave me only three months ago. The handmade red heart read, "Thank you for saving me. You are my hero, Maddie. I love you. J."

My flesh goose-pimpled from the cool air-conditioning, I swiveled around in my chair and reached for my cardigan off the quilted bed. I logged onto my virtual therapy session and accepted my therapist's video call.

"Hi, Alex."

"How are you today, Tina?"

I had been speaking with Alex since our move. Since I was unable to physically visit a therapist, video conferencing seemed like the next best option. It still felt a little awkward when she referred to me by my legal name, but it felt intimate and healthy to have a few people in my life that were a part of that small circle of people who knew Tina.

"Well, I'm struggling with a few things." I cleared my throat and glanced down to my hands, to the braided rope ring. I gazed at the way the light reflected off of the gold and toyed with the ring, rotating it around in circles.

"Let's talk about that," Alex offered, and I sighed. It was hard work, delving through the past, understanding our emotions, our actions, and creating new pathways. Sometimes it felt like more than I could bear, but that was why I had support.

"Well...I just got back from San Francisco. It was just really intense. I went to the Armory." I breathed, exhaling. Even saying the name out loud made my throat start to close up a bit.

35

I WALKED UP THOSE familiar castle stairs joined by a Femina Potens board member and a visiting artist from New York. The artist had a ravenous curiosity for the San Francisco Armory and the debauchery contained in those thick stone walls, so I agreed to accompany them on a guided tour of the Armory during his stay. In an effort to prove that the company had nothing to hide, it started offering an entertaining, guided tour similar to what you might expect at Disneyland or Universal Studios but with a pervy comedic twist. The guide joked about the padded cell and boiler room while leading us up the staircase to The Upper Floor. My stomach churned around every corner as I was reminded of so many disturbing memories.

Tourists giggled and blushed, but I felt like I was visiting a haunted mansion. Luckily, the tour guide hadn't recognized me, despite my having worked for KINK for a decade as a prominent model. I clocked over 150 scenes for the company. Now, as a ghost, I could float from floor to floor in the house I used to live in, now just a forgotten memory tucked somewhere among the archives.

As we entered the decadent dining room on The Upper Floor, I looked up at the wall and was surprised to find her likeness permanently stored, contorted in a back bend with thick, heavy steel restraints, in an oil painting surrounded by a gold frame—Sarah Chasm. I couldn't stomach her ball-gagged face, that troubled girl still filled me with anger and pain. I needed to get out of this room.

I stepped out onto the fire escape and closed my eyes. I let the anxiety wash over me. I acknowledged it, mindful of how it affected my body and, speaking softly, talked myself through the anxiety.

"It is only a space, only a castle, it is only as powerful as I allow it to be. This space has no power over me any more." The words dropped from my lips into the crisp San Francisco air.

There was nothing grand about the Armory, nothing spectacular. There were no princes and princesses here, regardless of titles and stage names and egos. These were all psychological constructs that we built and that the viewers, the performers, the public and even celebrities bought into and fed.

This wasn't my life any more. A few months calling a suburban desert home seem like a much-needed and even appreciated rehabilitation for all of us. I was letting the past go, ready to move forward, and so was James. We learned to do that in our own ways. We were slowly becoming rejuvenated, healing bit by bit, forgiving each other, and raising our family, flaws and all.

"I'M REALLY NERVOUS ABOUT finishing this book; my memoir. I've been working on it for so long. What if they crucify me? What if people hate it? People are going to hate me. Feminists won't understand why I stayed, why I believed in Daddy." I was finishing up the session with Alex and nervously digging my fingernail into the cuticle bed of my right thumb.

"People are flawed, Tina," Alex responded. "All of us. I think people will find it honest and brave and relatable." Alex seemed so confident, so much more confident than I.

"But don't people want a hero? I think people want a hero. They want to believe that there is someone out there that has it figured out. All I'm sure of is that...I don't." I released an exasperated sigh, covering my face with the palms of my sweaty hands.

"How is James?" Alex smiled, changing the subject.

"He's good. Going to meetings. We're good. It's like we're in love all over again. This time we have all of our flaws laid out on the table. Emma gives us a reason to be better people. We're not perfect, I don't think perfect really exists. We're in this together, and for us, that's huge." I swiveled around in my chair to gaze out at Daddy in the garden. He pushed on his wide-plated shovel, spearing the earth, making room for Emma's olive tree. It still has small, cream-colored tags strung on the branches with blessings for our daughter.

"Tell me more about that." Alex nudged and I glance at a lavender envelope on which Daddy had written: "Things I Love about You." The envelope was full of small inky notes that held phrases like: "I love the way you make me want to be a better person," "I love you for giving us Emma," and "I love the way you call me Daddy."

James—my partner, my hero, my lover, the father of my child, a humble man from Massachusetts with flaws and years of baggage who bravely left his own white picket fence behind years ago in search of a mythical father figure, a different kind of family. We aren't that different, but it's taken us many years to find each other. James fills a fatherly role in my life, a role that provides stability and comfort from a respected masculine elder. But James isn't my father and I don't need him to be. I have a father. My father is funny and charming in a goofy way. My father has a warm heart and is kind and loving, though he is not without flaws. We are all just people. Beautiful fallible creatures, regardless of the number of superhero capes in our closet, #1 Dad coffee mugs in the kitchen cupboard, or a young girl's unrealistic expectations. In this realization, through much love and exploration, I found myself. I found my Daddy, and I found the family that I had been searching for all this time that storybook fairytales had never prepared me for.

If I close my eyes and exhale the past, I'm only left with the present, this very moment: inhaling the spicy scent of Daddy's aftershave, my face nuzzled into Daddy's white ribbed A-frame, the strong thud of Daddy's heart pumping against my pink cheeks, Daddy's one hand fingering my red tangles of hair, his other planted firmly against my underside. Maybe we're all flawed and nowhere near perfection, but we are also perfectly human, aspiring toward our own inner truth, our own moments of heroism, our own moments of Daddy.

Afterword; Aftercare

LET'S TAKE A COLLECTIVE breath and sit with this moment. Pause. It's time for closure. It's time to say goodbye. It is the end of a book but also the end of an era. In the past two weeks I have witnessed the closure of San Francisco's Lusty Lady and the death of bondage pioneer and erotic engineer, Jeff Gord.

One, an iconic sexual institution which fought for labor rights and union worker rights for feminist sex workers. The other, a man who re-invented and re-invisioned the world of fetish and bondage with highly complex engineered creations which transformed the human form into living art.

Their voices will endure. The Lusty's contributions to the labor struggle and unionizing of worker owned cooperatives will remain a part of our feminist history. Their imprint is lasting, lasting longer than the now unemployed erotic dancers dwindling bank accounts. Jeff Gord's remains will be buried this week, but his contribution to the evolution of fetish and the sexual history of America is long documented, celebrated and will last. It will last longer than the orgasms catalyst from his ingeniously engineered mad scientist inventions.

And yet properties will be bought up by capitalist money hungry corporations and bodies will decompose.

Goodbyes are not easy. It is not easy to let go, acknowledge the passing of time, the passing of life, but still it passes, and we breathe. We must allow the moment to be what it is, to allow the moment to exist and know that moment will transform, transitioning into something new. Change is inevitable. We can count on that.

As we both discover our own closures, you and I, and make room for new beginnings, I invite you to treat yourself with gentle hands, with a gentle heart.

Instructions for Aftercare

1.   a) Draw a warm bath
     b) Add a few drops of luscious scented essential oil
     c) Soak body until your fingers and toes acquire zebra stripes

2.   a) Bake warm chocolate chip cookies
     b) Devour them straight from the oven
     c) Share them
     d) Give one to your love

3.   a) Drink water: All journeys require hydration

4.   a) Prepare a tea: chamomile-lavender-rose petals

5. a) Ask a friend or lover to hold you
    b) To stroke your hair

6. a) Call a friend
    b) Talk to a friend or don't talk to a friend, but allow them to be present with you

The journey we just experienced contained some intense moments and potentially triggering material. It has taken me thirty-three years to process and live through these moments. It's important to document our lives, to sink our hands deep into the cement as proof that we were here, that we existed. To purge the life that bubbles within us. Beautiful, beautiful, raw visceral life. You just ingested a small slice of my life, my love, one slice of many.

I am a feminist. I have pursued and chosen the life I live with the clearest of intentions. I understand my actions and choices and life are not the simplest to digest. But they are my choices, my truth, my humanity. I only hope—*wish*—for you to pursue your own truth.

May these pages be dog-eared and used often. May your life be rich and your stories be full of wonder and happiness. May you live each moment with a fullness and lustfulness that exemplifies your truest self.

—Madison Young

"We will all have so many incredible memories that most people only dream about."

—Jeff Gord (1946 -2013)

Acknowledgements

MY HEART IS FULL of gratitude to all of those who stood by me and supported me in my journey in writing this memoir, and in telling my story. I'd like to thank my mother for supporting me and standing by me, and for being such a strong pillar of womanhood and fierceness. You gave me courage, Mom. Thank you. Dad, I want to thank you for convincing Mom to let me go to performing art school and teaching me to dream big, lead with my heart, and believe in myself. I want to thank my fairy art mothers, Annie Sprinkle and Beth Stephens. I love you both dearly and you are a constant source of inspiration and strength, you are family and I love you both. Much gratitude to my tribe of bad ass queer performance artists and Queer X Tour alumnae: Wendy Delorme, DJ Metzgerei, Judy Minx, Mad Kate, and Sadie Lune. My close inner circle of friends and support: Henry Catalinich, Katy Chatel, Adria Lang, Mev Luna, Joe Freund, Brian Kidwell, Lydia Daniller. To the Queer Porn Mafia (Syd Blakovich, Jiz Lee, and Courtney Trouble). To all of the volunteers and interns who helped to make Femina Potens a reality. I couldn't have done it with out all of you. To all the mamas at Hacker Moms who cheerled me through the last few chapters of this book and helped in providing a creative DIY art space in which my child could engage in art while I was finishing my manuscript. To the artists, activists, and radicals in my life that continue to push the envelope and forge forward fearlessly: Carol Queen, Michelle Tea, Lee Harrington, Robert Lawrence, Nina Hartley, Tristan Taormino, Jennifer Lyon Bell, and Midori, you all inspire me. Thank you to Diane DiPrima for inspiring me and giving me courage to write. To my child, Em, I love you with all of my heart, you make my heart dance. To my Grandma Virginia: your courage, bravery and strength comfort me still. To all the folks at Barnacle Books that made this book a reality. Tyson, thank you for believing in me and this project. Dave Naz, thank you for helping me to find a home for my memoir. Manjula Martin, thank you for holding my hand, dotting my i's and crossing my t's. My gratitude extends to my fellow outsiders, the misfits, the sexual outlaws, the fringe seekers and boundary pushers, the gender benders, the queers, the femmes, the freaks, the artists, the daddies, and the little girls. And above all, thank you Daddy for taking this journey with me, for standing by my side and believing in me and my art. You inspire me in all you do. I looked forward to a life of collaboration with you, my papa bear.

MADISON YOUNG is an artist and activist dedicated to creating space for love. This sexpert grew up in the suburban landscape of Southern Ohio before moving to San Francisco, California in 2000. Since then this mid-western gal has dedicated her days to facilitating safe space to dialogue on the topic of fringe identities and cultures as well as documenting healthy expression of sexuality. Young's breadth of work in the realm of sexuality spans from documenting our sexual culture in her feminist erotic films to serving as the Artistic Director of the forward thinking non-profit arts organization, Femina Potens Art Gallery. Young values sexual education in her work and has taught workshops, lectures, and acted as a panelist on the topics of sexuality, feminist porn studies, and the politics of BDSM around the world including at Yale University, Hampshire College, Northwestern University, University of Toronto, University of Minnesota, and UC Berkeley. Her writings have been published in books such as *The Ultimate Guide to Kink*, *Baby Remember My Name*, *Rope, Bondage, and Power*, *Best Sex Writing of 2013*, and *John's Marks, Tricks, and Chickenhawks*. Madison Young lives in Berkeley, California with her partner James and child, Em. She is currently pursuing her doctorate in clinical sexology at the Institute of Advanced Studies for Human Sexuality.

CPSIA information can be obtained
at www.ICGtesting.com
Printed in the USA
JSHW022004220123
36468JS00002B/136